T0321482

SCALABLE SHARED MEMORY MULTIPROCESSORS

SCALABLE SHARED MEMORY MULTIPROCESSORS

Edited by

Michel Dubois
University of Southern California

and

Shreekant Thakkar
Sequent Computer Systems

KLUWER ACADEMIC PUBLISHERS
BOSTON/DORDRECHT/LONDON

Distributors for North America:
Kluwer Academic Publishers
101 Philip Drive
Assinippi Park
Norwell, Massachusetts 02061 USA

Distributors for all other countries:
Kluwer Academic Publishers Group
Distribution Centre
Post Office Box 322
3300 AH Dordrecht, THE NETHERLANDS

Library of Congress Cataloging-in-Publication Data

Scalable shared memory multiprocessors / edited by Michel Dubois and
    Shreekant Thakkar.
            p.   cm.
    Proceedings of a workshop held May 26-27, 1990, in Seattle, Wash.
    Includes bibliographical references.
    ISBN 0-7923-9219-1
    1. Multiprocessors--Congresses.   2. Memory management (Computer
science)--Congresses.   I. Dubois, Michel, 1953- .   II. Thakkar,
S. S.
QA76.5.S244   1991
004'.35--dc20   91-33013
                                                                              CIP

CONTENTS

Cache Protocols and Architectures

Distributed Shared Memory

PREFACE

The workshop on Scalable Shared Memory Multiprocessors took place on May 26 and 27 1990 at the Stouffer Madison Hotel in Seattle, Washington as a prelude to the 1990 International Symposium on Computer Architecture.

About 100 participants listened for two days to the presentations of 22 invited speakers, from academia and industry. The motivation for this workshop was to promote the free exchange of ideas among researchers working on shared-memory multiprocessor architectures.There was ample opportunity to argue with speakers, and certainly participants did not refrain a bit from doing so. Clearly, the problem of scalability in shared-memory multiprocessors is still a wide-open question. We were even unable to agree on a definition of "scalability".

Authors had more than six months to prepare their manuscript, and therefore the papers included in this proceedings are refinements of the speakers' presentations, based on the criticisms received at the workshop.As a result, 17 authors contributed to these proceedings. We wish to thank them for their diligence and care.   The contributions in these proceedings can be partitioned into four categories

1. Access Order and Synchronization
2. Performance
3. Cache Protocols and Architectures
4. Distributed Shared Memory

Particular topics on which new ideas and results are presented in these proceedings include: efficient schemes for combining networks, formal specification of shared-memory models, correctness of trace-driven simulations,synchronization, various coherence protocols, an evaluation of directory schemes, discussions on scalability, and updates on current projects such as the MIT Alewife, the CMU PLUS and the Rice University MUNIN projects.

We certainly hope that this book with contributions at the forefront of research in shared-memory systems, will be both informative and thought-provoking so as to create interest and generate new ideas in this critical technology of shared-memory multiprocessors. We wish to thank the Committee of the 1990 International Symposium on Computer Architecture for supporting the workshop as well as Anoop Gupta who did a superb job of taking care of the overall organization and local arrangements.

Michel Dubois
Shreekant Thakkar

August 1991

SCALABLE SHARED
MEMORY
MULTIPROCESSORS

Combining Windows
The Key to Managing MIMD Combining Trees

Philip Bitar

Aquarius Project
Computer Science Division
University of California
Berkeley, CA 94720
bitar@berkeley.edu

ABSTRACT

We develop the synchronization topic of *MIMD combining trees* — their motivation, their structure, their parameters — and we illustrate these principles using fetch-and-add. We define the concept of *combining window*, an interval of time during which a request is held in a combining node in order to allow it to combine with subsequent incoming requests. We show that the combining window is necessary in order to realize the dual forms of concurrency — execution and storage concurrency — that a combining tree is designed to achieve. *Execution concurrency* among the nodes of a combining tree enables the tree to achieve the *speed up* that it is designed to give. Without sufficient execution concurrency, the tree will not achieve the desired speed up. *Storage concurrency* among the nodes of a combining tree enables the tree to achieve the *buffer storage* that is necessary in order to implement the combining of requests. Without sufficient storage concurrency, node buffers will overflow. More specifically, the combining window shows how to bound node buffer size.

Key Words: Combining tree, combining window, fetch-and-add

CONTENTS

We develop the notion of combining tree for an MIMD architecture in a novel way and independent of physical implementation, in order to make the essential aspects clear and to make implementation options clear. The essential aspects may be explained in terms of *synchronization concepts* and in terms of *queuing constructs*.

1 BASIC CONCEPTS

Where do we start in trying to understand combining trees?

Consider an associative binary operation 'o' on i terms. A combining tree may be used to speed up this kind of computation through parallel execution, reducing the execution time from $\Theta(i)$ to $\Theta(\log i)$, as illustrated in Figure 1a. In addition, suppose that the operation is also commutative — such as addition — and that each CPU may contribute values at arbitrary times, requesting the addition of a local value x to y. Figure 1c illustrates the combining and decombining, while Figure 1b provides an abstract representation of Figure 1c.

Figure 1b represents the idea that each node of the tree combines requests flowing downward and decombines replies flowing upward. This defines *two conceptually distinct atomic operations* at each node: *a combining and possible downward sending operation*, and *a decombining and upward sending operation*. Specifically, when a node receives a request, if there is another request with which it can be combined in the combining buffer, the incoming request is combined with the other request, making a combined request that contains not only the combined value, but also identifies the original requests so that decombining will be possible. Then the combined request is either retained in the combining buffer for further combining, or else a corresponding request is sent down to the parent node, and the combined request is transferred to the decombining buffer to await the reply.

What was the original motivation for the combining tree?

The *fetch-and-add* paradigm was conceived by the Ultracomputer designers for incrementing a variable I that is used to derive index values for a FIFO queue implemented as a circular array (Gottlieb et al. 1983a [4], 1983b [5]; Almasi, Gottlieb 1989 [1]). Processes may concurrently obtain queue cells by incrementing I using the combining tree and then by taking the remainder modulo the queue size. This allows the processes to concurrently insert into the respective cells. This simple paradigm must, however, be accompanied by a busy-wait queue at each cell, since the cell indices will repeat themselves as I is incremented. Similar handling of a delete index D allows parallel deletions, but provision must be made for alternating inserts and deletes on each cell.

In addition, suppose it is desired that a delete request first detect if there is at least one occupied cell before continuing with the delete algorithm (and thus queuing at some cell to wait for an insert). To maintain the minimum number of occupied cells, a third variable *min* is incremented after each insert and decremented before each delete. Similarly, if it is desired that an insert request first detect if there is no more than some maximum number of occupied cells (such as the number of cells in the queue less one), a fourth variable *max* is incremented before each insert and decremented after each delete. The details of insert and delete algorithms are shown in Figures 2a and 2b, which provide an expression of algorithms proposed by Gottlieb et al. (1983b [5]). The authors also present other methods of handling busy wait at the cells.

What are hardware and software combining trees?

Hardware combining tree. The Ultracomputer designers envisioned using server synchronization in a tree implemented completely in hardware, yielding a hardware combining tree. By *server synchronization* we mean that an atomic operation on an object is implemented by a unique server processor (SP) for that object (Bitar 1990 [2]). The Ultracomputer designers used the configuration of Figure 3a with a multi-stage interconnect, and at each switch in the network they placed an SP having sufficient capability to implement fetch-and-add combining and decombining. The designers of the IBM RP3 took a similar strategy in an architecture like that of Figure 3c, but with SPs at the memory banks as in Figure 3a (Pfister et al. 1985 [10]).

Software combining tree. Yew et al. (1987 [14]), on the other hand, proposed implementing the atomic operations using server synchronization in Figures 3a and 3b with no combining in the network — just the SPs at memory execute atomic operations — and the tree itself is defined by software, yielding a software combining tree. They proposed this for busy-wait operations that create hot spots at memory, and hence bottlenecks in the network. An example of such an operation is polling a barrier count or a bit, waiting for it to become zero.

Using a software combining tree to implement general operations, such as fetch-and-add, would require greater complexity in the SPs in order to enable them to implement the combining and decombining operations illustrated in Figure 1b. In addition, the SPs would need to be able to communicate with each other, or else the CPUs would need to mediate inter-SP communication, notified by the SPs when appropriate.

Alternatively, notice that the pair of atomic operations of a software combining node (Figure 1b) may be implemented by the CPUs using *lock synchronization*. In this case, the tree is defined by the node buffers, without a unique SP at each buffer pair, and a CPU locks a node buffer in order to execute an atomic operation — combine, insert, or delete — on its contents.

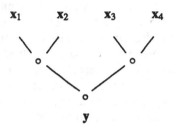

Figure 1a. Operation Tree.

$$y \; := \; x_1 \; o \; x_2 \; o \; x_3 \; o \; x_4$$

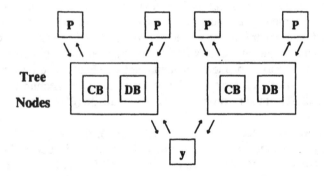

Figure 1b. Implementation Structure.

Down arrow = request {read y then add a value to y}
Up arrow = reply {a value of y}
CB = combining buffer, DB = decombining buffer

Figure 1. Combining Tree Structure and Function.
P = processor

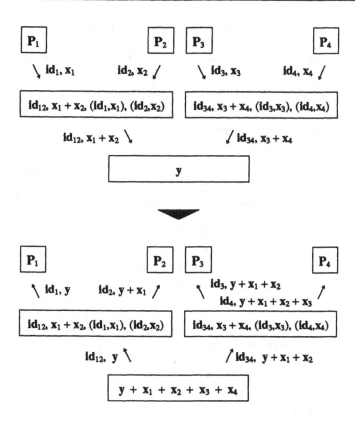

Figure 1c. Combining and Decombining.

Processor i request is fetch-and-add(x_i, y)

Fetch-and-add(x_i, y) = {read y then add x_i to y }

CB, DB are not distinguished. Address of y is implicit in request.

Figure 1 (continued). Combining Tree Structure and Function.

P = processor

Figure 2. Fetch-and-Add Queuing Algorithms.

Figure 2a. FIFO Enqueue (Insert) Using Fetch-and-Add.

Enqueue(input: *adr_entry;* output: *success_flag*):

global variable: *Q_size, max, min, I, Q[Q_size], Next[Q_size]*;
local, register variable: *my_I, cell, ticket*;

```
begin
    if max < Q_size  then                              /* queue not full */
    begin
        if fetch-and-add(max, 1) < Q_size  then        /* queue still not full */
        begin
            my_I := fetch-and-add(I, 1);

            /* now (in effect) divide my_I by Q_size */
            /* then take remainder to get cell, or truncate and multiply by 2 to get ticket */

            cell := remainder(my_I/Q_size );
            ticket := 2 * floor(my_I/Q_size );         /* 2 tickets/cell: */
                                                       /* 1 enqueue, 1 dequeue */
            while Next [cell] ≠ ticket  do null;        /* busy-wait for turn, */
            Q [cell] := adr_entry;                      /* could also delay retry */
            fetch-and-add(Next [cell], 1);
            fetch-and-add(min, 1);

            success_flag := 1;
            return;
        end;
        else                                           /* queue full */
            fetch-and-add(max, -1);
    end;
    success_flag := 0;                                 /* queue full */
end;
```

Notes for Figure 2.

1. The queue size, *Q_size*, is a power of 2 that is less than or equal to the capacity of *I* and *D*.

2. The variable *ticket* is used to implement FIFO busy-wait queuing at the cells. However, *I* and *D* must be large enough so that by the time they wrap around — and thus begin repeating *ticket* values — the same values of *ticket* from the previous iteration of *I* and *D* have been used, that is, the respective enqueues and dequeues have been completed.

Figure 2 (continued). Fetch-and-Add Queuing Algorithms.

Figure 2b. FIFO Dequeue (Delete) Using Fetch-and-Add.

Dequeue(output: *adr_entry, success_flag*):

global variable: *Q_size, max, min, D, Q[Q_size], Next[Q_size]*;
local, register variable: *my_D, cell, ticket*;

```
begin
      if min > 0 then                                   /* queue not empty */
      begin
            if fetch-and-add(min, -1) > 0 then          /* queue still not empty */
            begin
                  my_D := fetch-and-add(D, 1);

                  /* now (in effect) divide my_D by Q_size */
                  /* then take remainder to get cell, or truncate, multiply by 2, */
                  /* and add 1 to get ticket */

                  cell := remainder(my_D /Q_size);
                  ticket := 2 * floor(my_D /Q_size) + 1;    /* 2 tickets/cell: */
                                                            /* 1 enqueue, 1 dequeue */
                  while Next [cell] ≠ ticket  do null;       /* busy-wait for turn, */
                  adr_entry := Q [cell];                     /* could also delay retry */
                  fetch-and-add(Next [cell], 1);
                  fetch-and-add(max, -1);

                  success_flag := 1;
                  return;
            end;
            else                                        /* queue empty */
                  fetch-and-add(min, 1);
      end;
      success_flag := 0;                                /* queue empty */
end;
```

Notes for Figure 2.

1. The queue size, *Q_size*, is a power of 2 that is less than or equal to the capacity of *I* and *D*.

2. The variable *ticket* is used to implement FIFO busy-wait queuing at the cells. However, *I* and *D* must be large enough so that by the time they wrap around — and thus begin repeating *ticket* values — the same values of *ticket* from the previous iteration of *I* and *D* have been used, that is, the respective enqueues and dequeues have been completed.

Also observe that since the architecture of Figure 3c already has a CPU at each memory bank, it would be easy to implement a software combining tree in this architecture using the CPUs as the servers. This strategy would avoid the cost of the hardware combining nodes and the cost of the SPs, while retaining the flexibility of the software combining tree.

Generalized combining tree. We will characterize combining trees in a general manner that applies to both hardware and software trees. In this perspective, there is a combining tree for each combinable variable y, as in Figure 1b, and the m combining trees in the system share the system hardware, both the combining processors and their memories. Hence, a physical combining node must have sufficient processor power and memory space to accommodate all of the trees that it must process, which will be m or fewer trees.

2 PURPOSE

When are combining trees necessary?

Given their complexity, we would like to avoid combining trees if possible, so we ask when they are necessary. A combining tree is necessary when the respective computation is a *system bottleneck,* or when it creates a system bottleneck (as a memory hot spot creates in a network), and when the bottleneck can be relieved *only by the use of parallelism.*

In order to clarify the concept of bottleneck and how to design a combining tree that will relieve a bottleneck, let us conceptualize the execution of a program as a *closed queuing network,* and let us conceptualize an atomic operation as a *service center.* This is illustrated in Figure 4a for n processors. The request rate $\lambda(n)$ is the request rate generated by *an acceptable execution speed of the program,* where rate is the reciprocal of mean inter-request time. Keep in mind that since the system is closed, $\lambda(n)$ is a strictly increasing function of program execution rate. In particular, if program execution rate slows down due to congestion in the network, $\lambda(n)$ will slow down accordingly, and this dynamic balancing activity will lead to a processing state of the system that reflects the balanced, or steady, state averaged over time. In analytic terms, this corresponds to a solution to the balance equations for the queuing system. Underlying this slow down, a processor has a fixed number of contexts, and a context can have at most some fixed number of outstanding requests at a time, since its lookahead depth will be limited. Throughout our analysis, the parameters we consider will be time-average steady-state parameters.

It is evident that the atomic operation in Figure 4a will be a bottleneck if the request rate $\lambda(n)$ exceeds the operation service rate $\mu(n)$ for some implementation of the atomic operation. If the computation cannot be restructured to reduce $\lambda(n)$

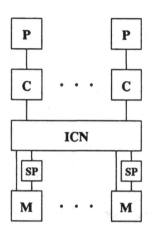

Figure 3a. Centralized Shared-Memory with Caches.

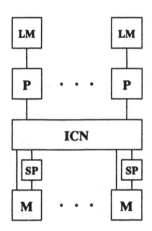

Figure 3b. Centralized Shared-Memory with Local Memories.

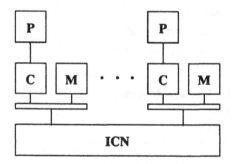

Figure 3c. Distributed Shared-Memory.

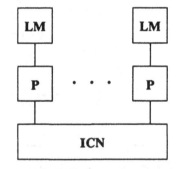

Figure 3d. Message Passing.

Figure 3. Major Architectural Configurations.
P = processor, C = cache, M = main memory, LM = local memory
SP = server processor, ICN = interconnect network

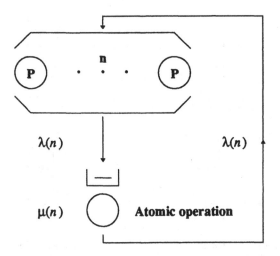

Figure 4a. Closed Queuing Network Model.

$\lambda(n)$ = steady-state request rate

$\mu(n)$ = operation steady-state service rate

Each processor has a fixed number of contexts.

Figure 4. Combining Tree Queuing Model.

P = processor

sufficiently while maintaining the acceptable execution speed of the program, then $\mu(n)$ must be sped up to match $\lambda(n)$. The service rate $\mu(n)$ could be sped up by speeding up the respective processor, memory, and network technologies. However, this will probably speed up the overall system — leaving it still unbalanced with $\lambda(n) > \mu(n)$ — and it will probably, thus, increase the acceptable program execution rate. *Given a fixed technology,* the solution is to speed up $\mu(n)$ by using parallelism, that is, by implementing the atomic operation as a combining tree, and this is possible in an MIMD architecture if the atomic operation is associative and commutative.

Another perspective on $\lambda(n)$ is its behavior when the system is scaled up. If the request rate grows arbitrarily large as the system is scaled, i.e., $\lambda(n) \rightarrow \infty$ as $n \rightarrow \infty$, then the operation service rate must also grow arbitrarily large, i.e., $\mu(n) \rightarrow \infty$ as $n \rightarrow \infty$, but the only means of achieving this is to use parallelism, that is, a combining tree.

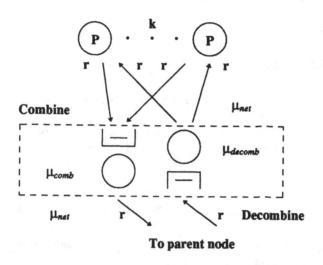

Figure 4b. Node Performance Parameters.

r = processor steady-state request rate, k = node fan-in

$$\mu_{comb} \geq kr, \ \mu_{net} \geq (k+1)r$$
$$1/r = \tau = \text{combining window size}$$

Figure 4 (continued). Combining Tree Queuing Model.

P = processor

Just the same, the idea that a program must be designed such that the request rate $\lambda(n) \rightarrow \infty$, for some object, seems questionable. To illustrate, the original motivation for fetch-and-add was concurrent access to a FIFO queue containing processes to run, or work to execute. If there is only a single queue to serve the respective function for the entire system, then certainly $\lambda(n) \rightarrow \infty$ for that queue. More generally, for $\lambda(n) \rightarrow \infty$, we are talking about a relatively small number of queues compared to the number of processors. For number of queues $q(n)$, we are saying that $n/q(n) \rightarrow \infty$, that is, that the number of processors per queue is unbounded — assuming that the single-processor access rate does not increase in n. However, strict FIFO is normally not necessary, so a more reasonable design would be to have one queue for every l processors, where l yields an acceptable request rate and occupancy level per queue: $q(n) = \lceil n/l \rceil$, making $n/q(n) \leq l$. When a processor wishes to access a queue, it would randomly select a queue for insertion (or else it would randomly select a queue for deletion).

3   PARAMETERS

How do we design a combining tree?

The designer must address the following parameters. The performance parameters are illustrated in Figure 4b. A rate is the reciprocal of mean inter-request time.

- Processor request rate r
- Node rates
  - □ Node combining rate μ_{comb}: The rate at which incoming requests can be combined.
  - □ Node decombining rate μ_{decomb}: The rate at which decombined requests can be produced. We assume $\mu_{decomb} = \mu_{comb}$.
  - □ Network request capacity μ_{net}: The rate at which the network can accept requests.
- Fan-in k
- Combining window size $\tau = 1/r$
- Buffer sizes
  - □ Buffer entry size
  - □ Combining buffer size (the buffer is associative by destination address)
  - □ Decombining buffer size (the buffer is associative by request i.d.)
- Number of combining trees m in the system
  - □ The foregoing parameters are determined per tree.

Regarding the number of combining trees m in the system, a physical combining node must have sufficient processor power and memory space to accommodate all of the trees that it must process, which will be m or fewer trees. If the number of concurrent trees varies over time, then m is the maximum of these numbers.

Regarding processor request rate r, we assume that the program structure is independent of the number of processors n. If a program is rewritten for a larger value of n, then we have a new program for which the combining trees must be reparameterized. Consequently, the processor request rate r — generated by an acceptable program execution speed — is independent of the number of processors n; in particular, r does not increase in n. Note that if $r \equiv r(n)$ could increase in n without bound, $r(n) \rightarrow \infty$, it would be impossible to design a scalable system, since node combining rate μ_{comb} would at some point be exceeded by its incoming request rate $k\, r(n) \to \infty$. Also, if the processor request rate is not the same for all processors, let r be the maximum rate over the processors.

Regarding node combining rate μ_{comb}, we divide the sojourn time of a combine request at a node into three successive intervals.

- *Entry time:* Time from the request's arrival at the node's hardware queue until the node enters the request in its combining buffer, combining it with a request already present (if any).

- *Window time:* Time for which the request is held in the node's combining buffer in order to allow combining with subsequent arrivals.

- *Exit time:* Time from the end of the window time until access to the network is obtained for routing the request to the parent node.

In addition, there are two alternatives for when to move a request from the combining buffer into the decombining buffer, thereby disallowing further combining of it.

- *Pre-exit move:* Move the request into the decombining buffer at the beginning of the exit time. This would be normal for a *software combining node,* for the user will manage the buffers, while the system will manage access to the network.

- *Post-exit move:* Move the request into the decombining buffer at the end of the exit time. This could be done in a *hardware combining node,* since the hardware will manage both the buffers and the network access.

We see, then, that the combining rate μ_{comb} is a node's processing capacity corresponding to the entry time — the rate at which a node can enter incoming requests into its combining buffer. The network request capacity μ_{net} corresponds to the exit time — the rate at which a node can gain access to the network to place outgoing requests into the network. From Figure 4b we see that the node combining rate μ_{comb} must accommodate the incoming request rate, and the network must allow an exit rate μ_{net} that matches the node request rate: we must have $\mu_{comb} \geq kr$, $\mu_{net} \geq (k+1)r$. Clearly the combining rate depends on the node design, so let us look more closely at node design now.

The highest-level decision in the node design is the choice between lock and server synchronization. *Under lock synchronization,* μ_{comb} will normally be affected by the network traffic, since a processor will normally not have a private connection to the memory bank containing a node's buffers. *Under server synchronization,* the primary decision is the choice between hardware and software combining nodes. Hardware combining nodes have the advantage of speed, but they have serious inflexibility disadvantages: inflexibility in the atomic operations they can perform, in the buffer resources they can use, and in the fan-in k. In contrast, implementation of a software combining tree in Figure 3c or 3d, using server synchronization, gives a combining node the power of a CPU, the flexibility of software, and the buffer capacity of a memory bank.

Regarding fan-in k, the fan-in k must be chosen so that the combined request rate of k processors does not exceed the combining rate μ_{comb}: as stated above, we must have $kr \leq \mu_{comb}$. Hence, combining rate μ_{comb} and fan-in k must be considered together in the design of the tree.

For a software combining tree, another consideration with respect to fan-in is *the tradeoff between tree depth and system balance:* greater fan-in k reduces tree depth, $(log_k n) - 1$, but also reduces system balance with respect to that tree since it concentrates the work on fewer physical nodes, namely, $(n-1)/(k-1) \approx n/(k-1)$ nodes. However, if different trees could be dispersed over different physical nodes, then system balance could be maintained across trees rather than within trees, thereby allowing larger k and hence smaller three depth. (The expressions assume that n is a power of k.) For simplicity, in the ensuing analysis we will assume that fan-in k is the same for all m trees.

Combining of requests requires their temporal proximity. Does the proximity need to be ensured?

Combining window. The answer is *yes*. In order to ensure the parallel execution, and hence speed up, that the combining tree is designed to give, it is necessary to observe a *combining window*, an interval of time during which a request is held in a combining node in order to allow it to combine with subsequent incoming requests.

At first glance, one might rebut, "But this will slow the computation down." In fact, it will not slow the computation down if the window has an appropriate size, but to fail to observe a combining window may slow the computation down. For without a combining window, sufficient combining may not occur at the wider levels of the tree (closer to the leaves), so the processing demands may be concentrated on the smaller number of nodes closer to the root. The result is that the request arrival rate at these nodes may exceed their service rate, so the combining tree may not be able to obtain the speed up that it is designed to achieve.

To see this, note that the combining window size appropriate for request rate r, as illustrated in Figure 4b, is $\tau = 1/r$. The window size τ is simply the mean time that it takes k requests to arrive at a node. From the point of view of combining, this allows a steady-state rate of k requests to be combined every $\tau = 1/r$ time units. From the point of view of flow rate through the tree, $\tau = 1/r$ maintains the node steady-state request rate of $r = 1/\tau$.

Now suppose that the combining window is not observed — the window time is zero. Then if two requests at a leaf do not arrive at the same time and if no combining occurs during the exit time, then the requests will not be combined, so the leaf will become invisible for those requests: the requests will pass right through to the parent node, subject to a transit delay through the leaf node.

COMBINING WINDOWS

To make the problem more explicit, let us focus on a group of k sibling processors, and assume that during a time interval I of size τ, each processor sends a request to the group's leaf, *but the requests are mutually staggered,* each arriving in a distinct subinterval of size τ/k. Assume that during the interval I, this also occurs for the other processor sibling groups in the system. Under this scenario, if the combining window is not observed and if no combining occurs during the exit time, then the leaf nodes become invisible (except for the transit delay), and a second-level node will receive requests at the rate of $k^2/\tau = k^2 r$ instead of at the rate of $k/\tau = kr$. This is a worst-case scenario, but it clarifies that if the combining window is not observed, the second-level nodes may receive requests at a rate that exceeds the rate on which the design is based. Specifically, we need τ such that $k/\mu_{comb} \leq \tau \leq 1/r$, but $\tau < 1/r$ wastes network bandwidth, so we want $\tau = 1/r$ in order to maintain system balance.

Continuing our scenario, due to the excessive request rate at the second-level nodes, more combining will occur there, and the third-level nodes will receive a reduced request rate, closer to the design rate kr. But then the third-level nodes will play a role like the leaf nodes, so the fourth-level nodes will receive an excessive rate. This alternation phenomenon will continue through the tree, and the tree will not be processing requests at the needed rate of $\lambda(n) = nr$, due to the loss of parallel execution. For example, the processing that should have occurred at the leaves, but occurs at the second level instead, will proceed at a rate k times slower than at the leaves.

Time/space duality. The problem of speed up that is solved by sufficient *parallel execution* has a dual problem: the problem of node buffer space, which is solved by sufficient *parallel storage*. That is, if the arrival rate at a node exceeds its service rate, not only will the processing rate be too slow, but the node must also store all of those requests, so its buffer space may be exceeded. Thus, the combining window allows us to bound node buffer size.

Window size. A combining window creates a batch request. But when a window closes, the batch may be empty due to the random inter-arrival times of requests. Since an empty batch will not generate a request for the parent node, we want window size, given that an empty window will be subsumed by the next window, to equal $\tau = 1/r$, and this implies that the unconditioned window size will be smaller than τ. Hence, what we really mean by window size τ is the conditioned window size, and for convenience we will continue to speak of window size τ with this implicit qualification.

Now the window sizes need not be constant. In general they are random with mean τ, where constant size is a special case. In particular, window size may be viewed in terms of the *time/space duality*, for mean window size of τ is equivalent to mean batch size of k; that is, each implies the other.

Constant batch size vs. *constant window size.* The simplest window discipline is to close a window every k requests, that is, to define windows by constant batch size. However, this introduces the problem of window-size variance, since it will take a variable amount of time for k successive requests to arrive at a node. From a high-level point of view, *constant batch size* will tend to propagate transient lulls and bursts in processor request rate through the tree, thereby increasing the queue-length variance and the transit-time variance, whereas *constant window size* will tend to smooth out lulls and bursts, thereby decreasing the variances. *Transit-time variance* is important, not only because of its effect on the variance of program execution time, but also due to its effect on the variance of decombining buffer size. We will see the relation between transit time and decombining buffer size below.

In short, we have a tradeoff between batch-size variance — a space variance — and window-size variance — a time variance: constant batch size gives us variable window size, while constant window size gives us variable batch size. Window-size variance, in turn, affects transit-time variance, which affects decombining buffer-size variance, a space variance.

How do we find an upper bound on node buffer size?

Using asymptotic notation, let us determine an upper bound on mean buffer size in terms of parameters n, m, k, r, and d_{root}, which is the distance of a node in question from the root. This is a much simpler task than obtaining the probability distribution, which we address in Bitar (1990 [2]). We will consider buffer entry size, combining buffer size, and decombining buffer size.

Buffer entry size. Let the buffer cell size accommodate c requests, $c \geq k$, and let us speak of cell size as c, ignoring a constant overhead component per cell. A batch entry will comprise some number of cells. Now if batch size is constant, cell size will be $c = k$, and an entry will comprise one cell. However, if batch size is not constant, we may want $c > k$, and more than c requests may arrive during a window. The overflow may be handled either by extending the *entry* — increasing the batch-size variance — or by extending the *window* — increasing the window-size variance. Under the first strategy, of extending the entry, at the arrival of a request $ic + 1$ within a window ($i = 1,2,...$), the entry will be extended, say by linking or rehashing. Under the second strategy, of extending the window, at the arrival of request $c + 1$ within a window, the current entry (containing c requests) will be completed and a new batch will be started, but the window of the new batch will be lengthened by the remaining, unused portion of the prior window. The first of the two strategies, which increases batch-size rather than window-size variance, will have greater effect in smoothing out bursts, and thus in reducing transit-time variance, but at the cost of the complexity of extending an entry. We express mean entry size in terms of k as $\Theta(k)$.

Combining buffer size. The combining buffer for a tree node needs only one entry, hence its mean size is $\Theta(k)$. However, the combining buffer for a physical combining node must, in general, handle multiple trees — m or fewer trees — giving a bound of $O(mk)$ on its mean size.

Decombining buffer size. We need to bound decombining buffer size in terms of the node's level in the tree, since the level will determine the bound, as follows.

- *Absolute bound:* The distance of a node *from the processors* determines the absolute upper bound on decombining buffer size.

- *Probabilistic bound:* The distance of a node *from the root* determines an upper-bound probability distribution for buffer size, and hence an upper bound on mean buffer size.

Now let us see why this is true. As stated earlier, let d_{root} be the distance of a node in question from the root, $0 \le d_{root} \le \lceil \log_k n \rceil - 1$, and let $d_{processor} = \lceil \log_k n \rceil - d_{root}$, which is the distance of the node from the processors. Let us consider the absolute bound, followed by the probabilistic bound.

Absolute bound. The absolute upper bound on decombining buffer size of a node may be determined from $d_{processor}$. Specifically, a processor has a fixed number of contexts, and a context can have at most some fixed number of outstanding requests at a time, since its lookahead depth will be limited. Thus, the absolute upper bound for distance $d_{processor}$ is

(max # requests/node) =

$$(\text{max \# requests/context}) \, (\text{\# contexts/processor}) \, (k^{d_{processor}} \text{ processors/node}) \quad (1)$$

The number of requests is then multiplied by the number of bits per request, but we will ignore this conversion.

Now if batch size were constant, ensuring k-fold combining, then setting $d_{processor} = 1$ in (1) would give us an absolute bound for all nodes. However, under non-constant batch size, k-fold combining for each window closure will not be guaranteed. Consequently, we must determine a probabilistic bound. In fact, even if $d_{processor} = 1$, if (1) is large, buffer size based on (1) may not be feasible, thus requiring a probabilistic bound anyway. Here we determine a bound on the mean, while in Bitar (1990 [2]) we address the probability distribution of buffer size.

Probabilistic/mean bound. Notice that after a combined request leaves a node for the parent node, the mean round-trip transit time to the root is a linear function of the number of tree nodes that must be visited: $2 a_n d_{root} + b$, for some a_n, b. The intercept b represents an adjustment for processing time at the root, so it is independent of n, assuming that processor requests are uniformly distributed across the memory banks, except for those handled by combining trees. The variable a_n is, analogously, a linear function of the mean number of communication links l_n between child and parent, with the coefficient being the mean sojourn time t_n at a link. Thus, the mean round-trip transit time to the root is $\Theta(t_n l_n d_{root})$.

But once a request has been sent, the mean number of additional combined requests that will be sent from the node until the reply for the original request returns is just the mean round-trip transit time divided by $\tau = 1/r$. Once a reply arrives and the original request is decombined, the request will be deleted from the decombining buffer. For if reliable delivery of decombined requests may be a problem, we assume that it will be handled by the network, which will handle each resulting component request individually.

This yields the following results for decombining buffer size. Note that $0 \le d_{root} \le \lceil \log_k n \rceil - 1$, and r_{max} is the maximum request rate over all m trees.

- Mean decombining buffer size

  □ For a tree node: $\Theta(k\, r\, t_n l_n d_{root}) = O(k\, r\, t_n l_n \log_k n)$

  □ For a physical combining node: $O(mk\, r_{max} t_n l_n d_{root}) = O(mk\, r_{max} t_n l_n \log_k n)$

- Absolute decombining buffer size, from (1): $\Theta(n/k^{d_{root}}) = O(n)$

Scalability. Observe that the bound on *mean* size *increases* in d_{root} since it increases in the round-trip transit time to the root, while the bound on *absolute* size *decreases* in d_{root} since it increases in distance from the processors. Thus, for a node at a fixed distance $d_{processor}$ from the processors, as $n \to \infty$, the bound on mean size goes to infinity, while the bound on absolute size remains constant.

On the other hand, for a node at a fixed distance d_{root} from the root, as $n \to \infty$, the bound on absolute size goes to infinity, while the bound on mean size depends on the physical transit time between child and parent in the tree. If this transit time is bounded independently of n, then mean buffer size for the node is bounded as $n \to \infty$, and the system becomes scalable. That is, if the system is scaled up by adding nodes at the leaves, leaving all prior nodes in place, *the buffers for the prior nodes may remain unchanged.* The buffers of the new leaves, however, must be sufficiently larger than the buffers of the prior leaves, in order to accommodate the longer round trip to the root. Notice that the absolute bound is irrelevant to scaling because when a new level is added to the tree, the absolute bound for all prior nodes increases by a factor of k.

Multistage interconnect. Let us illustrate the bound on mean size using a multistage interconnect having $k \times k$ switches. Let us assume that the number of memories is proportional to n, that processor request rate to the memory system is independent of n, and that processor requests are uniformly distributed across the memory banks, except for those handled by combining trees. This makes t_n independent of n, giving us the following bounds.

- For a software combining tree: l_n is $\Theta(\log_k n)$, yielding

  □ Mean size: $O(mk \; r_{max}(\log_k n) \, d_{root})$, which is $O(\log^2 n)$ with respect to n.

- For a hardware combining tree: l_n is one, yielding

  □ Mean size: $O(mk \; r_{max} d_{root})$, which is $O(\log n)$ with respect to n.

Eliminating the decombining buffer. In a system with caches, if coherence is maintained for a block by linking the cached copies into a list, as in the IEEE Scalable Coherent Interface (James et al. 1990 [7]), it is possible to eliminate the decombining buffer of a physical combining node by distributing the decombining information to the respective cache nodes. For software combining nodes, however, the distribution of information serves no useful purpose, since the combining trees should be distributed across the processor nodes in a balanced manner. For hardware combining nodes, one would expect the distribution strategy to incur a substantial performance cost due to the extra traffic and due to the decombining latency, thereby possibly eliminating the speed advantage of hardware combining trees over software combining trees.

How are the parameter values determined and implemented?

Software combining node. A software combining node is under software control, so processor request rate can easily be evaluated during the computation, and window size $\tau = 1/r$ may be incrementally modified, based on an initial estimate. With regard to implementing the combining window, a processor can set a timer trap, and if needed, it can keep additional timing information in a data structure that it consults when a timer trap goes off. The effect of fan-in k may also be evaluated, and k may be changed from execution to execution, as desired.

Note that under lock-synchronized nodes, each node is identified by its pair of buffers, and a processor must be designated as a supervisor for each node, in order to implement the combining window for the node. In order to achieve this, for each tree there would be a mapping from the set of memory banks to the set of processors, and each tree node would be assigned to the processor corresponding the node's memory bank.

Hardware combining node. For a hardware combining node, the situation is much more difficult due to the cost and the inflexibility of hardware implementation. It is necessary to design for an acceptable number of combining trees m, and then estimate the combining buffer size, which is $\Theta(mk)$, and the decombining buffer size having bound on its mean $O(mk \; r_{max} t_n l_n d_{root})$. Hence, the parameters must be determined by modeling and simulation.

In a hardware combining node, the exit time provides a *fortuitous combining window*. But if the mean batch size is less than k in using a fortuitous window, then an explicit window must be implemented. The constant batch-size discipline is the most attractive due to its simplicity. However, if it makes the variance of decombining buffer size too large, as discussed earlier, then a time-based window must be implemented. A time-based window may be implemented by augmenting a combining-buffer entry with a counter that maintains the age of the respective entry, decrementing the value from τ to zero. Since τ will, in general, differ from tree to tree, each request should carry a value of τ with it. A node would then send a request to a parent when the respective combining buffer of the node has an entry that is old enough — an entry with a counter equal to zero. Also notice that in this scheme a processor must dynamically estimate $\tau = 1/r$ for each tree, as in a software combining scheme, and store the information in an associative software table.

Finally, note that for both software and hardware combining nodes, the fraction of a node's busy time that is devoted to a tree is the tree's request rate r divided by the total request rate from a processor to the combining network that contains the node.

4   CONCLUSION

So what have we accomplished?

We have developed the notion of combining tree for an MIMD architecture in a novel way and independent of physical implementation, in order to make the essential aspects clear and to make implementation options clear. We have represented accesses to an atomic operation in terms of a closed steady-state queuing model (Figure 4a). This has enabled us to identify when a combining tree is necessary, and how to parameterize the tree nodes (Figure 4b).

In particular, the model led us to the concept of *combining window*, an interval of time during which a request is held in a combining node in order to allow it to combine with subsequent incoming requests. We then showed that the combining window is necessary in order to realize the dual forms of concurrency — execution and storage concurrency — that a combining tree is designed to achieve.

- *Execution concurrency* among the nodes of a combining tree enables the tree to achieve the *speed up* that it is designed to give. Without sufficient execution concurrency, the tree will not achieve the desired speed up.

- *Storage concurrency* among the nodes of a combining tree enables the tree to achieve the *buffer storage* that is necessary in order to implement the combining of requests. Without sufficient storage concurrency, node buffers will overflow.

More specifically, the combining window allows us to bound node buffer size. For n processors, m combining trees, and fan-in k, an upper bound on the mean decombining buffer size for a physical combining node at distance d_{root} from the root is $O(mk \; r_{max} t_n l_n d_{root})$, where l_n is the mean number of inter-node communication links, t_n is the mean sojourn time of a request at a communication link, and r_{max} is the maximum request rate over all m trees. We illustrated this for a multistage interconnect. In this case, the bound for a software combining node is $O(mk \; r_{max}(\log_k n) d_{root})$, which is $O(\log^2 n)$ with respect to n, while the bound for a hardware combining node is $O(mk \; r_{max} d_{root})$, which is $O(\log n)$ with respect to n.

What concepts relevant to windows have appeared in the literature?

In his dissertation, Ranade (1989 [12]) developed an SIMD combining scheme that is a realization of a concurrent-read-concurrent-write parallel random access machine (CRCW PRAM). The resulting node buffer size is $O(\log n)$, as shown in Chapter 5 of the dissertation. In Chapter 5, Ranade also briefly generalized his SIMD model to an MIMD system by introducing a time parameter τ, such that if a queue in level 0 of the interconnect is empty for time τ, then the respective node will send an end-of-stream message to the next level. The end-of-stream messages propagate through the interconnect.

The effect of the end-of-stream message would be the same as that of a combining window in our scheme if the message were sent whether or not queues were empty. Even so, without the queuing model, it is impossible to determine what the value of τ should be, for it is impossible to quantify its role with respect to overall system performance. Ranade suggests that τ might be as small as the network can handle. Our model clarifies that for one combinable variable, we need $k/\mu_{comb} \leq \tau \leq 1/r$, but $\tau < 1/r$ wastes network bandwidth, so we want $\tau = 1/r$ in order to maintain system balance. In addition, our model clarifies that each combinable variable has its own τ, so ideally each request will carry the τ of its variable and be managed accordingly.

There has been very little published on the topic of combining tree performance evaluation since the original study by Pfister and Norton (1985 [11]), in which they identified the problem of *tree saturation*. In a non-combining network, tree saturation occurs when the buffers of nodes along a pathway to a memory hot spot overflow, forcing the nodes to stop accepting requests. This problem, along with the additional problem of decombining buffer overflow, can occur in a combining network under insufficient combining.

Several papers (Dias, Kumar 1989 [3]; Ho, Eager 1989 [6]) proposed discarding, rather than combining, requests in order to reduce the request rate to a hot spot. While this can alleviate tree saturation, it will slow down program execution speed since the request rate $\lambda(n)$ to the atomic operation will be reduced (Figure 4a). If the negative feedback strategy of Scott and Sohi (1990 [13]) were applied to combine requests, the effect would be similar.

Only one author that we are aware of has identified the issue of degree of combining, pointing out that if the degree of combining is not great enough, then the request rate to parent nodes will exceed their service rate, as we explained in Section 3 (Lee et al. 1986 [8]; Lee 1989 [9]). However, Lee did not provide the general perspective that we have provided in terms of a queuing network; hence, he did not identify the need for combining windows. Lee addressed combining in hardware combining nodes using, what we call, *fortuitous combining windows*. In this context, he pointed out that if buffer entry size is fixed (to keep the hardware simple and fast), the entry size must be larger than fan-in k in order to compensate for the fact that k-fold combining will not occur for some requests due to lack of temporal proximity. Lee also used an open system model, and pointed out that decombining buffer size at the leaves is unbounded as $n \rightarrow \infty$.

We have gone beyond Lee's work to identify the duality of execution and storage concurrency in a combining tree, and to develop the concept of combining window, which solves the dual concurrency problems. In particular, the combining window solves the problem of node buffer overflow by ensuring sufficient combining, and thereby showing how to bound decombining buffer size as a function of distance d_{root} of a node from the root. Here we presented a bound on the mean in terms of asymptotic notation. In Bitar (1990 [2]), we find a bounding probability distribution for buffer size using an M/M/1-based analytic queuing model. We are carrying this research on, developing more realistic analytic models, as well as simulation models, in order to obtain the distribution of node buffer size, and in order to determine the effects on execution speed and node buffer size of different window disciplines.

ACKNOWLEDGEMENTS

I appreciate the support of Al Despain and Vason Srini, directors of the Aquarius research group, as well as my colleagues in the group. I thank Michel Dubois for his criticism, insight, and encouragement of my work. I thank Prof. Ronald Wolff for his comments. This research was partially funded by the Defense Advanced Research Projects Agency (DoD) and monitored by Office of Naval Research under Contract No. N00014-88-K-0579.

REFERENCES

[1] Almasi, G.S., Gottlieb, A. 1989. "The NYU Ultracomputer." Section 10.3.6 in *Highly Parallel Computing*. Benjamin/Cummings, Redwood City, CA, 1989, 430-450.

[2] **Bitar, P. 1990.** "MIMD Synchronization and Coherence." November 1990, Version 90/12/22. Tech. Report UCB/CSD 90/605, Computer Science Division, U.C. Berkeley, Berkeley, CA 94720.

[3] **Dias, D.M., Kumar, M. 1989.** "Preventing congestion in multistage networks in the presence of hotspots." *18th Int'l Conf. on Parallel Processing*, 1989, I-9 - I-13.

[4] **Gottlieb et al. 1983a.** Gottlieb, A., Grishman, R., Kruskal, C.P., McAuliffe, K.P., Rudolph, L, Snir, M. "The NYU Ultracomputer — designing an MIMD shared memory parallel computer." *IEEE Trans. Computers*, C-32(2), February 1983, 175-189.

[5] **Gottlieb et al. 1983b.** Gottlieb, A., Lubachevsky, J., Rudolph, L. "Basic techniques for the efficient coordination of very large numbers of cooperating sequential processes." *ACM Trans. Prog. Lang. and Sys.*, 5(2), April 1983, 164-189.

[6] **Ho, W.S., Eager, D.L. 1989.** "A novel strategy for controlling hot spot congestion." *18th Int'l Conf. on Parallel Processing*, 1989, I-14 - I-18.

[7] **James et al. 1990.** James, D.V., Laundrie, A.T., Gjessing, S., Sohi, G.S. "Scalable Coherent Interface." *Computer*, 23(6), June 1990, 74-77.

[8] **Lee et al. 1986.** Lee, G., Kruskal, C.P., Kuck, D.J. "The effectiveness of combining in shared memory parallel computers in the presence of hot spots." *15th Int'l Conf. on Parallel Processing*, 1986, 35-41.

[9] **Lee, G. 1989.** "A performance bound of multistage combining networks." *IEEE Trans. Computers*, C-38(10), October 1989, 1387-1395.

[10] **Pfister et al. 1985.** "The IBM research parallel processor prototype (RP3): Introduction and architecture." *14th Int'l Conf. on Parallel Processing*, 1985, 764-771.

[11] **Pfister, G.F., Norton, V.A. 1985.** "Hot spot contention and combining in multistage interconnection networks." *IEEE Trans. Computers*, C-34(10), October 1985, 943-948.

[12] **Ranade, A.G. 1989.** "Fluent Parallel Computation." Ph.D. dissertation, May 1989. Tech. Report 663, CS Dept., Yale U., 10 Hillhouse Avenue, New Haven, CT 06511.

[13] **Scott, S.L., Sohi, G.S. 1990.** "The use of feedback in multiprocessors and its application to tree saturation control. *IEEE Trans. Parallel and Distributed Sy.*, 1(4), October 1990, 385-398.

[14] **Yew et al. 1987.** Yew, P.-C., Tzeng, N.-F., Lawrie, D.H. "Distributing hot-spot addressing in large-scale multiprocessors." *IEEE Trans. Computers*, C-36(4), April 1987, 388-395.

Formal Specification of Memory Models

Pradeep S. Sindhu, Jean-Marc Frailong
Xerox Palo Alto Research Center
Palo Alto, CA 94304
and
Michel Cekleov
Sun Microsystems, 1501 Salado Avenue
Mt. View, CA 94043

Abstract

We introduce a formal framework for specifying the behavior of memory systems for shared memory multiprocessors. Specifications in this framework are axiomatic, thereby avoiding ambiguities inherent in most existing specifications, which are informal. The framework makes it convenient to construct correctness arguments for hardware implementations and to generate proofs of critical program fragments. By providing a common language in which a range of memory models can be specified, the framework also permits comparison of existing models and facilitates exploration of the space of possible models. The framework is illustrated with three examples: the well-known Strong Consistency model, and two store ordered models TSO and PSO defined by the Sun Microsystem's SPARC architecture. The latter two models were developed using this framework.

1. Introduction

A multiprocessor consists of some number of processors connected to a memory system. Processors typically interact with the memory system using Loads, Stores, and other synchronization operations such as atomic Load-Store. When running a program, processors execute other operations, such as adding one register to another, or performing a subroutine call, but these operations are irrelevant to the behavior of the memory system as observed by processors. This behavior as observed by processors is called the **memory model**. A **specification** of the memory model is a description of how the memory system *ought* to behave. The main purpose of such a specification is to allow hardware designers and programmers to work independently, while still ensuring that any program will work as intended on any implementation. Ideally, a specification should be formal so conformance to specification can be verified at some level. In practice, however, specifications are informal or worse nonexistent, in which case a particular hardware implementation becomes the specification by default.

This paper introduces a formal framework for specifying memory models. A specification in this framework uses axioms to define the semantics of memory operations, and to establish constraints on the order in which memory operations appear to be executed given the order in which they were issued by processors. The formal nature of such a specification establishes a precise contract between hardware and software, fulfilling its main purpose. The framework makes it convenient to construct correctness arguments for hardware implementations, a property that will be increasingly important as memory models and hardware implementations get more complex in the search for higher performance. It also allows correctness proofs to be generated for short, critical program fragments. Finally, and perhaps most importantly, the framework provides a uniform language to describe a range of memory models from strong to weak, making it easier to compare models and to explore the space of possible models.

The paper begins with the question of why a formal framework is interesting. It then presents the formalism on which the framework is based, and goes on to illustrate the framework by presenting three separate memory models: the familiar Strong Consistency model, and two store ordered models called Total Store Ordering, and Partial Store Ordering. The latter two models define the standard memory model for Sun Microsystem's SPARC architecture [12], and were in fact developed within the framework to be described. Many real system issues, such as dealing with non-coherent caches, code modification, process migration, and incorporating IO locations therefore had to be addressed within the framework. These issues will not be presented in this paper for lack of space, but are mentioned for completeness. The interested reader may find the details in [12].

2. Background

The memory model provided by a shared memory multiprocessor may range anywhere from Strong (or Sequential) Consistency [9], to any of a number of flavors of weak consistency [2], [5], [6], [7]. Strong Consistency is the memory model most people are familiar with. In this model, the memory operations of all processors appear to execute in a single global order that is compatible with the issuing order of individual processors. While this model is intuitively appealing and generally understood, it is also the one that provides the worst performance, especially when the number of processors is large.

Weaker models were developed precisely to allow more efficient implementations of scalable multiprocessors. Unfortunately, weak models are more difficult to understand than Strong Consistency, and all of them constrain the way in which parallel programs can be written. Thus, implementing weaker models requires considerably more care on the part of hardware designers, and using them requires conscious effort on the part of programmers to avoid thinking in terms of the mental model provided by Strong Consistency. For both hardware designers and programmers, informal or unwritten specifications that were barely adequate for Strong Consistency break down for the more complicated weak models.

In spite of these drawbacks, weak models are generally specified for the most part in informal, human language terms. Many specifications make the implicit assumption of global real time without realizing the pitfalls this assumption represents [8]. The potential for making subtle programming or hardware implementation errors exists even with a formal specification. It is considerably greater when the model is specified informally. Thus informal specifications fail to meet their principal goal, which is to permit independent development of virtually error-free components. An added difficulty with informal specification is that it is hard to compare two models to know if they are related to one another in interesting ways. For example, is one model strictly stronger or weaker than the other or are the models equivalent? The ability to compare models in this way is interesting from a theoretical standpoint since it provides structure to the space of memory models. It also has practical utility, because choosing a memory model involves making a compromise between having a model that is strong enough to minimally restrict software yet one that is weak enough to be implemented efficiently; this is a process that invariably requires comparing models with regard to their semantics. Finally, the ability to compare models easily is also helpful in determining whether a given program is portable across different models.

Others have recognized the need for formal specification, but the frameworks used have been either too general [3], [10] making them cumbersome to use for the specific purpose of specifying memory models, or too specialized [11], making them unsuitable for describing a range of models. Both fail to serve as a convenient vehicle for exploring the space of possible models.

We believe that a framework that has as basis partial orders defined over the sets of memory operations provides the appropriate level of generality and specificity for the purpose of specifying memory models. Specifications in such a framework are both easier to understand and easier to manipulate. The use of partial orders gives a specific handle on the problem of verifying machine implementations: physical interpretations of each order can usually be found in the hardware, permitting a one-to-one correspondence to be established between behavior permissible by the hardware and that required by the model. The use of partial orders also appears to be natural in constructing correctness proofs for small, critical program fragments.

3. The Formalism

The formalism that underlies our framework consists of three sets of objects: the set of memory operations, a set of orders defined over the memory operations, and a set of axioms that define the semantics of operations or constrain the possible operation sequences that are legal. The formalism will be illustrated with particular operations, orders, and axioms for the sake of specificity, but it should be understood that the intent is not to limit the framework to just the examples described here.

3.1 Set of Operations

The set of operations consists of all the operations supported by the memory system to be modeled. Typically, this includes Load, Store, and one or more synchronization operations such as atomic Load-Store or Conditional Store.

We will use the memory operations for the SPARC architecture [12] as an example to introduce the notation used for the remainder of the paper. In addition to Load and Store this architecture defines the operations Swap and Stbar (Store barrier). This latter operation has no effect on the contents of memory locations, but is used to maintain the ordering of Stores. Data Loads and Stores are denoted by L and S, respectively. Swaps are denoted by $[L ; S]$, where [] represents atomicity. Stbar is denoted by $\mathcal{S}$. Instruction fetches are denoted by IF. Superscripts on L, S, $\mathcal{S}$, and IF refer to processor numbers, while subscripts on L, S and IF refer to memory locations; $\mathcal{S}$ does not carry subscripts because conceptually it applies to all memory locations. A #n after an S refers to the value written by the S. Thus,

S_a^i #0   denotes a Store of 0 to location a by processor P^i.

L_a^i denotes a Load from location a by processor P^i.

$[L_a^i ; S_a^i$ #1]   denotes a Swap of 1 to location a by P^i.

$\mathcal{S}^i$ denotes an Stbar by processor P^i.

In the axioms that follow, L's and S's refer both to ordinary Loads and Stores and those done as parts of Swap. The value returned by an L or IF or stored by an S is denoted by **Val**[]. **Val** is not defined for $[L ; S]$ as a whole, or for $\mathcal{S}$. Thus,

Val$[L_a^i]$ denotes the value returned by L_a^i.

Val$[S_a^i]$ denotes the value stored by S_a^i.

Op is used to denote either L or S. Note that Op specifically *does not* denote a Swap. Finally, $(Op;)\infty$ denotes the infinite sequence of Op.

3.2 Set of Orders

Order relationships are fundamental to the formalism, so it is useful to define them. A relation $\rightarrow$ is an **order** over a set S if it is

transitive: $(a \rightarrow b) \wedge (b \rightarrow c) \Rightarrow a \rightarrow c$

reflexive: $a \rightarrow a$, and

antisymmetric: $(a \rightarrow b) \wedge (b \rightarrow a) \Rightarrow a = b$

where a, b, and c are elements of S. The order is **total** if for all pairs (a, b) in S either $(a \rightarrow b)$ or $(b \rightarrow a)$, otherwise it is **partial**.

The formalism uses three types of orders defined over the set of memory operations:

- A single partial order $\leq$ called the **memory order**. Intuitively, this order conforms to the order in which operations are performed by memory in real time. The order is partial because not all operations can be compared.

- For each location a a **per-location** total order $\leq_a$ that denotes the order in which operations to location a are performed by the memory system. The existence of these orders places a restriction on the weakest model that can be represented with this notation. We call this restriction single-variable consistency. These orders are not necessary for expressing the three models described in this paper, but are useful for weaker models.

- A per-processor total order $;^i$ that denotes the sequence in which processor i logically executes instructions (for example, as defined by the ISP [1]). This is called the **program order**. The order is total because the instructions corresponding to *all* memory operations of processor i are related by $;^i$. Note that $A ; B$ does not mean that A and B are necessarily consecutive. Also note that unlike the other two orders, this order is not defined directly over the set of memory operations but over the instructions corresponding to these operations. Thus, for example, the notation $S^i ; S^i$ means P^i executed Instruction[S^i] before it executed Instruction[S^i]. The superscript on $;^i$ is dropped when i is obvious from context (the usual case).

3.3 Set of Axioms

The set of axioms describes the semantics of memory operations for a particular model and constrains the possible behaviors that can be observed for the model. As an example, consider the three axioms below:

$$(S_a^i \leq S_b^j) \vee (S_b^j \leq S_a^i)$$

$$L_a^i ; Op_b^i \Rightarrow L_a^i \leq Op_b^i$$

$$\text{Val}[L_a^i] = \text{Val}[\underset{\leq}{\text{Max}} \ \{S_a^k \mid S_a^k \leq L_a^i\}]$$

(We avoid the use of quantifiers where possible, since these are usually obvious from context and would not add to clarity.) The first axiom says that any two Stores must be ordered by ≤. The second axiom says that if a processor does a Load to location a followed in program order by any other memory operation, then these two operations must be ordered by ≤. The third simply provides the intuitive definition of memory, which is that a Load returns the value stored by the "latest" Store to that location. Note that "latest" here has a precise definition provided by the order ≤. Note also that this particular set of three axioms does not necessarily result in a useful model.

4. Specification of Strong Consistency

The Strong Consistency (SC) model is widely understood, so it provides a good first candidate for illustrating our framework. In this model, the Loads, Stores, and Swaps of all processors appear to execute serially in a single global order that conforms to the individual program orders of the processors. Five axioms describe the complete semantics of the Strong Consistency model:

Order states that the partial order ≤ is total over all L's and S's.

$$(Op_a^i \le Op_b^j) \vee (Op_b^j \le Op_a^i)$$

Atomicity says that a Swap is atomic with respect to other S's. That is, no other S can intervene between the L and S parts of a Swap.

$$[L_a^i ; S_a^i] \Rightarrow (L_a^i \le S_a^i) \wedge (\forall S_b^j : S_b^j \le L_a^i \vee S_a^i \le S_b^j)$$

Termination states that all Stores and Swaps eventually terminate. This is formalized by saying that if one processor does an S and another processor repeatedly does L's to the same location, then there will be an L that is after the S in ≤.

$$S_a^i \wedge (L_a^j;)\infty \Rightarrow \exists \text{ an } L_a^j \text{ in } (L_a^j;)\infty \text{ such that } S_a^i \le L_a^j$$

Value states that the value of a Load is the value written by the most recent Store to that location.

$$\text{Val}[L_a^i] = \text{Val}[\underset{\le}{\text{Max}} \ \{S_a^k \mid S_a^k \le L_a^i\}]$$

OpOp states that if two operations appear in a particular order in ; then they must appear in the same order in ≤.

$$Op_a^i ; Op_b^i \Rightarrow Op_a^i \le Op_b^i$$

Figure 1 shows this model graphically for comparison with the axiomatic specification. The memory system consists of a single-port memory that is able to service exactly one operation at a time, and a switch that connects this memory to one of the processors for the duration of each operation. The order in which the switch is thrown from one processor to another determines the global order of operations.

FIGURE 1. The Strong Consistency Model.

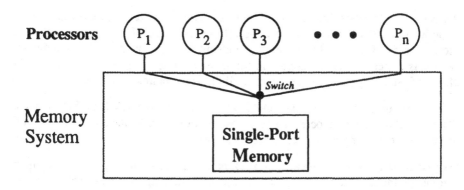

5. Specification of Total Store Ordering

Total Store Ordering (TSO) is one of the two models defined for the SPARC architecture. This model is weaker than SC, and it guarantees that the Stores and Swaps of all processors appear to be executed by memory serially in the memory order $\le$ and that the sequence of operations in $;^i$ is the same as that in $\le$. Before presenting the axioms, we will use Figure 2 to provide an intuitive description of TSO.

FIGURE 2. The Total Store Ordering Model.

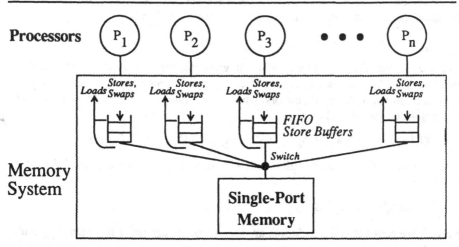

Stores and Swaps issued by a processor are placed in a dedicated store buffer for the processor, which is FIFO. Thus the order in which memory executes these operations for a given processor is the same as the order in which the processor issued them. As for SC, the memory order corresponds to the order in which the switch is thrown from one processor to another.

A Load by a processor first checks its store buffer to see if it contains a Store to the same location. If it does, then the Load returns the value of the most recent such Store. Otherwise, the Load goes directly to memory. Since not all Loads go to memory, Loads in general *do not* appear in the memory order. A processor is logically blocked from issuing further operations until the Load returns a value.

A Swap behaves both like a Load and a Store. It is placed in the Store Buffer like a Store, and it blocks the processor like a Load. In other words, the Swap blocks until the store buffer is empty and then proceeds to memory.

Six axioms describe the semantics of TSO. Note that the Atomicity and Termination axioms are identical to those for SC and for the remaining axioms there is a strong parallel.

Order states that the partial order $\leq$ is total over all S's.

$$(S_a^i \leq S_b^j) \vee (S_b^j \leq S_a^i)$$

Atomicity says that a Swap is atomic with respect to other S's. That is, no other S can intervene between the L and S parts of a Swap.

$$[L_a^i ; S_a^i] \implies (L_a^i \leq S_a^i) \wedge (\forall S_b^j : S_b^j \leq L_a^i \vee S_a^i \leq S_b^j)$$

Termination states that all Stores and Swaps eventually terminate. This is formalized by saying that if one processor does an S and another processor repeatedly does L's to the same location, then there will be an L that is after the S in $\leq$.

$$S_a^i \wedge (L_a^j;)\infty \implies \exists \text{ an } L_a^j \text{ in } (L_a^j;)\infty \text{ such that } S_a^i \leq L_a^j$$

Value states that the value of a Load is the value written by the most recent Store to that location. Two terms combine to define the most recent Store. The first corresponds to Stores by other processors, while the second corresponds to Stores by the processor that issued the Load.

$$\text{Val}[L_a^i] = \text{Val}[\underset{\leq}{\text{Max}} \ [\{S_a^k \mid S_a^k \leq L_a^i\} \cup \{S_a^i \mid S_a^i ; L_a^i\}]]$$

LoadOp states that if an operation follows a Load in ; then it must also follow the Load in $\leq$.

$$L_a^i ; Op_b^i \implies L_a^i \leq Op_b^i$$

StoreStore states that if two Stores appear in a particular order in ; then they must also appear in the same order in $\leq$.

$$S_a^i ; S_b^i \implies S_a^i \leq S_b^i$$

6. Specification of Partial Store Ordering

Partial Store Ordering (PSO) is a performance enhanced version of TSO. This model guarantees that the Stores and Swaps of all processors appear to be executed by memory serially in the memory order $\le$. However, the order of such operations in $;^i$ and $\le$ is not required to be the same in general. Conformance between the two orders is respected only when the two Stores or Swaps are separated in $;^i$ by an Stbar operation. As for TSO, we will first provide an intuitive description of PSO before presenting the axioms.

FIGURE 3. The Partial Store Ordering Model.

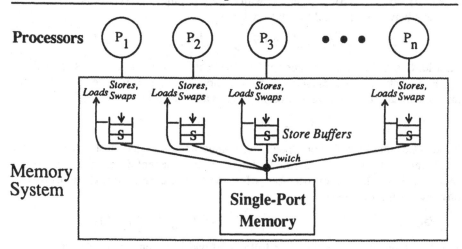

Stores and Swaps issued by a processor are placed in a dedicated store buffer for the processor. This buffer is not guaranteed to be FIFO as it was for TSO; it does maintain the order of Stores and Swaps to the same location, but otherwise it is ordered only by the occurrence of Stbar operations. These operations are shown in the figure as S. Thus the order in which memory executes two Stores or Swaps separated by an Stbar for a given processor is the same as the order in which the processor issued them. As for SC and TSO, the memory order corresponds to the order in which the switch is thrown from one processor to another.

Loads first check the store buffer of the issuing processor to see if it contains a Store to the same location. If it does, then the Load returns the value of the most recent such Store. Otherwise, the Load goes directly to memory. Since not all Loads go to memory, Loads in general *do not* appear in the memory order. A processor is logically blocked from issuing further memory operations until the load returns a value.

A Swap behaves both like a Load and a Store. It is placed in the Store Buffer like a Store, and it blocks the processor like a Load. In other words, the Swap blocks until the store buffer is empty and then proceeds to memory.

Seven axioms describe the semantics of PSO. Note that the Order, Atomicity, Termination, Value, and LoadOp axioms are identical to those for TSO. The only difference is that the StoreStore axiom now splits into two axioms: StoreStore and StoreStoreEq.

Order states that the partial order $\leq$ is total over all S's.

$$(S_a^i \leq S_b^j) \vee (S_b^j \leq S_a^i)$$

Atomicity says that a Swap is atomic with respect to other S's. That is, no other S can intervene between the L and S parts of a Swap.

$$[L_a^i ; S_a^i] \implies (L_a^i \leq S_a^i) \wedge (\forall S_b^j : S_b^j \leq L_a^i \vee S_a^i \leq S_b^j)$$

Termination states that all Stores and Swaps eventually terminate. This is formalized by saying that if one processor does an S and another processor repeatedly does L's to the same location, then there will be an L that is after the S in $\leq$.

$$S_a^i \wedge (L_a^j;)\infty \implies \exists \text{ an } L_a^j \text{ in } (L_a^j;)\infty \text{ such that } S_a^i \leq L_a^j$$

Value states that the value of a Load is the value written by the most recent Store to that location. Two terms combine to define the most recent Store. The first corresponds to Stores by other processors, while the second corresponds to Stores by the processor that issued the Load.

$$\text{Val}[L_a^i] = \text{Val}[\underset{\leq}{\text{Max}} \ [\{S_a^k \mid S_a^k \leq L_a^i\} \cup \{S_a^i \mid S_a^i ; L_a^i\}]]$$

LoadOp states that if an operation follows a Load in ; then it must also follow the Load in $\leq$.

$$L_a^i ; Op_b^i \implies L_a^i \leq Op_b^i$$

StoreStore states that if two Stores are separated by an Stbar in ; then the Stores must appear in the same order in $\leq$.

$$S_a^i ; \mathcal{S} ; S_b^i \implies S_a^i \leq S_b^i$$

StoreStoreEq states that if two Stores to a given location appear in a particular order in ; then they must also appear in the same order in $\leq$. This reflects the fact that memory executes Stores to a given location in the order in which they were issued by a processor even though the processor did not separate them by an Stbar.

$$S_a^i ; S'_a{}^i \implies S_a^i \leq S'_a{}^i$$

7. Proof Examples

We will use three examples to show how short, critical program fragments can be proven correct in the framework just described. The three fragments are *Critical Sections*, *Indirection Through Processors*, and *Dekker's Algorithm*. Each program fragment is first shown as it would be written for Strong Consistency and then for PSO, followed by the proof for PSO.

It is convenient to use graphical notation to illustrate the proofs. If two memory operations A and B have the relationship $A \leq B$ then we will show this as a directed graph with A and B as points connected by an arc *from A to B*. Also, we will label arcs derived via the axioms with the names of the axioms used in the derivation.

7.4 Critical Sections

This example consists of two processors P^1 and P^2 trying to enter a critical section. The variable x is used to protect the critical section, and a and b are variables referenced inside the critical section. What we show below is the execution sequence for the two processors in the case where each processor is successful in entering the critical section. Thus both Swaps observe 0 on entry.

P^1	P^2
Swap #1, x	Swap #1, x
Load b	Load a
Store #1, a	Store #1, b
Store #0, x	Store #0, x

We want to guarantee that the effect of any interleaving of these sequences is the same as if either (i) all the operations of P^1's critical section are executed before any of the operations of P^2's critical section, or (ii) all the operations of P^2's critical section are executed before any of the operations of P^1's critical section. This is the classical correctness requirement for critical sections, and it is satisfied by the above code when the memory model is strongly consistent.

7.4.1 Execution Sequence for PSO

P^1	P^2
$[L_x^1 ; S_x^1$ #1] $(Val[L_x^1]=0)$	$[L_x^2 ; S_x^2$ #1] $(Val[L_x^2]=0)$
L_b^1	L_a^2
S_a^1	S_b^2
S^1	S^2
S_x^1 #0	S_x^2 #0

7.4.2 Proof

We begin by assuming that the L's and S's shown above are the only memory operations in the universe. Without this assumption, nothing can be proved because spurious Stores could violate any correctness criterion. The initial value of x is 0 before either $\mathbf{P}^1$ or $\mathbf{P}^2$ is started. Also, recall that since these each processor's sequence represents successful entry, the initial value of x seen by each Swap is 0; that is, $\mathbf{Val}[L_x^1]=0$ and $\mathbf{Val}[L_x^2]=0$. From the code of the two processors, we can directly derive the relations shown in Figure 4 via solid arcs.

FIGURE 4. Illustration for Proof of Critical Sections.

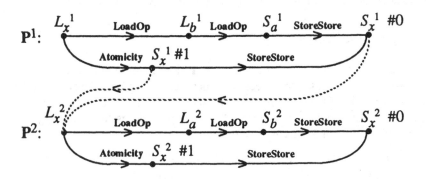

From **Order** and **Atomicity** we can derive that the L's and S's of Swaps are ordered by $\le$ such that either $(L_x^1 \le S_x^1 \,\#1 \le L_x^2 \le S_x^2 \,\#1)$ or $(L_x^2 \le S_x^2 \,\#1 \le L_x^1 \le S_x^1 \,\#1)$. If the L's and S's were not so ordered, we would violate **Atomicity** because the S of one of the Swaps would lie between the L and S of the other Swap. Without loss of generality, we can assume that $(L_x^1 \le S_x^1 \,\#1 \le L_x^2 \le S_x^2 \,\#1)$. The central part of this relation is shown in the above figure as the leftmost dotted arc.

From **Atomicity**, we know that $(S_x^1 \,\#0 \le L_x^2) \vee (S_x^2 \,\#1 \le S_x^1\#0)$. Assuming that the second term is true leads us to conclude that $\mathbf{Val}[L_x^2]$ is 1, which contradicts the assertion $\mathbf{Val}[L_x^2]=0$. Thus the first term must be true, or $(S_x^1 \,\#0 \le L_x^2)$. This relation is shown by the rightmost dotted arc in Figure 4.

By transitivity of $\le$ we conclude that $S_a^1 \le L_a^2$, and so from **Value** that $\mathbf{Val}[L_a^2] = \mathbf{Val}[S_a^1]$.

We show $\mathbf{Val}[L_b^1] \ne \mathbf{Val}[S_b^2]$ by contradiction: If we assume that the values are equal, we can apply **Value** to conclude that $S_b^2 \le L_b^1$. This causes a circularity in the relation $\le$, which we know to be impossible. Therefore $\mathbf{Val}[L_b^1] \ne \mathbf{Val}[S_b^2]$.

This completes the proof.

7.5 Indirection Through Processors

This example involves communication between two processors P^1 and P^3 that occurs indirectly through another processor P^2. Initially, $a=b=c=0$.

P^1	P^2	P^3
Store #1, a	Load b	Load c
Store #1, b	Store #1, c	Load a
		Load b

P^1 does two Stores; P^2 waits for b to become 1 before issuing the Store c; and P^3 waits for c to become 1 before issuing the Loads to a and b. As before, we do not show wait loops, but only the execution sequence for the successful case. For Strong Consistency, the only legal values for a and b in P^3 are $a=b=1$, and this is our correctness condition.

7.5.1 Code Sequence for PSO

P^1	P^2	P^3
S_a^1 #1	L_b^2 (Val[L_b^2]=1)	L_c^3 (Val[L_c^3]=1)
S^1	S_c^2 #1	L_a^3
S_b^1 #1		L_b^3

7.5.2 Proof

As before, we assume that the L's and S's shown above are the only memory operations in the universe. From the execution sequences of the three processors, we can directly derive the relations shown in Figure 5 via solid arcs.

FIGURE 5. Illustration for Proof of Indirection Through Processors.

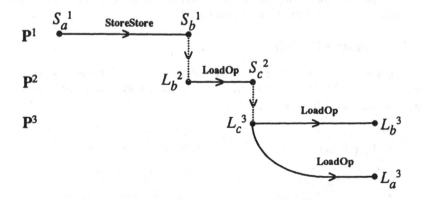

Since $\text{Val}[L_b{}^2] = \text{Val}[S_b{}^1]$, and $\text{Val}[L_c{}^3] = \text{Val}[S_c{}^2]$, we can use **Value** once for each equality to derive that

$$S_b{}^1 \le L_b{}^2 \text{ and } S_c{}^2 \le L_c{}^3$$

These new relations are shown by dotted arcs in the above figure. By transitivity of $\le$ we have

$$S_a{}^1 \le L_a{}^3 \text{ and } S_b{}^1 \le L_b{}^3$$

Finally, by applying **Value** we have $\text{Val}[L_a{}^3] = \text{Val}[S_a{}^1]$ and $\text{Val}[L_b{}^3] = \text{Val}[S_b{}^1]$. This completes the proof.

7.6 Dekker's Algorithm

Dekker's algorithm is the classical sequence for synchronizing entry into a critical section for two processors using only Loads and Stores [4]. We show the execution sequences for successful entry for two processors $\mathbf{P}^1$ and $\mathbf{P}^2$. Initially $c=d=0$. Note that the execution sequence consists of *only* the instructions used for entry; the instructions used for exit are *not* present.

$\mathbf{P}^1$	$\mathbf{P}^2$
Store #1, c	Store #1, d
Load d (observes 0)	Load c (observes 0)
\<begin critical section\>	\<begin critical section\>

We want to show that the effect of any interleaving of these sequences is identical to what would have happened had the processors taken an exclusive lock to enter the critical section (see the Critical Section example). $\mathbf{P}^1$ enters its critical section only if it finds $d=0$ and $\mathbf{P}^2$ enters its critical section only if it finds $c=0$. Thus we want to show that we can never have $\text{Val}[L_c]=0$ and $\text{Val}[L_d]=0$.

Once this is proved, we can use this primitive in place of Swap in the entry sequence of a critical section as, for example, in Section 7.4.

7.6.1 Code Sequence for PSO

It is not possible to implement Dekker's algorithm in PSO using just Loads and Stores because PSO is too weak. However, if we replace the Stores by Swaps, then Dekker's works as in Strong Consistency.

$\mathbf{P}^1$	$\mathbf{P}^2$
$[L_c{}^1 ; S_c{}^1 \ \#1]$	$[L_d{}^2 ; S_d{}^2 \ \#1]$
$L_d{}^1 \ (\text{Val}[L_d{}^1]=0)$	$L_c{}^2 \ (\text{Val}[L_c{}^2]=0)$
\<begin critical section\>	\<begin critical section\>

Note that the value returned by the Swap is discarded, so we are using Swap just for its blocking semantics.

7.6.2 Proof

As usual, we assume that the L's and S's shown above are the only memory operations in the universe. From the code of the two processors, we can directly derive the relations shown in Figure 6 by solid arcs.

FIGURE 6. Illustration for Proof of Dekker's Algorithm.

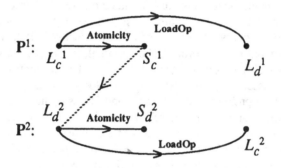

From **Order** and **Atomicity** we can derive that the L's and S's of Swaps are ordered by $\leq$ such that either $(L_c^1 \leq S_c^1 \ \#1 \leq L_d^2 \leq S_d^2 \ \#1)$ or $(L_d^2 \leq S_d^2 \ \#1 \leq L_c^1 \leq S_c^1 \ \#1)$. If the L's and S's were not so ordered, we would violate **Atomicity** because the S of one of the Swaps would lie between the L and S of the other Swap. Without loss of generality, we can assume that $(L_c^1 \leq S_c^1 \ \#1 \leq L_d^2 \leq S_d^2 \ \#1)$. The central part of this relation is shown in the above figure as a dotted arc.

By transitivity of $\leq$ it follows that $S_c^1 \leq L_c^2$. Now, from **Value** and the fact that there is no other S_c, we can deduce that

$$\text{Val}[L_c^2] = \text{Val}[S_c^1].$$

Similarly, by assuming that $(L_d^2 \leq S_d^2 \ \#1 \leq L_c^1 \leq S_c^1 \ \#1)$ we can show that

$$\text{Val}[L_d^1] = \text{Val}[S_d^2].$$

Thus we have shown that either $\text{Val}[L_c^2]=1$ or $\text{Val}[L_d^1]=1$, or both. In other words, we cannot have L_c^2 observing $c=0$ and L_d^1 observing $d=0$, which completes the proof.

8. Conclusion

We have presented a formal framework for specifying memory models for shared memory multiprocessors. Three memory models were specified in this framework for purpose of illustration: the familiar Strong Consistency model, the SPARC Total Store Ordering model, and the SPARC Partial Store ordering model. The framework was shown to be formal enough to carry out proofs of small, but critical program fragments.

Four system level issues that have been addressed within the framework were not presented in this paper for lack of space. The first of these is that for a specification to be useful to a programmer, the axioms must be stated in terms of "processes" not "processors". To do this, we must have a process switch sequence and show that for each axiom we can replace every occurrence of ; by the process switch sequence, while maintaining the axiom true. In order to be practical, this process switch sequence must also be reasonably efficient in terms of the number of memory operations required. The second issue is the incorporation of IO locations into the memory model. IO locations present a problem because Loads and Stores to them typically have side effects in addition to, or even in lieu of, the normal semantics of Load and Store. Moreover, the semantics are typically different for different locations. The third issue is code modification. For loading code, for placing breakpoints, and for dynamically replacing procedures during run time it is essential to have precise semantics of Stores or Swaps to instructions. In the SPARC architecture synchronization of code modification is accomplished through the use of the FLUSH instruction for which detailed semantics are provided in the TSO and PSO models in [12]. Finally, the framework has also addressed the issue of how to incorporate pipelined processors and processors with non-coherent internal caches. Again, the interested reader is referred to the SPARC architecture manual for details.

During the development of the TSO and PSO models, we examined a number of weak models, some of which were considerably weaker than PSO and others which were in between PSO and TSO. These models were not presented here for reasons of space, but they provide an indication of the expressive power of the framework.

We have also used our framework to sketch out correctness arguments for machine implementations of TSO and PSO. As alluded to earlier, the key idea is to establish a correspondence between the model's behavior and the machine's by using the various orders in the framework. The techniques used will be the subject of a future paper.

Finally, as weaker and more complex memory models begin to be used more widely in the search for higher performance, we expect formal specification of models to become more popular once the limitations of informal techniques are realized. This paper offers a powerful, yet simple framework within which many of these models can be described, yielding most of the benefits of formal specification.

9. Acknowledgments

The development of this framework was helped by discussions with Cesar Douady, Eric Jensen, Steve Kleiman, and Mike Powell. We thank them for their contributions.

10. References

[1] C. G. Bell and A. Newell, "Computer Structures: Readings and Examples", McGraw-Hill, N.Y., 1971.

[2] S.V. Adve and M.D. Hill, "Weak Ordering - A new definition", *Proceedings of the 17th International Symposium on Computer Architecture, 1990.*

[3] W. Collier, "Principles of architecture for systems of parallel processes", Tech. Report TR00.3100, IBM T.J. Watson Research Center, Yorktown Heights, N.Y., March 1981.

[4] E. Dijkstra, "Solution of a problem in concurrent programming control", *CACM*, Vol 8, No 9, September 1965.

[5] M. Dubois, C. Scheurich, and F. Briggs, "Synchronization, Coherence and Ordering of Events in a Multiprocessor", IEEE Computer, Vol 21, No 2, February 1988.

[6] K. Gharacharloo, D. Lenoski, J. Laudon, P. Gibbons, A. Gupta, and J. Hennessy, "Memory Consistency and Event Ordering in Scalable Shared-Memory Multiprocessors", *Proceedings of the 17th International Symposium on Computer Architecture, 1990.*

[7] J. Goodman, "Cache consistency and sequential consistency", Tech. Report 61, IEEE SCI Committee P1596.

[8] L. Lamport, "Time, Clocks, and the Ordering of Events in a Distributed System", CACM, Vol 21, No 7, July 1978.

[9] L. Lamport, "How to make a multiprocessor computer that correctly executes multiprocess programs", IEEE *Trans on Computers*, C-28(9), September 1979.

[10] B. Lampson, "Specifying Distributed Systems", Tech. Report, Cambridge Research Laboratory, Digital Equipment Corp, November 1988.

[11] J. Misra, "Axioms for Memory Access in Asynchronous Hardware Systems", ACM TOPLAS, Vol 8, No 1, January 1986.

[12] "SPARC Architecture Reference Manual V8", Sun Microsystems, December 1990.

An Example of Correct Global Trace Generation *

Mark A. Holliday and Carla S. Ellis
Department of Computer Science
Duke University
Durham, NC 27706
holliday@cs.duke.edu and carla@cs.duke.edu

Abstract

The memory reference trace of a parallel program is strongly
dependent on the memory architecture and memory management
policy environment. A change in that environment can change the
addresses in the trace as well as the interleaving of the addresses.
We have examined the issue of ensuring that the generated global
trace is correct for the new environment. In this paper we summarize the key results and informally illustrate the proposed method
using an example parallel program.

INTRODUCTION

An important technique in computer architecture and operating system
performance evaluation is trace-driven simulation using address references [2]. In uniprocessor trace-driven simulation a workload of application programs and, sometimes, operating system code is executed and
its address reference trace collected. The trace is then used as input
to a simulator that considers alternative system features (such as cache
sizes). In the uniprocessor context the validity of the trace under the
alternative system features is generally not an issue [6].

In the multiprocessor case, however, trace validity is much more of
an issue. To understand the problem we first introduce some terminology. We assume that the system being simulated is synchronous in that

---

*This work was supported in part by the National Science Foundation (Grants
CCR-8721781 and CCR-8821809).

all activity is divided into clock cycles. The activity of interest is the sequence of *loads* and *stores* that each process generates as memory references. We consider three significant points in the lifetime of a load or store: the clock cycle at which it is *issued* by its processor, the clock cycle at which the operation is *performed* at the memory, and the clock cycle at which the operation *completes*. The operation completes at the cycle when the processor is notified that the operation has been performed. We also assume that loads and stores are synchronous in the sense that a processor cannot issue another load or store until its previous load or store has completed.

In order to make the definition of being performed at a given cycle meaningful, we further assume that the system is *sequentially consistent* (the extension to non-sequentially consistent environments is discussed elsewhere [3]). A system environment is sequentially consistent if "the result of any execution is the same as if the operations of all the processors were executed in some sequential order, and the operations of each individual processor appear in this sequence in the order specified by its program." [4]. This allows a load or store to be viewed as taking effect atomically with respect to all other references to the same address.

Figure 1 shows the framework we assume for a multiprocessor trace-driven simulator. The code that a particular process instantiates is its *process program*. The trace of a single process's address references is its *process trace*. A traditional process trace contains the sequence of loads and stores issued by that process and the number of clock cycles between the completion of one reference and the issue of the next reference. The interleaving of process traces that occurs in a particular environment is called the *global trace*. The simulator generates the global trace using the process traces, the *environment parameters*, and the current *global trace prefix*. Environment parameters include any feature of the system that can change the time between issuing consecutive references for a process. Such features can be architectural (processor speed, network access time) or operating system-based (the policy that determines which memory contains a particular address). The global trace prefix is the portion of the global trace up to the current cycle. This prefix includes the state of issued references that have not completed.

For such a deterministic simulation, there exists a single, reproducible global trace for a fixed set of data inputs to the process programs and a

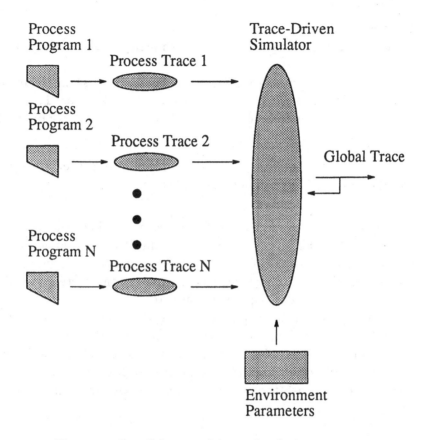

Figure 1: Parallel trace-driven simulation.

fixed environment (given some consistent ordering convention for events occurring within the same clock cycle). When simulating an environment, E, different from the one in which the process traces were collected, an important issue is whether the generated global trace is correct in that it is the same as the global trace that results from executing the parallel program in environment E. It is straightforward to have changes in environment parameters cause the global trace to change in that the relative ordering of the memory operations change. Such changes can be accounted for in the simulator.

The serious problem is that it is possible for the addresses in the load/store sequence of a process trace to change. This problem we have named the *global trace problem* [3]. As an example consider the program fragment in Figure 2. Whether or not process 1 has already set the variable *flag* at statement B when process 0 executes its statement A

Process 0			Process 1		
shared	int	flag=0;	shared	int	flag=0;
A:		if flag = 1 goto C;	A:		< something >
B:		<something>	B:		flag := 1;
C:		<something else>	C:		< something else >

Figure 2: A race condition makes the address sequence in the process trace of process 0 environment dependent.

determines the next address issued by process 0. The relative timing of the accesses to the variable *flag* is environment-dependent; for example, it might depend on the placement of *flag* in memory. This problem is not simply one of interleaving, so constructing the correct global trace for a new environment requires further steps.

In a companion paper [3] we identify the global trace problem and present a solution. In this paper we illustrate that solution method using an example parallel program. In the next section we summarize the proposed method for the sequentially consistent case. In the third section, we illustrate the method on an example program. Finally, we summarize.

METHOD

In this section we summarize the main points about the solution method in the sequentially consistent case. See the companion paper [3] for the details and extensions. Our summary divides into three subsections: characterizing the aspects of a program that cause the global trace problem, the *intrinsic trace* extension of the traditional process trace, and the actions taken by the simulator to decide what references to issue during a given cycle.

Causes of the Global Trace Problem

We consider programs that can be expressed in a certain three-address intermediate code format [1]. This format is quite general and does not significantly restrict the class of programs considered. The traditional binary and unary operators exist including *TestAndSet(x)* which, as an atomic unit, sets the value of x to 1 and returns the previous value of x. Statement forms include assignment statements, unconditional branch statements, conditional branch statements, indexed assignment statements, and address and pointer assignment statements. Each intermediate code statement corresponds to a sequence of load and stores. The sequence of load and stores is needed by the simulator. However, we primarily discuss programs at the more readable intermediate statement level which can be done without substantive restrictions on the programs considered.

The first step is to characterize the aspects of a parallel program that can cause the global trace problem. It would be desirable to define an *address change point(ACP)* to be an instance of the issue of a reference by a process if the address to be issued is environment-dependent. Within our intermediate code format, it is clear that such an ACP can only occur within three intermediate code statements: conditional branch statements, indexed assignment statements, and pointer assignment statements. However, it is not clear how, in general, to determine if a reference is environment-dependent. Consequently, we define an ACP in terms of a somewhat broader class that is easier to identify.

A variable is called a *shared variable* if it is possible that during some execution, more than one process will reference it. Variables that are not shared variables are called *private variables*. A private variable is said to *depend* on a shared variable if there exists at least one execution in which a change in the value of the shared variable causes a change in the value of the private variable. If the index of an indexed assignment statement or the pointer of a pointer assignment statement is a shared variable or a private variable that depends on a shared variable, then the load or store using the contained address is an ACP. The index or pointer involved is called an *ACP operand*. If one of the operands to the relational operator of a conditional branch statement is a shared variable or a private variable that depends on a shared variable, then there is said to be an ACP immediately after the loads and stores of the branch (more precisely, at the issue of the next instruction fetch). The operands that cause there to be an ACP are called ACP operands.

Recall a few terms from compiler optimization theory [1]. The *def-*

inition of a variable x is an intermediate code statement that assigns a value to x. A definition d *reaches* an intermediate code statement p if d might be the place at which the value of x used at p was last defined. Each *use* of a variable has a *use-definition chain* or a *ud-chain* which is a list of all the definitions that reach that use.

We use the concept of ud-chains to identify the *address affecting points (AAPs)* that are associated with a particular ACP. Still at the intermediate code level, we introduce the *affects* relation. We say that a definition of a variable y at a statement p_1 *directly affects* a definition of a variable x at statement p_2 (x might be y) if that definition of x is also a use of the variable y and the definition of y at statement p_1 is in the ud-chain of that use of variable y at statement p_2. If we view *directly affects* as a relation between statements p_1 and p_2, then we define the *affects* relation as the transitive closure. The affects relation is translated to the load/store trace level by considering loads as uses and both loads and stores as definitions (since a load may constitute the definition of a value in a register).

We say that the set of AAPs associated with an ACP A consists of the performs of the loads and stores that are in the affects relation for at least one definition that is in the ud-chain of an ACP operand of A. Note that a statement containing an AAP need not be in the same process program as the statement containing its associated ACP. The usefulness of AAPs is discussed in the next subsection.

Intrinsic Traces

Now that we have identified what causes the global trace problem, we want to propose a solution that allows the use of trace-driven simulation with assurance of correctness. In a strict sense, a solution is not possible in that a traditional process trace as a sequence of addresses references is inadequate. A required step, consequently, is to generalize the traditional process trace so as to allow a solution. We contend that the key concept of trace-driven simulation is to decouple program execution (which generates the trace) from simulation in the new environment. Consequently, our generalization of traces, called *intrinsic traces*, is the modification to traditional traces that allows a solution to the global trace problem while maximizing the decoupling of program execution from simulation.

In analogy with the compiler concepts of a *basic block* and a *flow graph*, we define the *address basic blocks* and the *address flow graph* of a process program. An address basic block (ABB) is a sequence of intermediate code statements that is started either at the statement after a conditional branch statement that has an ACP or is started at the target statement of such a branch statement. The address basic block ends with a conditional branch statement that is an ACP or the instruction before the target statement of such a branch statement. Each process program can be viewed as a directed graph of address basic blocks. This directed graph is called the address flow graph for that process program. During one execution of a parallel program each process follows one *path* through the address flow graph of that process.

The intrinsic trace of a process consists of the ABBs organized into the address flow graph. For an ABB three classes of information are kept. First, is the trace of loads and stores that an execution of the ABB generates including the actual addresses when those are known. The only unknown addresses are at the ACPs for the array component of an indexed assignment and the pointer address in a pointer assignment (the direction taken at ACP conditional branches are implicitly unknown addresses). Second, is the inter-reference durations for a given processor speed. Third, is a marker at each AAP and a *path expression* at each ACP.

For a given environment and data inputs, the next address to issue at an ACP is determined by the current global trace prefix. One can enumerate the set of global trace prefixes possible at a particular ACP and partition them according to the corresponding next address. Listing all the global path prefixes associated with each possible next address at each ACP is clearly unattractive. AAPs are of interest because this enumeration-based approach can be replaced by a simpler one defined in terms of the AAPs.

The *process path prefix* of a process is the sequence of load and store performs by that process before the current cycle. The set of process path prefixes, one per process, at a given cycle is the *global path prefix (GPP)* at that cycle. For an ACP, the *complete path prefix (CPP)* is the union of the global path prefixes at the cycle its process was at this ACP (meaning about to issue the address) and at the cycles when the various processes involved were at the AAPs (that is, the cycle at which the load or store was performed) for this ACP. Note that if a particular process executes a particular AAP multiple times, then the GPP of each of the instantiations is in the CPP.

As discussed in the companion paper any two global trace prefixes that map to the same complete path prefix, also have the same next address. Thus, the enumeration of sets of global trace prefixes at an ACP can be replaced by the enumeration of sets of complete path prefixes. As a further simplification, a *path expression* can replace the explicit enumeration of sets by a formalism using regular expression notation. In the companion paper we formally introduce this regular expression notation. Because of space constraints, in this paper we use an informal prose version of the path expressions in the development of the example program.

Simulator Actions

The steps taken by the simulator are straightforward. For a given environment the simulator starts processing each process's process trace to produce a global trace. Between ACPs the process traces are address reference sequences that are issued with timing and interleaving influenced by the environment. When an AAP of an ACP is encountered that is used in that ACP's path expression, then the parts of the AAP's complete path prefix used in the path expression are saved. When an ACP is reached, the parts of its complete path prefix that are used in its path expression have been saved or are current knowledge. That information is used to determine which partition this prefix is in. The next address associated with that partition is issued.

In the above method the difficult part is the static construction of the path expressions. For a given partition of complete path prefixes, one aspect is finding a succint regular expression that describes that partition. The second and more difficult aspect is determining what complete path prefixes are associated with different next addresses and what those next addresses are. For this second aspect, one approach that always works is to reexecute the program or the needed subset of the program. This of course defeats the purpose of trace-driven simulation (to avoid program reexecution for each environment). In some cases, the possible next addresses and their associated complete path prefixes can be determined by inspection of the program. In our opinion, it is not clear, how to formalize the distinction between when inspection at an ACP is adequate (which we call *graph-traceable* ACPs) and when it is not.

EXAMPLE PROGRAM

Our example program uses the *microtasking* approach. In this approach the main thread adds a set of work items to a work queue and then forks a thread onto each processor. Each thread executes a loop that repeatedly takes an item from the work queue and processes it until all the work items are processed. The source code (loosely based on an example in [5]) for the example program is shown in Figure 3 in the C programming language. The point of the program is to find the distance (say, along a railroad line) between each city in the *cities* array and a given city, *Durham*. The city closest to *Durham* is also identified. All the cities processed by the same processor are linked together by the *next* fields. The intermediate code for the *find_dist* function is shown in Figure 4. The load/store sequence for the statement H is shown in Figure 5.

The address basic blocks are *AB, CDEF, GH, IJ, K, L, MNO, PQ, RSTU*. In Table 1 each of the ACPs is listed, divided into those due to conditional branches and those due to array assignments (there are no pointers in the program). For each ACP, its AAPs and its path expression code are listed. In listing the AAPs recall that each process has a copy of this code. Consequently, the AAPs also refer to those statements in the copies executed by other processes. For example, consider the ACP in statement *H*. A private variable, *local_loop*, is assigned in this process's statement *C* or *R*. That definition of *local_loop* is a use of the shared variable *loop*. That use of *loop* could have been defined by statement *D* or *S* of any process. Those statements also only use *loop* so they have themselves as their definitions all the way back to the initialization of *loop*.

Table 2 lists informal prose descriptions for each path expression code. These descriptions can be formalized; however, the prose is adequate for the intuitive understanding sought in this paper. The complexity of the path expressions varies. The simplest are (1) and (3) where the complete path prefix at the ACP is sufficient; that is, the path pre-

```
shared    int      closest = 9999.0;
shared    int      loop_lock = 0;
shared    int      short_lock = 0;
shared    int      durham;
shared    int      loop = 0;
shared    int      cities[MAX_CITIES];
shared    char     city_names[MAX_CITIES][MAX_NAME];

main()
{
m_fork(find_dist, cities);
printf("%s is closest to Durham.", city_names[closest]);
}

void find_dis(cities)
struct location cities[];
{
int       local_loop;
int       last_local_loop = NIL;
int       city_dist[MAX_CITIES];
int       city_next[MAX_CITIES];

m_lock(loop_lock);
local_loop = loop++;
m_unlock(loop_lock);
if (local_loop < MAX_CITIES) {
        city_dist[local_loop] = cities[local_loop] - durham;
        m_lock(short_lock);
        if (city_dist[local_loop] < closest)
                closest = city_dist[local_loop];
        m_unlock(short_lock)
        city_next[last_local_loop] = local_loop;
        last_local_loop = local_loop;
        m_lock(loop_lock);
        local_loop = loop++;
        m_unlock(loop_lock);
}
```

Figure 3: Source code for the example program.

```
shared    int        loop_lock = 0;
shared    int        short_lock = 0;
shared    int        loop = MAX_CITIES;
shared    int        closest = 9999.0;
shared    int        city_dist[MAX_CITIES];
shared    int        cities[MAX_CITIES];
shared    int        city_next[MAX_CITIES];
shared    int        durham;
shared    int        loop = 0;
          int        val;
          int        local_loop;
          int        last_local_loop = NIL;
```

```
find_dis(cities)
A:        val = TestAndSet(loop_lock);
B:        if val = 1 goto A;
C:        local_loop = loop;
D:        loop = loop + 1;
E:        loop_lock = 0;
F:        if local_loop >= MAX_CITIES goto V;
G:        val = cities[local_loop] - durham;
H:        city_dist[local_loop] = val;
I:        val = TestAndSet(short_lock);
J:        if val = 1 goto I;
K:        if city_dist[local_loop] >= closest goto M;
L:                closest = city_dist[local_loop];
M:        short_lock = 0;
N:        city_next[last_local_loop] = local_loop;
O:        last_local_loop = local_loop;
P:        val = TestAndSet(loop_lock);
Q:        if val = 1 goto P;
R:        local_loop = loop;
S:        loop = loop + 1;
T:        loop_lock = 0;
U:        if local_loop < MAX_CITIES goto G;
V:
```

Figure 4: Intermediate code for the *find_dis* function.

HA: L val; (wait 1 cycle)
HB: L local_loop; (wait 2 cycle)
HC: S city_dist + local_loop; (wait 1 cycle)

Figure 5: Load/store sequence for statement H with inter-reference durations.

ACPS	AAPs	Code
Conditional Branch ACPs		
after B	$A_{all}, E_{all}, P_{all}, T_{all}$	(1)
after F	$C_{local}, D_{all}, S_{all}$	(2)
after J	I_{all}, M_{all}	(3)
after K	$C_{local}, D_{all}, R_{local}, S_{all}, L_{all}$	(4)
after Q	$P_{all}, T_{all}, A_{all}, E_{all}$	(1)
after U	$C_{local}, D_{all}, R_{local}, S_{all}$	(2)
Array Assignment ACPs		
G,H,K,L	$C_{local}, D_{all}, R_{local}, S_{all}$	(5)
N	$O_{local}, C_{local}, D_{all}, R_{local}, S_{all}$	(6)

Table 1: The ACPs of the example program along with the associated AAPs and path expression codes.

fixes at the associated AAPs are not needed. The next simplest are (2) and (5) which are the same except that (2) returns a boolean value and (5) returns a count. In (2) and (5) the complete path prefix at the last instantiation of an AAP is needed. The AAP in question happens to be in this process's code. The next is (6) which is similar to (2) except that the AAP needed is further back in the *affects* relation and that the instance of that AAP needed is not the last one, but the previous to last one.

 The path expression (4) is quite different from the others. A path expression can be complex in two independent senses. One is in the combination of path prefixes needed to specify the next address. In this sense path expression (6) is more complex than (2) and (5) (which in turn are more complex than (1) and (3)) because it requires more extensive

Code	Explanation
(1)	another process is in a *loop_lock* critical section
(2)	as of the last time *local_loop* was assigned to, the total number of times processes have gone through statements incrementing *loop* is at least MAX_CITIES
(3)	another process is in a *short_lock* critical section
(4)	the set of assignments to the *city_dist* array so far does include a city closer to *Durham* than the current city
(5)	the total number of times processes have gone through statements incrementing *loop*, as of the last time *local_loop* was assigned
(6)	the total number of times processes have gone through statements incrementing *loop*, as of the time the *local_loop* was assigned to what was used in the last assignment to *last_local_loop*

Table 2: Explanation of path expression codes.

history. The second sense is that the mapping from global path prefixes to next addresses may be difficult to do without program reexecution. It is in this sense that (4) is more complex than the other expressions. Whether "*city_dist[local_loop]* $>=$ *closest*" depends on which indices of the *city_dist* array have already been updated and on the values in the *city_dist* array components (this is for given input values). A path expression mapping between the set of indices that have been updated and the conditional branch to be taken can be formulated. However, determining the mapping seems to require having done the subtractions for each set of indices that might have been updated. These subtractions can be viewed as a partial program execution.

Assume the architecture has two processors, a shared bus, and a single shared memory. A bus transfer takes one cycle and a memory access takes one cycle. Assume all inter-reference durations are one cycle. A possible fragment of the global trace prefix is shown in Figure 6. Prior to cycle 5, the statement A has been fetched by each process. Between cycles 8 and 17 each process stores into its copy of the *val* variable and fetches statement B.

Suppose that the simulator is at the point of issuing the next address

Cycle	Process	Reference	Stage
5	0	$TestAndSet_A(loop\_lock)$	issue
6	0	"	perform
6	1	"	issue
7	0	"	complete
7	1	"	perform
8	1	"	complete
⋮			
17	0	$Load_B(val)$	issue
18	0	"	perform
18	1	"	issue
19	0	"	complete
19	1	"	perform

Figure 6: Fragment of a simulation.

for process 0 after completing the access for the conditional branch, statement B, in cycle 19. This is an ACP so it has a complete path prefix listing the path prefix of each process at the ACP and each AAP of this ACP. As described in Tables 1 and 2, the path expression for this ACP, in prose, is "another process is in a *loop_lock* critical section". For this two process case, a more precise statement of this path expression is "Process 1 acquired *loop_lock* at statement A and has not yet released it (the perform of the $TestAndSet_A$ by process 1 preceded the perform of the $TestAndSet_A$ by process 0 and process 1 has not yet done the perform of $Store_E$) OR Process 1 acquired *loop_lock* at statement P and has not yet released it (the last perform of $TestAndSet_P$ by process 1 preceded the most recent (if any) perform of $TestAndSet_A$ by process 0 AND process 1 has not yet done the perform of the subsequent $Store_T$)". For the global trace prefix of Figure 6, this predicate is not satisfied and the simulator generates a fetch of instruction C for process 0, allowing it to enter the critical section. This illustrates how the global trace prefix can be used to determine the next address at an ACP.

SUMMARY

Global trace generation of a parallel program in a shared memory multiprocessor is challenging because the address sequences of the process traces may be environment-dependent. We propose a method of ensuring that the global trace correctly reflects environment changes. For process traces, traditional traces are replaced by intrinsic traces. The intrinsic trace is composed of address basic blocks in the address flow graph. Each address basic block identifies its address change points (ACPs) and associated address affecting points (AAPs). At each ACP is a path expression mapping possible complete path prefixes to next addresses. At each ACP during the simulation, the simulator uses the path expression to determine the address references to issue.

References

[1] A. V. Aho, R. Sethi, and J. D. Ullman. *Compilers: Principles, Techniques, and Tools.* Addison-Wesley, Reading, MA, 1986.

[2] M.A. Holliday. Techniques for cache and memory simulation using address reference traces. *Int. Journal of Computer Simulation.* to appear.

[3] M.A. Holliday and C.S. Ellis. Accuracy of memory reference traces of parallel computations in trace-driven simulation. Technical Report CS-1990-8, Dept. of Computer Science, Duke Univesity, Durham, NC, July 1990. submitted for publication.

[4] L. Lamport. How to make a multiprocessor computer that correctly executes multiprocess programs. *IEEE Transactions on Computers,* C-28(9):690–691, September 1979.

[5] Sequent Computer Systems, Inc. *Balance 8000 Technical Summary.* Sequent Computer Systems, Inc., 1986.

[6] A. Smith. Cache evaluation and the impact of workload choice. In *Proceedings of the 12th Annual International Symposium on Computer Architecture,* Boston, MA, June 1985.

Locks, Directories, and Weak Coherence - a Recipe for Scalable Shared Memory Architectures *

Joonwon Lee 　　　*Umakishore Ramachandran*

College of Computing
Georgia Institute of Technology
Atlanta, Georgia 30332 USA

Abstract

Bus based multiprocessors have the limitation that they do not scale well to large numbers of processors due to the bus becoming a bottleneck with the current bus technology. Lock-based protocols have been suggested as a possible way of mitigating this bottleneck for single bus systems with snooping ability. In this research, we are interested in extending lock-based protocols to general interconnection networks. Directory based cache coherence schemes have been proposed for such networks. We are investigating a combination of locking with directory based schemes. Further, most protocols in the literature until now, assume a strong coherence requirement. However, recent research has shown that it is possible to weaken this coherence requirement. Such an approach is expected to reduce the coherence overhead even further, making it an appealing one for building scalable systems.

1 Introduction

In shared memory multiprocessors there is a need for defining a consistency model that specifies the order of execution of memory accesses

*This work is supported in part by NSF grant MIP-8809268

from multiple processors. Lamport [Lam79] has proposed sequential consistency as the ordering constraint for correct execution of a multiprocess program: The multiprocessor execution of the program should have the same effect as a sequential execution of any interleaving of the operations of all the processes (that comprise the program). The allowed interleavings are those that preserve the program order of operations of each individual process. With the sequential consistency model, read and write operations are sufficient to implement synchronization operations correctly. However, this model is inherently inefficient since it imposes a strong ordering constraint for all memory accesses regardless of the usage of shared data. Further, each memory access has to wait until the previous memory access is completed. Thus large scale shared memory multiprocessors are expected to incur long latencies for memory accesses if this ordering constraint is imposed, leading to poor performance. Further, such long latencies seriously hamper the scalability of shared memory multiprocessors.

In parallel program design, it is not unusual to use synchronization operations to enforce a specific ordering of shared memory accesses. Based on this observation Dubois et al. [DSB86] have proposed *weak ordering* that relaxes the ordering constraint of sequential consistency by distinguishing between accesses to synchronization variables and ordinary data. Their model requires (a) that sychronization variables be strongly consistent, (b) that all global data accesses be globally notified before synchronization operations, and (c) that all global data accesses subsequent to the synchronization operation be delayed until the operation is globally performed. Thus this model requires strong consistency of global data accesses with respect to synchronization variables.

A synchronization operation usually consists of *acquire* and *release* steps, e.g. lock and unlock, P and V of semaphores, barrier-request and barrier-notify. The acquire step (such as P or lock) need not be strongly consistent with respect to global memory accesses issued before it. Likewise, global memory accesses following the release step (such as V or unlock), need not wait until the synchronization operation is globally performed. This observation enables several extensions [AH90, CLLG89] to weak ordering, and thus provides more flexibility in machine design.

Private caches significantly reduce memory latencies and network contention in shared memory multiprocessors, provided an efficient cache coherence scheme is devised. For bus-based multiprocessors snooping cache protocols have been popular since they provide the sequential consistency model without much overhead. However, snooping caches rely on a fast broacast capability, not available in more scalable interconnections such as a multistage interconnection network. However, private caches are indispensable for reducing memory latencies, despite the fact that scalable interconnections complicate coherence maintenance. Because of their scalability, directory-based cache coherence protocols have been proposed for large scale shared memory multiprocessors [CGB89, CFKA90]. Until recently, such protocols implement the strong sequential consistency constraint used in the snoopy cache protocols. However, given that global operations such as invalidation and updates are expensive in scalable interconnects, it is important to incorporate weak consistency models in such protocols.

In this paper, we present a directory-based caching scheme based on a consistency model in which strong consistency is enforced only for cache lines accessed by lock operations. Other accesses are deemed to be for private data. This protocol is similar to write-broadcast protocol [TS87, McC84] with the difference that updates are only sent to processors that request them. Lock requestors wait in a FCFS queue organized with pointers in each cache line and the directory[1]. In the next section we consider the effect of caching schemes on consistency models. The motivation for and applications of our new caching scheme are presented in Section 3. Section 4 describes our cache protocol and its implementation issues. Finally, the performance potential of our scheme is discussed in Section 5.

2 Cache Consistency

For the purposes of this paper the multiprocessor model is a uniform shared memory one: each processor has a private cache; an intercon-

---

[1]Similar ideas have been proposed in our previous work [LR90], and IEEE SCI protocol [IEE89]

nection network connects the processors with the memory module(s); and a cache coherence scheme assures consistency using some consistency model. The sequential consistency model for cache coherence is the most straightforward one to comprehend from the point of view of programming. This model parallels the database transaction model of single copy serializability in the way it ensures correctness of concurrent execution of operations. Therefore, it is easy to see that this consistency model relieves the programmer from having to worry about the order of execution of individual operation in writing parallel programs. Thus, until recently multiprocessor cache coherence schemes have used this consistency model.

The implementation cost (in time, network traffic, and circuit complexity) of a cache protocol depends on the choice of interconnection network. When the interconnection network is a single shared bus it is relatively easy to implement the sequential consistency model for cache coherence since (a) each processor has the ability to observe the (read/write) events from all the other processors by *snooping* on the bus, and (b) the bus provides a fast broadcast capability. This observation has led to a group of cache coherence protocols often referred to as *snooping cache* protocols [Goo83, KEW+85, PP84, KMRS88, TS87, McC84, LR90] for bus-based systems. The snooping ability of the processors allows the directory information to be distributed among the private caches.

It is fairly well-known that single bus systems are incapable of scaling to very large numbers of processors due to the bus becoming a bottleneck beyond a few processors [AB86]. Therefore, there has been a resurgence of interest in developing efficient cache coherence schemes for more scalable interconnection networks [MHW87, GW88, Wil87, BW87]. While some of these have been extensions of single bus snooping cache protocols to multiple buses, some researchers have been investigating an alternative approach, namely, *directory-based protocols*. In this approach, the directory information is centralized at the memory module(s) instead of being distributed in the private caches, thus making it is possible to implement the sequential consistency model for non bus-based networks. However, the lack of a fast broadcast capability in such networks leads to an inefficient implementation of the sequential consistency model.

All of the protocols until recently have used the sequential consistency model for assuring correctness. However, recently researchers have observed that the sequential consistency model is too strong, and have developed weaker models of consistency [SD87, AH90, LS88, HA89, ABM89]. Researchers have shown that it is possible to achieve a more efficient implementation of multiprocessor cache protocols with weaker models of consistency [ABM89, AH90, CLLG89].

3 Consistency and Synchronization

The evolution of multiprocessor cache protocols has three distinct aspects: development of different models of consistency, study of tradeoffs between centralized and distributed directories, and innovation in the choice of cache primitives. We discussed the first two aspects in the previous section. In this section we discuss the motivation for developing new cache primitives. Early cache protocols assumed the traditional uniprocessor interface between the processor and the cache, namely, the cache responds to read and write requests from the processor. However, in a multiprocessor data is potentially shared between processors. To account for this, the cache protocols extend the functionality of the private caches for read/write accesses from other processors via the network, satisfying some chosen model of consistency.

However, when there is sharing there is synchronization that usually governs such sharing. By ignoring the synchronization aspect, most of the early protocols treated the coherence problem for shared data in isolation. In reality, synchronization and data coherence are intertwined. Realizing this, researchers have proposed primitives for synchronization via the caches [GW88, BD86, LR90].

The data accesses from a processor can be grouped into three categories: access to private data, access to synchronization variables, and access to shared data. If permission to access to shared data is acquired through some synchronization mechanism then strong coherence would be required only for the access to the synchronization variables. Synchronization operations may be used in a program for one of three purposes:

- Case 1 The operation guarantees the atomicity of a set of operations (transaction) on shared data. A lock is usually associated with the shared data for this purpose. The lock governs access to the shared data.

- Case 2 The operation provides mutual exclusion to a critical section in the program.

- Case 3 The operation signals the completion of an epoch of a computation to other processes (e.g. barrier synchronization).

In each case the synchronization operation itself requires strong coherence enforcement. If the cache is capable of recognizing a synchronization request distinct from other requests, then it is relatively straightforward to enforce the strong coherence requirement: stall the processor until the synchronization operation is performed globally. However, once the synchronization operation is performed globally there is lattitude in how other accesses are performed. For instance in case 1, if the hardware has knowledge of the shared data associated with each lock then it can "batch" the global propagation of all the updates to shared data that happened in this transaction upon release of the lock. Similarly, in case 2 the synchronization variable governing access to the critical section needs to be strongly coherent but accesses inside the critical section need not be globally notified until exit from the critical section. Case 3 is similar to case 2 in that accesses done during the epoch of the computation need not be globally propogated until the notification phase (similar to exiting a critical section) of the barrier operation. These arguements are along the lines of those put forward by Scheurich et al. [SD87], and Adve and Hill [AH90] for justifying weak ordering.

Thus if the hardware is capable of recognizing a set of synchronization operations, then subsequent data accesses can be treated as not requiring any consistency. Therefore, any cache protocol that performs consistency maintenance for *all* shared accesses is doing more work than it has to. This arguement is the motivation for our cache coherence protocol that is described in the next section.

In the discussion thus far we have assumed that a process always acquires permission to access data or code through some synchronization mechanism. This need not always be true. There are applications in which it may be sufficient that a read of a shared location return the most recent value. Further it may not be necessary that the value be updated or invalidated if other processors write that location subsequently. An example is a monitoring process that wants to read the value just once. Parallel game programs are another example where it may be sufficient to perform the updates more *lazily*. Once again any such optimizations to reduce the network traffic requires that the hardware (cache controller) support additional primitives, and that the software be written to take advantage of such primitives. Needless to say such optimizations allow the scalability of such machines by reducing the network traffic.

Our proposed cache protocol (to be described next) has four features: (a) it provides hardware recognized locking primitives to handle all three cases discussed above; (b) it exploits the weak ordering principle by performing updates to shared locations more lazily; (c) it distinguishes between a read (that returns the value once) and a read-update (that returns the value and provides updates); and (d) it uses a centralized directories for update propagation and distributed directories in the caches for lock implementation.

4 Protocol Description

In this section, we present a directory-based cache protocol based on the consistency requirements discussed in section 3. Our scheme assumes cooperation with the software in generating appropriate requests for the desired consistency.

The cache entertains seven commands from the processor: read, read-update, write, read-lock, write-lock, unlock, and flush. Read and write are regarded as requests for private data requiring no consistency maintenance. Read-update is similar to read except that it requests updates for the cache line. This is a dual to the write-update schemes [TS87, McC84] in that the updates are receiver initiated as opposed to sender initiated. Read-lock, write-lock, and unlock requests combine processor synchronization with data coherence. Read-lock provides the requesting processor with a non-exclusive copy of the cache line that is guaranteed by the protocol not to change. Similarly, an exclusive copy of the cache line is

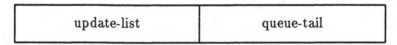

update	$d_1 d_2 \ldots d_k$	lock-status	previous	next

a. Tag fields of a cache line

update-list	queue-tail

b. Tag fields of a directory entry

Figure 1: Tag fields of a cache line and a directory entry

provided to the write-lock requester. The processors have to explicitly perform unlock to release the cache lines acquired under a lock. The flush operation purges a cache line updating memory words that are modified in the cache line. The main memory, in turn, sends updates of this line to other processors if need be.

Figure 1-a illustrates tag fields of a cache line. The *update* bit of a cache line indicates whether updates have been requested for this line. The next k bits denote the modified word(s) of the cache line respectively , where k is the number of words per cache line. Only the modified words are written back to memory when the cache line is replaced. The *lock-status* denotes if the cache line is locked, and if so, the kind (read or write) of lock. The next two fields are pointers which are used to construct a doubly-linked list for processors waiting for the same lock. If the lock-status is not locked and the *previous* pointer is not null, this cache line is waiting for a lock. If the *next* pointer is null, this processor is at the *tail* of the queue.

Figure 1-b shows tag fields of a directory entry. The first field, *update-list*, consists of n bits, one for each of the n processors in the system. Each processor has a designated bit in this field which is set when it makes a read-update request, and reset when the cache line is replaced

update-list	tail	L	prev	next	L	prev	next	L	prev	next
. . .			. .			. .			. .	
	3	r	null	2	r	1	3		2	null
. . .			. . .			. . .			. . .	

| Directory of the main memory | P_1 Cache | P_2 Caches | P_3 Caches |

Figure 2: A waiting queue: doubly linked list

by the processor. Upon write backs to main memory, this field is checked and the updated cache line is sent to processor i if the i-th bit of the update-list is set. The *queue-tail* field is a pointer to a processor which was the last lock requester for the memory block. If queue-tail is *null* this memory block is currently unlocked.

For a read request, if the requested data is in the cache, the cache provides the data regardless of the state of the cache line. If the data is not in the cache, the request is forwarded to the main memory. Regardless of the state of the corresponding directory entry, the main memory sends the data to the requesting cache. A read-update request can be serviced by the cache if the update bit of the cache line is set. Otherwise, this request is forwarded to the main memory. The main memory provides the requested data and sets the appropriate bit in the update-list. Once this bit is set, the processor will be supplied with the new data whenever the memory block is written back by another processor. The write backs occur when a cache line is replaced, unlocked, or flushed.

Upon a lock request it is sent to the main memory and the directory entry is investigated. If the memory block is not locked, the address of the requester, say P_i, is stored in the queue-tail field of the directory entry. The memory block is sent to the requester and the cache sets the lock status of the cache line according to the type of the lock. If the memory block is locked, the lock request is forwarded to the processor addressed by the current queue-tail field and P_i becomes the new queue-tail field of the directory entry. The next pointer of the current queue-tail processor is now made to point to P_i. P_i's lock request is granted if the cache line of the tail processor is currently holding a read-lock, and P_i's request is also a read-lock. Figure 2 illustrates a queue for a series of lock requests, P1:read-lock, P2:read-lock, P3:write-lock. P1 and P2 currently hold read-locks while P3 is waiting for a write-lock. For more details on this lock-based protocol the reader is referred to a companion paper [LR90].

Upon an unlock request, the cache controller releases the lock to the next waiting processor (if any), and writes the cache line to the main memory (if necessary). When a write-lock is released there could be more than one processor waiting for a read-lock. The lock release notification goes down the linked list until it meets a write-lock requester (or end of the list), and thus, allows granting of multiple read-locks. When a processor unlocks a read-lock and the processor is not the sole lock owner, the list is fixed up similar to deleting a node from a doubly-linked list. When a lock is released by a tail processor, the main memory marks the tail pointer null. Note that the unlocking processor is allowed to continue its computation immediately, and does not have to wait for the unlock operation to be performed globally.

Replacing a cache line that is a part of the list of lock requesters is a bit more complicated. The most simple and straightforward solution is to disallow replacement of such a cache line. However, this solution may be feasible only if a fully associative or a set-associative caching strategy is in use. If a direct mapped caching scheme is in use it is necessary to modify the tag handling mechanism of cache controllers. When a locked cache line is replaced, the cache controller preserves the lock status and the two pointer fields in the tag memory of the cache line, i.e., only the data part and address tag part of the line is evicted. We assume that the compiler allocates at most one lock variable to a cache line. Since the new line to occupy this evicted cache line is for ordinary data, it does not interfere with the list structure for the lock (guranteed by the compiler). Cache controllers do not perform address tag matching for link update operations to allow the operations to be performed correctly even after the locked cache line is replaced. A subsequent access (read, write or unlock) to the lock variable will reload the replaced cache line.

However, restricting one locking process per processor at a time may be too restrictive. Since a processor holds (or waits for) only a small number of locks at a time, a small seperate fully-associative cache for lock variables can be an efficient method to eliminate the restriction. This cache has tag fields as shown in Figure 1. Other ordinary shared or private data are stored in another cache which does not have tag fields for locks such as lock-status, previous, and next.

Another hardware requirement for our protocol is a write buffer. The flush operation is suposed to write back all the updated cache lines. However, detecting updated cache lines cannot be done by a compiler statically since shared data may be referenced throufh pointers. Searching all the cache lines by hardware is very inefficient. So, our protocol needs a write buffer which holds updated data until they are globally performed.

5 Performance Analysis

In this section, we present a simple performance analysis of our cache protocol. We compare ours with a write-back invalidation full-map directory (WBI) protocol that uses the sequential consistency model. First, we analyze the performance of each scheme for lock and ordinary memory accesses. Based on this analysis, cache schemes are compared for common structures of parallel programs such as task queue model, and static scheduling model.

5.1 Lock Operations

First, we derive expressions for time and network message complexity for acquiring a mutually exclusive lock to enter a critical section for the WBI protocol. Recall that with the sequential consistency model, read and write operations are sufficient to implement synchronization operations correctly. An implementation of synchronization operations can be more efficient with an atomic test&set primitive which most architectures provide. However, implementation of the test&set on traditional cache schemes can create additional penalties due to the *ping-pong* effect [DSB88]. Since the 'set' part of the test&set primitive involves a write to a piece of shared data, a spin-lock may cause each contending processor to invalidate (or update) other caches continually with the sequential consistency model. The following test-test&set method avoids the ping-pong effect by busy-waiting on the cache memory without modification.

```
repeat
    while(LOAD(lock_variable) = 1) do nothing;
    /* spin without modification */
until(test&set(lock_variable) = 0);
```

But, this method still generates considerable network traffic when a lock is released since all the waiting processors try to modify the cache line, thus invalidating (or updating) the corresponding cache line of the other caches.

Figure 3 shows a timing diagram for the case when n processors execute test-test&set at the same time. The lock variable is assumed to be initially in the dirty state in a peer cache. t_{nw} denotes the message transit time on the network. For simplicity of analysis, we assume the same time for all types of network messages: request to the main memory, query from the main memory to a cache, acknowledgment, and block transfer. Let t_m be the memory access time; t_D and t_C denote directory checking time of the main memory and the cache memory, respectively. In this analysis, we assume requests to memory are queued by order of arrival if the memory is busy. Figure 3-a shows the parallel execution of load instruction of test-test&set by n processors. n read requests are issued at the same time (t_{nw}). For the first request (top time line in Figure 3-a), the main memory performs a directory checking (t_D) and sends a request for the block to the cache which has the dirty copy (t_{nw}). After checking the cache directory (t_C), the cache controller sends the block to the main memory (t_{nw}). Once the requested data arrives it is written to the main memory (t_m), and sent to the requester (t_{nw}).

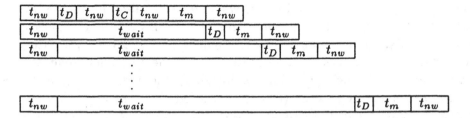

a. Time lines for the load part of test-test&set

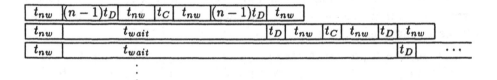

b. Time lines for the test&set part of test-test&set

| t_{nw} | $(n-1)t_D$ | t_{nw} | t_C | t_{nw} | $(n-1)t_D$ | t_{nw} |

c. reset

Figure 3: Timing diagram for parallel exclusive locks for WBI protocol

After these steps the main memory has a valid copy. So, subsequent read requests require just directory checking (t_D) , wait for memory (t_{wait}), memory read (t_m), and block transfer (t_{nw}). Note that memory operations cannot be overlapped.

Assuming that the lock-variable is 0, all the processors are going to execute test&set operations next. But these test&set requests can be serviced only after the last load request finishes. These requests can be serviced by the memory only after the last t_m request of Figure 3-a finishes. Referring to the top line in Figure 3-b, the first test&set operation (t_{nw}) invalidates valid copies which were acquired by the above load operations by $n-1$ processors. Sending $n-1$ invalidation messages is a sequential operation for the main memory $((n-1)t_D + t_{nw})$. After invalidating local copies (t_C), all these $n-1$ cache controllers send acknowledgments to the main memory. Receiving these acknowledgments is also a sequential operation $((n-1)t_D)$. After that, memory acknowledges the test&set of the first processor (t_{nw}), allowing it to complete successfully. For the next test&set operation (second time line in Figure 3-b) the main memory requests the block from the cache that has a dirty copy after checking its directory ($t_D + t_{nw}$). The block is transferred to the main memory from the cache ($t_C + t_{nw}$), and then to the test&set requester ($t_D + t_{nw}$).

Among the n processors executing the test&set operation, only one completes it successfully. The remaining $n-1$ processors re-execute the load operation and busy-wait on cached copies of the lock variable until the lock variable is reset by the lock owner. Since all the waiting processors have valid copies (in their caches), the reset operation invalidates $n-1$ copies. Now, $n-1$ processors compete for the lock simultaneously with one dirty copy in the resetting processor's cache, which is the initial condition that was assumed when n processors competed for the lock. This parallel lock contention is repeated n times, with one less contender in every round, until all the requesters get serviced.

Since the performance of large-scale multiprocessors depends on the amount of traffic on the interconnection network, the number of messages generated by a cache protocol can be used as a metric for evaluating the performance of cache protocols. Let $f_m(n)$ be the number of messages generated for granting a lock to one processor when n processors are competing simultaneously. Then $f_m(n)$ is computed as the sum of (refer to Figure 3): $4 + 2(n-1)$ for load operations, $2 + 2(n-1)$ for the first test&set, $4(n-1)$ for the next $n-1$ test&sets, $4 + 2(n-2)$ for $n-1$ re-loads, and $2 + 2(n-1)$ for reset. Therefore, $f_m(n) = 12n - 2$, and the total number of messages for servicing n lock requests is

$$\sum_{i=1}^{n} f_m(i) = 6n^2 + 4n$$

For measuring the execution time for the n parallel lock requests, we made the following assumptions: a) Lock contention of other processors do not delay the memory accesses of a processor holding the lock. b) The sojourn time inside the critical section is long enough so that the reset operation comes after all the test&sets and re-loads are completed. c) The network transit time is a constant independant of switch contentions. From Figure 3-a, load operations take $3t_{nw}+t_C+t_D+t_m+(n-1)(t_D+t_m)$ until the last memory operation completes. The first test&set takes $2(n-1)t_D + 3t_{nw} + t_C$ before successfully entering the critical section. Let t_{cs} be the processing time in the critical section, and t_1 be the time at which the first lock holder completes unlock operation. Then t_1 can be expressed as a function of n,

$$
\begin{aligned}
t_1 = f_t(n) \quad &= \quad 3t_{nw} + t_C + t_D + t_m + (n-1)(t_D + t_m) + & (1) \\
&\quad 2(n-1)t_D + 3t_{nw} + t_C + & (2) \\
&\quad t_{cs} + & (3) \\
&\quad 2(n-1)t_D + 4t_{nw} + t_C & (4) \\
&= \quad t_{cs} + 10t_{nw} + 3t_C + nt_m + (5n-4)t_D & (5)
\end{aligned}
$$

where the first line is for n loads, the second line is for test&set, the third line is for a critical section, and the fourth line is for unlock. Since $t_i = t_{i-1}+f_t(n-i+1)$ for $2 \le i \le n$, the completion time for n processors executing the critical section is

$$
\begin{aligned}
t_n \quad &= \quad \sum_{i=1}^{n} f_t(i) \\
&= \quad nt_{cs} + 10nt_{nw} + 3nt_C + \frac{n(n+1)}{2}t_m + \frac{(5n-4)(5n-3)}{2}t_D
\end{aligned}
$$

For our scheme, the timing diagram for acquiring a mutually exclusive lock (write-lock) is shown in Figure 4. The first lock operation (top time line of Figure 4-a) requires one network message for lock request (t_{nw}), a directory check at the memory (t_D), memory read (t_m), and a network message for granting the lock (t_{nw}). For each subsequent request, the memory does a directory check (t_D), sends a message to the current tail (t_{nw}), which updates its directory (t_C), sends an acknowledgment

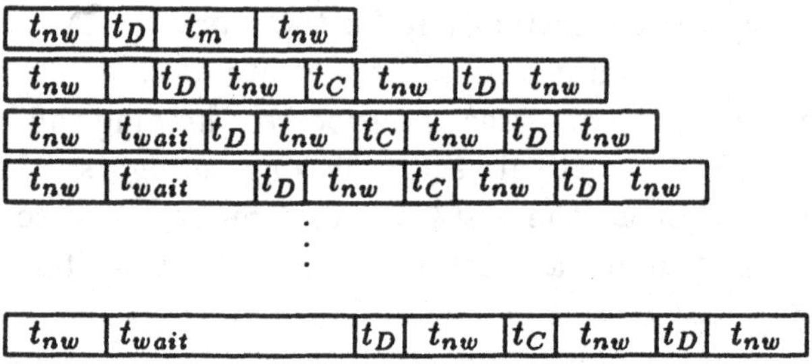

t_{nw}	t_D	t_m	t_{nw}

t_{nw}		t_D	t_{nw}	t_C	t_{nw}	t_D	t_{nw}

t_{nw}	t_{wait}	t_D	t_{nw}	t_C	t_{nw}	t_D	t_{nw}

t_{nw}	t_{wait}		t_D	t_{nw}	t_C	t_{nw}	t_D	t_{nw}

$\vdots$

t_{nw}	t_{wait}		t_D	t_{nw}	t_C	t_{nw}	t_D	t_{nw}

a. Time lines for n parallel locks

t_{nw}	t_D	t_{nw}

b. Time line for unlock

Figure 4: Timing diagram for parallel exclusive locks for the proposed lock-based scheme

(t_{nw}), which is received by the memory (t_D), and results in a message from the memory to the new tail (t_{nw}). For n lock operations, $2+4(n\text{-}1)$ messages are issued. Each unlock operation generates 2 messages (See Figure 4, one for unlock, and one for waking up the next requester). So, for servicing n lock requests, total number of messages generated is

$$2 + 4(n - 1) + 2n - 1$$
$$= \ 6n - 3$$

And, for the completion time,

$$t_1 \ = \ 2t_{nw} + t_D + t_m + t_{cs} + 2t_{nw} + t_D$$
$$t_i \ = \ t_{i-1} + t_{cs} + 2t_{nw} + t_D \qquad (2 \le i \le n)$$

Therefore,

$$t_n \ = \ t_1 + (n - 1)(t_{cs} + 2t_{nw} + t_D) - t_{nw}$$
$$= \ nt_{cs} + (2n + 1)t_{nw} + (n + 1)t_D + t_m$$

The subtraction of t_{nw} in the above equation accounts for the last unlock operation in which the main memory does not send a wake-up message.

The other extreme of lock competition to the parallel lock is when all the n processors are serialized, i.e., only one processor requests the lock at a time. For the WBI protocol, each lock requester generates 4 messages for load, 4 messages for test&set, and 0 message for reset since the cache has a dirty copy of the lock variable. Thus, n processors generate $8n$ messages. The time spent by each processor is $4t_{nw} + t_D + t_C + t_m$ for loading, $4t_{nw} + t_C + 2t_D$ for test&set, and t_{cs} for the critical section. Since lock requests are occurring serially, the time for executing the critical section with the WBI protocol for each processor is $8t_{nw} + t_{cs} + 2t_C + 3t_D$. With our scheme, the time for each processor to execute the critical section serially is $3t_{nw} + t_D + t_{cs}$; with 2 messages for acquiring the lock and one message for releasing the lock.

5.2 Barrier Synchronization

Barrier requires all participating processors to synchronize at a certain point (the barrier). Since the barrier counter can be a hot-spot several approaches [YTL87, Bro86] have been proposed for distributing the contention. However, we assume a traditional implementation using a counter with lock operations on the counter for the performance analysis. The cost for a barrier-request is the cost for lock request plus the cost for accessing the counter. So, the performance of the barrier depends on the arrival pattern. For the WBI protocol, the barrier-notify step causes $n - 1$ simultaneous read requests. If we assume serial arrivals for a barrier-request, each processor generates 8 messages for a serial lock, 8 messages for reading and writing the counter variable, 2 messages for reading a flag variable. The time taken for a barrier-request is $8t_{nw} + 3t_D + 2t_C$ for a lock, $8t_{nw} + 3t_D + 2t_C$ for incrementing the counter, and $2t_{nw} + t_D$ for reading the flag variable, where the time for incrementing the counter and the time for checking conditions are not included. So, each barrier request takes $18t_{nw} + 7t_D + 5t_C$ time, and generates 18 messages.

The barrier-notify is a write to the flag variable on which all the waiting processors busy-wait. This write causes invalidations of all the

$n-1$ copies. So, messages generated by a barrier-notify are 1 write request, $n-1$ invalidation signals to caches, $n-1$ acknowledgments, 1 acknowledgment to the writer, $n-1$ re-load requests, and $n-1$ block transfers. So, a barrier-notify generates a total of $5n-3$ messages. The time spent for a barrier-notify is t_{nw} for a write request, $(n-1)t_D + t_{nw}$ for sending $n-1$ invalidations, t_C for invalidation at the caches, $(n-1)t_D + t_{nw}$ for receiving $n-1$ acknowledgments, and t_{nw} for sending an acknowledgment to the barrier-notifier, resulting in a total time of $4t_{nw} + 2(n-1)t_D + t_C$.

With our scheme, the barrier can be implemented by lock and read-update primitives. The counter is secured by lock operations and the busy-waiting is implemented by the read-update primitive. Processors arriving at the barrier increment the counter. If it is less than n, the processor issues a read-update for the flag variable. The processor that arrives last at the barrier sets the flag variable and notifies this update using the flush primitive. A barrier-request generates one message for write-lock and one for unlock. Both write-lock and unlock each take $t_{nw} + t_m$ time. When the flag is written and flushed by a processor, $n-1$ processors waiting for updates will receive the update. So, it generates 1 flush request and $n-1$ word transfers, and takes $t_{nw} + (n-1)t_D + t_{nw}$ time.

synchronization operation	WBI protocol	Our Scheme
parallel lock	$6n^2 + 4n$	$6n - 3$
serial lock	8	3
barrier request	18	2
barrier notify	$5n - 3$	n

Table 1: Number of messages generated by synchronization operations.

Summary of the costs for each synchronization scenario with the WBI protocol and ours is presented in Table 1 and 2.

synchronization operation	WBI protocol	Our Scheme
parallel lock	$nt_{cs} + 10nt_{nw} +$ $n(n+1)/2t_m +$ $5n(5n-1)/2t_D$	$nt_{cs} + (2n+1)t_{nw} +$ $(n+1)t_D + t_m$
serial lock	$8t_{nw} + 5t_D + t_m + t_{cs}$	$3t_{nw} + t_D + t_{cs}$
barrier request	$18t_{nw} + 12t_D$	$2(t_{nw} + t_m)$
barrier notify	$4t_{nw} + (2n-1)t_D$	$2t_{nw} + (n-1)t_D$

Table 2: Time taken by synchronization operations. t_C is replaced by t_D for simplicity. Costs for serial lock and barrise request are for one processor.

5.3 Shared Variables

While the performance of the invalidation-based directory scheme is sensitive to the sharing pattern of memory accesses, our scheme is independent of the sharing pattern since strong coherency is enforced only for lock requests. In this subsection, we analyze the time taken for accessing private/shared data during an epoch of computation for the WBI protocol. The analysis is based on two basic assumptions: the mean time between shared accesses is exponentially distributed, and shared accesses are uniformly distributed over k shared variables. Following are the parameters used:

N : total number of memory accesses
k : the number of shared variables in words
h : cache-hit ratio
sh : ratio of shared accesses
r : ratio of read accesses
w : ratio of write accesses, i.e., $1 - r$
t : mean time between memory requests

The total time for accessing data can be divided into two components: private accesses and shared accesses. For both types of accesses, we assume the same hit-ratio. However, the cache-hit ratio may be decreased for shared lines by interferences from other processors such as invalidations and external reads of a dirty cache line. So, we develop the following equations;

$$
\begin{aligned}
total-time &= N((1-sh)t_{private} + sh*t_{shared}) \\
t_{private} &= h*t_C + (1-h)2t_{nw} \\
t_{shared} &= r*t_{shared-read} + w*t_{shared-write} \\
t_{shared-read} &= (h*P_{invalid} + 1 - h)(t_{read-miss}) + h(1-P_{invalid})t_C \\
t_{shared-write} &= (h*P_{not-dirty} + 1 - h)(t_{write-miss}) \\
&\quad + h(1 - P_{not-dirty})t_C
\end{aligned}
$$

where t_X is a time needed for an X-type memory access. $P_{invalid}$ is the probability that a shared variable in the cache of a given processor has been invalidated since it was last accessed by the same processor. This invalidation(s) results in changing the state to invalid, which would have been valid otherwise. Likewise, $P_{not-dirty}$ is the probability that there has been an external access(s) to a shared variable after the last write to the variable by a given processor. This external access(es) results in changing the dirty state to valid or invalid, thus causing a write miss.

The time interval between two shared accesses from a given processor is t/sh and the probability that another processor issues a shared write during the time interval is $1 - e^{-\lambda t/sh}$ where λ is the mean arrival rate of shared writes from a given processor, i.e., $sh*w/t$. Since there are k shared variables which can be accessed by any processor, the probability that the write is to the same shared variable is $1/k$. Since the invalidation can be from any of $n-1$ processors,

$$
P_{invalid} = 1 - (1 - \frac{1}{k}(1 - e^{-w}))^{n-1}
$$

Similarly, the time interval for two consecutive writes from a processor is $t/(sh*w)$ and the mean arrival rate of shared accesses is sh/t. Therefore,

$$
P_{not-dirty} = 1 - (1 - \frac{1}{k}(1 - e^{-1/w}))^{n-1}
$$

If false sharing is considered both $P_{invalid}$ and $P_{not-dirty}$ would be higher.

The time for servicing a read-miss, $t_{read-miss}$, is $2t_{nw} + t_D$ if the main memory has a valid block, and $4t_{nw} + 2t_D + t_C$ otherwise. The main memory has a valid copy if the last global operation on that block was a read. So,

$$t_{read-miss} = r(2t_{nw} + t_D) + w(4t_{nw} + 2t_D + t_C)$$

On the other hand, $t_{write-miss}$ is $4t_{nw} + 2t_D + t_C$ if the block is in dirty state in another cache, and $2t_{nw} + t_D + v(2t_{nw} + 2t_D + t_C)$ if there exist v valid copies. So,

$$t_{write-miss} = r(2t_{nw} + t_D + v(2t_{nw} + 2t_D + t_C)) + w(4t_{nw} + 2t_D + t_C)$$

Let m_X be a number of messages generated by a X-type memory access. Then we can get the following equations by the same way as for the timing analysis.

$$
\begin{aligned}
total - messages &= N((1 - sh)m_{private} + sh * m_{shared}) \\
m_{private} &= 2(1 - h) \\
m_{shared} &= r * m_{shared-read} + w * m_{shared-write} \\
m_{shared-read} &= (hP_{invalid} + 1 - h)m_{read-miss} \\
m_{shared-write} &= (hP_{not-dirty} + 1 - h)m_{write-miss} \\
m_{read-miss} &= 2r + 4w \\
m_{write-miss} &= r(2v + 2) + 4w
\end{aligned}
$$

In the following subsections, we apply the cost functions developed thus far to several widely used structures of parallel programs.

5.4 Performance for Different Program Structures

In this subsection, we analyze the performance of cache schemes for programming paradigms which have been widely accepted in the parallel programming community. The first model represents a dynamic

Parameters	value
h	0.95
r	0.70
t_{nw}	log_2N
t_D, t_C	1
t_m	4 (=B)
v	2

Table 3: Fixed parameters

scheduling paradigm believed to be the kernel of several parallel programs [Pol88]. The basic granularity is a task. A large problem is divided into atomic tasks, and dependencies between tasks are checked. Tasks are inserted into a work queue of executable tasks honoring such dependencies. If a new task is generated as a result of the processing, it is inserted into the queue. All the processors execute the same code until the task queue is empty or a predefined finishing condition is met. A barrier is used to synchronize all the processors after executing a task. Correct queue operations require each queue access be atomic, and thus lock operations are needed for accessing the queue. Since all the processors are synchronized by the barrier, these lock requests are generated at the same time. The second model is the same as the first one except that the barrier synchronization is not used. The third model represents a static scheduling paradigm. In this model, the computation consists of several phases and each phase depends on the result of previous phase. Therefore, a barrier is used between phases. Table 3 shows values for fixed parameters.

Figure 5-8 show the effect of sh, k, N, and n on the completion time and the number of network messages for the WBI protocol and our scheme. In the legends, QB denotes the task queue with a barrier model, Q is the task queue without a barrier model, and S is the static scheduling case. Figure 5 shows that the completion times of both schemes are not affected much by sh, the degree of sharing. The WBI protocol is inferior to our scheme in all the tested cases. The completion time for the WBI protocol increases as sh increases because it takes longer time for accessing shared variables than accessing private variables. But our scheme is not affected by sh since coherency maintenance is not necessary for shared variables. The huge performance gap between two cache schemes for the task queue with a barrier model comes from the overhead of parallel locks. The task queue alone (Q) or the barrier alone (S) does not hamper the performance that much.

Figure 6 shows the effect of different k values. As k, the number of shared variables, is decreases, the contention for share variables increase. The WBI protocol shows a slight decrease in the completion time and the number of messages generated as the value of k increase. For a fixed set of parameter values ($sh = 0.3, k = 30, N = 300 and n = 32$), time for accesing shared variables is 1315 and the total time for memory accesses is 1619.62 while the total execution time is 3294 for Q model. That shows almost half the execution time is spent for synchronization activities. Therefore, even the memory access time is affected considerably by k, the total execution time is not. The execution time of QB model is worse: more than 80% of the execution time is spent for synchronization.

The effect of the size of granularity in Figure 7 shows that the time is increased less than linearly and the number of messages increases slightly. That confirms the fact that the execution time is governed by synchronization overhead not by ordinary memory accesses. Otherwise the time should have increased linearly. The less increase in the number of messages can be explained by the fact that the ordinary memory accesses generate only a small portion of (usually, 3%for QB, 40% for Q and S) the total messages generated.

The question of scalability is answered in Figure 8. As the number of processors increases, the QB model shows sharp increases in both the completion time and the number of messages. That is because the QB model incurs $O(n^2)$ overhead for both the metrics (see Table 1 and 2. For our scheme the QB model generates $O(n^2)$ messages and $O(n)$ takes completion time. That explains the steep increase in the number of messages for our scheme.

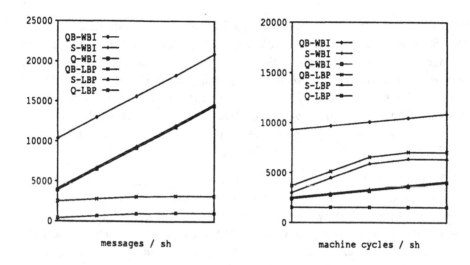

Figure 5: Effect of *sh*

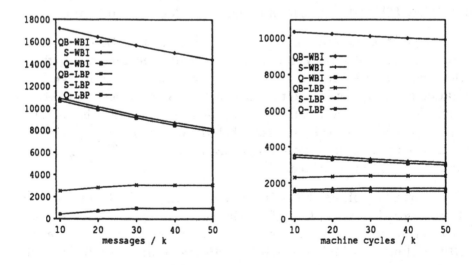

Figure 6: Effect of *k*

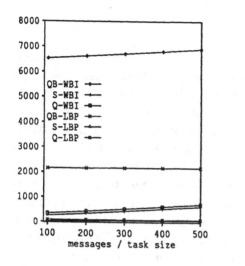
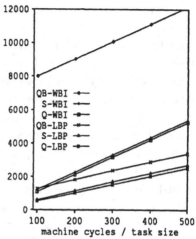

Figure 7: Effect of N

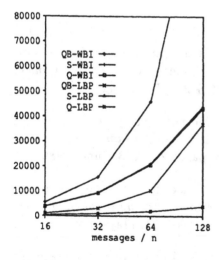
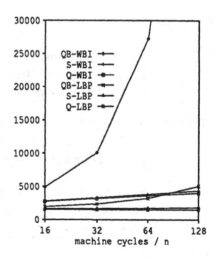

Figure 8: Effect of n

6   Concluding Remarks

For multiprocessors to be scalable, they should be able to tolerate large memory latencies as well as hop-spot contention. This paper shows that the most scalability issues can be handled by coherent private caches. The weak coherence model reduces global accesses and makes fast the execution of critical sections. And, thus the overall memory latencies are reduced. The memory latencies are enlarged if the load on the interconnection network becomes large. Reader-initiated coherence minimizes the transactions required to maintain the cache consistency. Thus, coupled with the cache-based lock scheme, the new cache scheme will enable the system to scale to a large number of processors. Most of the new cache primitives of our cache scheme will be used by the compiler or the programmer. Thus, the future research includes the program analysis for detecting the need for our primitives. Trace-driven simulation is also being performed to verify the analytical model used for performance evaluation.

References

[AB86]   J. Archibald and J. Baer. Cache coherence protocols: evaluation using a multiprocessor model. *ACM Transactions on Computer Systems*, pages 278–298, Nov. 1986.

[ABM89] Y. Afek, G. Brown, and M. Merritt. A lazy cache algorithm. In *Proceedings of the 1989 ACM Symposium on Parallel Algorithms and Architectures*, pages 209–223, June. 1989.

[AH90]   S. V. Adve and M. D. Hill. Weak ordering - a new definition. In *Proceedings of the 17th Annual International Symposium on Computer Architecture*, pages 2–11, May 1990.

[BD86]   P. Bitar and A. M. Despain. Multiprocessor cache synchronization : Issues, innovations, evolution. In *Proceedings of the 13th Annual International Symposium on Computer Architecture*, pages 424–433, June 1986.

[Bro86]   E. D. Brooks. The Butterfly barrier. *International Journal of Parallel Programming*, pages 295–307, Aug. 1986.

[BW87]   J. Baer and W. Wang. Architectural choices for multi-level cache hierarchies. In *Proceedings of the 1987 International Conference on Parallel Processing*, pages 258–261, 1987.

[CFKA90]   D. Chaiken, C. Fields, K. Kurihara, and A. Agarwal. Directory-based cache coherence in large-scale multiprocessors. *IEEE Computer*, 1990.

[CGB89]   D. A. Cheriton, H. A. Goosen, and P. D. Boyle. Multi-level shared caching techniques for scalability in VMP-MC. In *Proceedings of the 16th Annual International Symposium on Computer Architecture*, pages 16–24, June 1989.

[CLLG89]   K. Charachorloo, D. Lenoski, J. Laudon, and A. Gupta. Memory consistency and event ordering in scalable shared-memory multiprocessors. Technical Report CSL-TR-89-405, Stanford University, Computer Systems Laboratory, Nov. 1989.

[DSB86]   M. Dubois, C. Scheurich, and F. Briggs. Memory access buffering in multiprocessors. In *Proceedings of the 13th Annual International Symposium on Computer Architecture*, pages 434–442, June 1986.

[DSB88]   M. Dubois, C. Scheurich, and F. Briggs. Synchronization, coherence, and event ordering in multiprocessors. *IEEE Computer*, pages 9–21, Feb. 1988.

[Goo83]   J. R. Goodman. Using cache memory to reduce processor-memory traffic. In *Proceedings of the 10th Annual International Symposium on Computer Architecture*, pages 124–131, June 1983.

[GW88]   J. R. Goodman and P. J. Woest. The Wisconsin Multicube: a new large-scale cache-coherent multiprocessor. In

Proceedings of the 15th Annual International Symposium on Computer Architecture, pages 422–431, June 1988.

[HA89]   P. Hutto and M. Ahamad. Slow memory: Weakening consistency to enhance concurrency in distributed shared memory. Technical Report GIT-ICS-89/39, Georgia Institute of Technology, Oct. 1989.

[IEE89]   IEEE P1596 - SCI Coherence Protocols. *Scalable Coherent Interface*, March 1989.

[KEW⁺85] R. H. Katz, S. J. Eggers, D. A. Wood, C. L. Perkins, and R. G. Sheldon. Implementing a cache consistency protocol. In *Proceedings of the 12th Annual International Symposium on Computer Architecture*, pages 276–283, June 1985.

[KMRS88] A. R. Karlin, M. S. Manasse, L. Rudolph, and D. D. Sleator. Competitive snoopy caching. *Algorithmica*, 3:79–119, 1988.

[Lam79]   L. Lamport. How to make a multiprocessor computer that correctly executes multiprocess programs. *IEEE Transactions on Computers*, C-28(9):690–691, September 1979.

[LR90]   J. Lee and U. Ramachandran. Synchronization with multiprocessor caches. In *Proceedings of the 17th Annual International Symposium on Computer Architecture*, pages 27–37, May 1990.

[LS88]   R. J. Lipton and J. S. Sandberg. PRAM: A scalable shared memory. Technical Report CS-TR-180-88, Princeton University, September 1988.

[McC84]   E. McCreight. *The Dragon Computer System: An early overview*. Xerox Corp., Sept. 1984.

[MHW87]   T. N. Mudge, J. P. Hayes, and D. C. Winsor. Multiple bus architectures. *Computer (USA)*, 20(6):42–48, June 1987.

[Pol88]   C. D. Polychronopoulos. *Parallel Programming and Compilers*, pages 113–158. Kluwer Academic Publishers, 1988.

[PP84]   M. Papamarcos and J. Patel. A low overhead solution for multiprocessors with private cache memories. In *Proceedings of the 11th Annual International Symposium on Computer Architecture*, pages 348–354, June 1984.

[SD87]   C. Scheurich and M. Dubois. Correct memory operation of cache-based multiprocessors. In *Proceedings of the 14th Annual International Symposium on Computer Architecture*, pages 234–243, June. 1987.

[TS87]   C. P. Thacker and L. C. Stewart. Firefly: A multiprocessor workstation. In *Proceedings of the Second International Conference on Architectural Support for Programming Languages and Operating Systems*, pages 164–172, Oct. 1987.

[Wil87]   A. W. Wilson. Hierarchical cache/bus architecture for shared memory multiprocessors. In *Proceedings of the 14th Annual International Symposium on Computer Architecture*, pages 244–252, June 1987.

[YTL87]   P. C. Yew, N. F. Tzeng, and D. H. Lawrie. Distributing hotspot addressing in large-scale multiprocessor. *IEEE Transactions on Computers*, pages 388–395, April 1987.

WHAT IS SCALABILITY?*

Mark D. Hill

Computer Sciences Department
1210 West Dayton St.
University of Wisconsin
Madison, Wisconsin 53706
markhill@cs.wisc.edu

Abstract

Scalability is a frequently-claimed attribute of multiprocessor systems. While the basic notion is intuitive, scalability has no generally-accepted definition. For this reason, current use of the term adds more to marketing potential than technical insight.

In this chapter, I first examine formal definitions of scalability, *but I fail to find a useful, rigorous definition of it.* I then question whether scalability is useful and conclude by challenging the technical community to either (1) rigorously define scalability or (2) stop using it to describe systems.

INTRODUCTION

Even though *scalability* has no generally-accepted definition, it is often used without elaboration to describe multiprocessor systems. This practice imparts a positive feeling toward a system without providing any new information and therefore has no place in technical literature.

---

*The work is supported in part by the National Science Foundation's Presidential Young Investigator and Computer and Computation Research Programs under grants MIPS-8957278 and CCR-8902536, A.T. & T. Bell Laboratories, Cray Research, Digital Equipment Corporation, Texas Instruments, and the graduate school at the University of Wisconsin–Madison. This work is also scheduled to appear in *ACM SIGARCH Computer Architecture News, 18(4), December 1990.*

The attribute *scalability* can be made technically useful by rigorously defining it so that questions like the following can be answered:

- Is my architecture scalable?

- Are all architectures that avoid buses and broadcasts scalable?

- Can some architectures be more scalable than others?

- Does the intended workload affect an architecture's scalability?

- Does cost affect scalability?

- Is an architecture scalable with respect to a uniprocessor version of itself or a theoretical multiprocessor?

- Does a scalable architecture imply that all, some, or at least one implementation of it are scalable?

- When is an implementation scalable?

- How does one adjust for physical limitations (e.g., bounded fan-in/out and the speed of light)?

- Should a system builder design for scalability or speed?

- Who must consider scalability?

In this chapter, I will try and fail to formalize scalability, question whether scalability is important. and conclude by asking others to define scalability or to stop using it.

A FORMAL DEFINITION OF SCALABILITY?

An intuitive notion of scalability is that it implies a favorable comparison between a larger version of some parallel system with either a sequential version of that same system or a theoretical parallel machine. If we choose to compare with a sequential version, it seems natural to define scalability with *speedup* [Eager *et al.*, 1989]. Let $time(n, x)$ be the time required by an n-processor system to execute a program to solve a of problem of size x.[1] The speedup on a problem of size x with n processors is the execution time on one processor divided by the time on n processors, or:

$$speedup(n. x) = \frac{time(1, x)}{time(n, x)}.$$

Related to speedup is *efficiency*, which is speedup divided by the number of processors, or:

$$efficiency(n, x) = \frac{speedup(n, x)}{n} = \frac{time(1, x)/n}{time(n, x)}.$$

In general, the best possible efficiency is one,[2] implying the best speedup is linear, $speedup(n, x) = n$. Clearly a system that achieves linear speedup matches an intuitive notion of scalability. Therefore, a restrictive definition of scalability is:

> A system is scalable if $efficiency(n, x) = 1$ for all algorithms, number of processors n and problem sizes x.

This definition is not useful, however, because it precludes any system from being called scalable. First, many parallel algorithms have a sequential (or at least not completely parallel) component, yielding poor efficiencies for a sufficiently large number of processors [Amdahl, 1967].[3] Second, if problem size is held constant (as with benchmarks), efficiencies will be poor for sufficiently large systems, for example, when the number of processors nears or exceeds the problem size [Francis and Mathieson, 1988]. Third, if problem size is increased for larger systems, then the rate of increase must be specified. Gustafson sparked considerable debate with his proposal that execution time rather than problem size be held constant for larger systems [Gustafson, 1988, Zhou, 1988,

---

[1] *Problem size* is the amount of memory necessary to specify the input to the problem. In serial complexity theory, it is usually denoted with n rather than x. We use x since n has already been used to denote the number of processors. Many notations for speedup omit mention of problem size, usually implying that it is large and held constant.

[2] Super-linear speedups occasionally occur, primarily due to interactions with a system's memory hierarchy.

[3] A recent paper [Karp and Flatt, 1990] even advocates using the lack of variability in experimental measures of a program's sequential fraction as an indicator of scalability.

Heath and Worley, 1989]. Others propose to follow the lead of sequential complexity theory and examine only asymptotic efficiencies, requiring the number of processors to increase without bound and the problem size to grow at an even faster rate (i.e., $n \to \infty$ and $x/n \to \infty$) [Almasi and Gottlieb, 1989].

While one can imagine a list of caveats to make the above definition more useful (but less elegant), its fundamental deficiency is that a definition of system scalability should exercise systems, not algorithms. One way to factor out the effect of algorithms is to define the efficiency of a real parallel system a second way: with respect to a theoretical parallel machine rather than with respect to a real sequential system. Let $time^*(n, x)$ be the time required by an n-processor theoretical machine to execute the same algorithm as used by the real machine to solve a problem of size x. An alternative definition of efficiency is:

$$efficiency^*(n, x) = \frac{time^*(n, x)}{time(n, x)}.$$

One candidate theoretical machine, at least for shared-memory MIMD multiprocessors, is a *parallel random access machine* (PRAM) [Fortune and Wyllie, 1978]. An n-processor PRAM has a single globally-addressable memory and n processors that operate on a lock-step read-memory, compute, write-memory cycle. PRAMs differ in whether they allow simultaneous reads of the same location (concurrent read (CR) versus exclusive read (ER)), whether they allow simultaneous writes of the same location (CW versus EW), and what value remains in a location written by simultaneous writers (COMMON – all simultaneous writes store the same value; ARBITRARY – any one of the values written may remain; and MINIMUM – the value written by the lowest numbered processor remains) [Snir, 1982, Fich and Ragde, 1984].

A problem with using $efficiency^*(n, x)$ is that theoretical machines and real machines exist in different worlds, making comparisons between $time^*(n, x)$ and $time(n, x)$ difficult. Theoretical machines operate with hypothetical cycle times, occupy no space, and are not limited by technological constraints. Real machines, on the other hand, have cycle times determined by numerous practical factors, and have global communication limited by the propagation of light and the bounded fan-in and fan-out of most real technologies [Almasi and Gottlieb, 1989]. Implementing systems in three-space means global communication must eventually slow down with the cube-root of system size, while bounded fan-in and fan-out introduces a logarithmic factor. The multiplicative effect of these constraints can yield a second definition for scalability:

A system is scalable if $efficiency^*(n, x) = O([n^{1/3}logn]^{-1})$ for all algorithms, number of processors n and problem sizes x.

Another problem with using a theoretical machine is that one must be selected. Unfortunately, different theoretical machines have different asymptotic execution times for the same problem. For example, there exist problems for which a CREW (concurrent-read-exclusive-write) PRAM takes a factor of log n longer than a CRCW-COMMON PRAM, and other problems where the latter machine can take take log n longer than a CRCW-MINIMUM PRAM [Fich and Ragde, 1984]. Thus, the best the above definition allows is for an architecture to be called scalable or not scalable with respect to a particular, explicitly-mentioned theoretical machine.

A final problem with the above definition of scalability is that it is too much work (for systems architects and implementors). While it is time-consuming to compute $efficiency^*(n, x)$ for one algorithm, it is worse to do so for all algorithms. Perhaps it is more appropriate to call a machine scalable for a particular algorithm.

IS SCALABILITY IMPORTANT?

An implicit assumption of the previous section is that scalability is important and worth defining. Here I examine this assumption.

Scalability is important if it is useful. Whether it is useful depends on who is using it, what their purpose is, and how it is defined. Potential users are theoreticians, academic paper-writers, academic system-builders, industrial visionaries, industrial systems architects, industrial systems builders, product marketing, and customers.[4] Purposes for using scalability include gaining insight about mathematical models of large systems, designing new computer architectures, implementing new machines, marketing products,[5] and selecting new computers to purchase.

---

[4] These categories are not mutually exclusive.

[5] One company even calls its instruction set architecture scalable.

Definitions of scalability range from considering performance relative to a PRAM to brainstorming about a somewhat larger system.

I view scalability, even without a rigorous definition, as being useful for providing insight. Contemplating large systems enable researchers to discover approaches not presently necessary or practical. Designers of the NYU Ultracomputer [Gottlieb *et al.*, 1983], for example, invented *combining* for handling situations where the rate of requests to a single memory word increases with system size. While combining hardware is still not necessary in today's systems, the ideas have evolved to affect commercial systems (e.g., Sequent Symmetry [Graunke and Thakkar, 1990].

I do not view scalability, especially asymptotic scalability, as being useful for selecting between design options or for describing an architecture or implementation. I see no reason to believe that the best software and hardware for an arbitrarily large number of processors is best for smaller systems. Engineering factors are important. The best interconnection network for ten or hundred processors may be a bus or 2-D torus, respectively. Does it matter whether either is asymptotically optimal?

Systems architects probably want to design a system to work well over a size range of ten to twenty times, while implementors should be concerned with a smaller range, say two to four times. Thus, a company designing a new architecture for which initial, low-end systems that will have four processors may wish to consider ramifications for 80-processor systems when making architectural decisions, but should probably implement the first system with a bus. Furthermore, systems implementors should consider using ugly, unscalable things (e.g., buses and broadcast) if such things simplify the design, reduce system cost, and improve performance.

CONCLUSIONS

In this chapter, I examined aspects of scalability, but did not find a useful, rigorous definition of it. Without such a definition, I assert that calling a system "scalable" is about as useful as calling it "modern". I encourage the technical community to either rigorously define scalability or stop using it to describe systems.

95

Acknowledgements

The ideas in this chapter evolved from ideas appearing in [Goodman et al., 1989] through discussions with Jim Goodman, Mary Vernon, Phil Woest and others and through feedback from a talk I gave at the *Scalable Shared-Memory Architectures* workshop in Seattle on May 26, 1990. I would like to thank Michel Dubois and Shreekant Thakkar for organizing the workshop. Finally, I wish to thank Sarita Adve, Anant Agarwal, Sue Dentinger, Rajiv Jauhari, Ross Johnson, Richard Kessler, James Larus, Dan Nussbaum, Diana Stone, and Mary Vernon for reading and improving drafts of this chapter.

References

[Almasi and Gottlieb, 1989] G. S. Almasi and A. Gottlieb. *Highly Parallel Computing*. Redwood City, CA, Benjamin / Cummings Publishing Company, Inc., 1989.

[Amdahl, 1967] G. M. Amdahl. Validity of the single-processor approach to achieving large scale computing capabilities. In *AFIPS Conference Proceedings*, pages 483–485. April 1967.

[Eager et al., 1989] Derek L. Eager, John Zahorjan, and Edward D. Lazowska. Speedup versus efficiency in parallel systems. *IEEE Trans. on Computers*, C-38(3):408–423, March 1989.

[Fich and Ragde, 1984] Faith E. Fich and Prabhakar L Ragde. Relations between concurrent-write models of parallel computation. In *Proc. Principals of Distributed Computing*, pages 179–190, August 1984.

[Fortune and Wyllie, 1978] Stephen Fortune and James Wyllie. Parallelism in random access machines. In *Proc. Tenth ACM Symposium on Theory of Computing*, pages 114–118, 1978.

[Francis and Mathieson, 1988] R. S. Francis and I. D. Mathieson. A benchmark parallel sort for shared memory multiprocessors. *IEEE Transactions on Computers*, 12:1619–1626, December 1988.

[Goodman et al., 1989] James R. Goodman, Mark D. Hill, and Philip J. Woest. Scalability and its application to multicube. Technical report,

Univ. of Wisconsin, March 1989. Computer Sciences Technical Report #835.

[Gottlieb et al., 1983] Allan Gottlieb, Ralph Grishman, Clyde P. Kruskal, Kevin P. McAuliffe, Larry Rudolph, and Marc Snir. The nyu ultracomputer–designing an mimd shared memory parallel computer. *IEEE Trans. on Computers*, C-32(2):175–189, February 1983.

[Graunke and Thakkar, 1990] Gary Graunke and Shreekant Thakkar. Synchronization algorithms for shared-memory multiprocessors. *IEEE Computer*, 23(6):60–69, June 1990.

[Gustafson, 1988] John L. Gustafson. Reevaluating amdahl's law. *Communications of the ACM*, 31(5):532–533, May 1988.

[Heath and Worley, 1989] Michael Heath and Patrick Worley. Once again, amdahl's law. *Communications of the ACM*, 32(2):262–264, February 1989.

[Karp and Flatt, 1990] Alan H. Karp and Horace P. Flatt. Measuring parallel processor performance. *Communications of the ACM*, 33(5):539–543, May 1990.

[Snir, 1982] Marc Snir. On parallel search. In *Proc. Principals of Distributed Computing*, pages 242–253, August 1982.

[Zhou, 1988] Xiaofeng Zhou. Bridging the gap between amdahl's law and sandia laboratory's result. *Communications of the ACM*, 31(8):1014–1016, August 1988.

Measuring Process Migration Effects Using an MP Simulator

Andrew Ladd, Trevor Mudge, and Oyekunle Olukotun

Advanced Computer Architecture Lab
Department of Electrical Engineering and Computer Science
University of Michigan
Ann Arbor, Michigan

Abstract

This chapter examines multiprocessors that are used in throughput mode to multiprogram a number of unrelated sequential programs. This is the most common use for multiprocessors. There is no data sharing between the programs. Each program forms a process that is scheduled to execute on a processor until it blocks because its time-slice expires or for I/O. The process can migrate among the processors when its turn to resume occurs. The degree of process migration can dramatically impact the behavior of caches and hence the throughput of the multiprocessor. This chapter investigates the behavior of cache misses that can result from different degrees of process migration. The degree of migration is varied by assigning each process an affinity for a particular processor. An efficient multiprocessor cache simulator is described that is used in the study. The study is restricted to shared-bus multiprocessors and two contrasting cache consistency protocols, write update and invalidate.

INTRODUCTION

In today's computing environment, multiprocessors are playing a greater role than ever before. Originally, multiprocessors were intended to accelerate single program execution through parallel processing. However, their most common use to date has been as "throughput" machines in multiprogramming environments. These systems typically consist of 2 to 32 processors connected by a common backplane bus. Memory units are also attached to this backplane such that all processors have equal access to memory. This is commonly referred to as a tightly-coupled shared-memory system.

Programs are selected to execute on the processors of the machine by the operating system scheduler. In a typical case, the scheduler takes a program (process) from a common run queue and sends it to one of the available processors. When the process' time-slice expires or it blocks on a system call (for example when waiting on I/O), it is removed from its processor and another process from the run queue takes its place. This is characteristic of a preemptive scheduler. When the process is ready to execute again it is placed back on the run queue and waits its turn for execution. In a straightforward round-robin type of scheduling, there is no guarantee which processor this process will execute on next. With respect to cache performance, the best processor for it to execute on next is most likely the one it executed on last. There is a much greater likelihood that the process will find more of its initial memory references in the cache of the processor it executed on last, thereby reducing the number of instructions and data that must initially come from memory[1]. This gives the process an affinity for the cache of the processor it last left [2]. On the other hand, if the process is scheduled on a processor it has never executed on, it will have no footprint (matching data and instruction lines) in that processor's cache. In this case it will have to bring in all the instructions and data it initially needs from memory, making an initially cold cache warm to the process [3]. Bouncing a process from processor to processor in this manner is termed process migration and can have a detrimental affect on the overall cache performance and bus traffic in a computer system. Process migration also increases the interference of a migrating process' address references with the cache footprints of other processes. This interference will displace cache lines from previously executed processes, thus reducing the cache footprint of those processes.

An understanding of these process migration effects on system performance is important for the operating system designer. If better scheduling algorithms can send a process to a warm cache (one that the process left recently) then the cache hit rate is improved and bus traffic is lowered during the initial execution of the process. Transient or compulsory misses, initial misses that result from warming up a cache to a process, are reduced if the process is scheduled to a cache which is already warm to it. Steady state misses are cache misses that result from memory references displacing valid cache lines of the executing process [4]. Process migration tends to increase the transient miss behavior of caches in the system while leaving the steady state miss behavior unaffected. Other aspects of the design can also benefit from understanding process migration effects. For instance, cache and bus designers should consider the impact of how process migration effects could degrade system behavior.

A method to keep the caches consistent is required because processes migrate from processor to processor. This is especially important when actual data sharing occurs between processes because each processor needs to have equal access to the shared data. In tightly-coupled shared-memory systems there are two basic types of consistency algorithms: invalidate and update based. The invalidate protocol is based on eliminating shared data in other processor's caches when one processor modifies its copy of that data. The update protocol updates shared data in other caches upon each modification of the data in the expectation that it will be reused.

The choice between using physical caches or virtual caches has many tradeoffs. Virtual cacheing does not require the translation of the virtual address in the TLB (Translation Lookaside Buffer) before accessing the virtual cache. This significantly reduces the cache access time after the generation of the virtual address [3]. Cache line synonyms can cause problems in a virtual cache. Synonyms occur when two cache lines indexed by different virtual addresses refer to the same physical address.

A problem arises when a processor tries to modify one of the synonym lines because it is difficult to identify the other synonyms for the required modification. Virtual caches also create added complexity in the bus watching of the consistency protocols. A reverse TLB is required to map physical bus addresses into virtual addresses because the references on the system bus are physically addressed.

The trend in cache design for processors has been to increase cache size as processor speeds have increased. This is to compensate for the growing gap between main memory speeds and processor speeds. Main memory cycle times (and intrinsic bus delays) have not decreased at the pace of processor cycle times. This makes memory references that miss the local caches even more costly. The easiest method to reduce this cost is to make the local caches larger. In most designs the first level cache (primary cache) is limited to the amount of chip area the CPU designers can set aside. One solution is to create a secondary level of cacheing that can alleviate the high cost of references missing the first level cache. The secondary cache is usually made up of standard SRAM parts assembled on the board in close proximity to the CPU and is typically slower than the primary cache. A secondary cache built this way is usually an order of magnitude larger than the primary cache. It is for these large cacheing systems that longer address tracing is crucial. Effectively analyzing these large caches requires a large address stream to measure its steady state behavior [5]. Address streams that are too short may only measure the initial warming of the cache (i.e., transient behavior).

The experiments conducted in this study examine cacheing behavior in a multiprocessing environment. Only process migration effects are considered, therefore processes do not share data between other processes. This restriction was made to simplify the tools and to focus on "throughput" environments. The tools used include an address trace generator and a multi-cache simulator. These tools provide fast and accurate measurements of cacheing behavior with respect to scheduling algorithms, consistency algorithms, and cache characteristics.

Method	references	slow-down	abstraction
Analytical	>1M	-	Yes
Trace Driven	>1M	10X	No
RTL	~10K	1000X	No

Table 1: Comparisons of Cache Analysis Methods.

Previous Studies

Many studies have focused on the sharing between parallel processes. These studies [6, 7, 8, 9, 10] are interested, primarily, in exploring the effects of cache consistency or coherency where there is shared data. Although some of these studies account for process migration, the central theme they explore is somewhat different from characterizing process migration effects on multiprocessor caches.

Some of these studies [6, 7, 8] use analytical models to simulate address streams. While they can produce results very quickly and have the most flexibility, their results are an abstraction of real system behavior. At the other end of the spectrum are studies [10] which completely simulate each processor in some form of detailed register transfer level. While this method produces the most accurate results, it is far too slow to capture large multiprogrammed address traces. Trace driven simulations offer a compromise between the two. They take real address traces from targeted programs and run them through a high level cache simulator. Trace driven methods are considerably faster than detailed models but still simulate "real" system behavior. Faster methods are becoming increasingly desirable because cache sizes are growing. As cache sizes grow, the need for longer traces is crucial to accurately measure the behavior of these large caches. Table 1 illustrates a comparison of these methods.

This study uses a high level cache simulator driven by address traces extracted from benchmark programs. The size of the traces excluded register transfer simulation from consideration due to the time required for RTL simulations. Analytical models were not considered due to their inaccuracies.

SCHEDULING

A key aspect to examining process migration effects is to set up a multi-programming model that is sufficiently realistic yet deterministic enough to allow the resimulation of the same sequence of scheduling events through various cache configurations. When studying migration effects, it is important to identify which address stream is produced by which process (program). Without this identification it is difficult to isolate cacheing behavior affected by process migration.

Not only is process identification important but so is finding an accurate algorithm to interleave the multiple processes (scheduling). One approach is to let the host system schedule the multiple programs with its native scheduler and have each program send its results to the same cache simulator. The simulator then processes the address streams as they are received. In this way, the cache simulator analyzes the address traces generated in a manner consistent with the host machine's scheduler. This provides a straightforward method to utilize a real scheduling algorithm [5]. One drawback to having scheduling performed by the host is that it is sensitive to traced code side-effects, since the host scheduler cannot account for the annotated code. Another drawback is that the traced code would rarely schedule the same way between separate executions due to the uncertainty of system loading.

An alternative scheduling approach is to take a known scheduling algorithm, or statistical measurement of one, and apply that directly to the programs which are executed. This approach can compensate for some of the tracing side-effects by altering the algorithm appropriately. It also allows repeatable scheduling for different executions of the programs.

Closely related to program interleaving is processor scheduling. As with interleaving, an algorithm is needed to schedule each processor in the multiprocessor set. This problem is less severe since a new context can start execution on any idle processor or the first that becomes available. Since measuring the effects of process migration and affinity is the topic of this chapter, the scheduler must be flexible enough to study various scheduling algorithms and their impact on system performance.

CACHE COHERENCY

A method to keep the caches consistent is required because processes migrate from processor to processor. This is especially important when actual data sharing occurs between processes. Since this study does not examine data sharing, why should cache coherency matter at all? To answer this question, one only has to note that the context of a process must be consistent with past contexts of that process. For example: if process A was on processor 1 and referenced location X, then location X is valid in that processor's cache. Now assume process A is swapped out of processor 1 and is later scheduled on processor 2. While executing on processor 2 it writes to location X. Without a consistency protocol, processor 1's cache line for X will not be updated or invalidated. Now if process A is re-scheduled back to processor 1 and reads X it will receive a stale value.

Since cache coherency is an important consideration with process migration, valuable insight can be gained by measuring different coherency effects on caches. Cache coherency algorithms have been studied at great length. Many papers have been devoted to the comparison of coherency based on directory schemes and snoopy protocols [6, 7, 8, 9, 10]. Although these studies focus primarily upon the sharing of data, valuable conclusions are drawn as to when each scheme is beneficial over the others. Directory schemes are ideally suited for a distributed bus type of organization while snoopy schemes are more suited for centralized shared bus organizations. Distributed bus organizations, and thus directory based coherency, are more applicable with large numbers of processors where a centralized bus cannot support the necessary bandwidth for the communication traffic between processors and memory. Centralized buses on the other hand are simpler and less costly to implement and are therefore suited for a modest number of processors. Although the directory mechanisms tend to reduce the bus traffic bottleneck they usually cause a bottleneck at the memory modules because memory must maintain the coherency tables. Both the directory and snoopy based schemes can support invalidation or update protocols.

Finally, software approaches keep caches coherent without causing bus or memory bottlenecks. This is done by flushing a processor's cache at each context switch. Their primary drawback is the reduction of usable cached data because a process is guaranteed to enter a cold cache at each context switch.

ADDRESS TRACE GENERATION

Before a cache analysis of "real" multiprocessing system can begin, accurate address traces must be generated. Ideally the address trace contains the complete set of address streams as seen by each processor in a multiprocessor system, or the equivalent information. This allows a cache simulator to process addresses exactly as they occurred. There are many factors that prevent the generation of an ideal set of address traces. Such factors include the side-effects of generating or extracting the traces, the performance degradation between the traced code and the actual code, and the difficulties of tracing certain kernel routines.

One major deviation from the ideal is that in many instances one cannot acquire address trace data from all instructions executing on a particular CPU. The particular method used may restrict tracing only to user programs and ignore the tracing of kernel code. This is particularly burdensome when trying to measure how context switching affects caches since various kernel procedures are likely to execute repeatedly on each processor.

Another deviation is the intrusion of the tracing method on the traced program. Tracing is usually done by inserting code between load, store, and program control instructions to record memory references. The program control instructions provide basic block boundaries which identify program flow changes. Whether the code is inserted into microcode [9] or inserted into program code [5, 11, 12], it still only executes when a program is traced. This extra code obviously creates side-effects and behavior that is never seen in the original untraced code. Memory management side-effects are examples of abnormal behavior which manifest themselves from the added code. The added calls to the inserted code to record addresses could cause page faults and displace TLB entries not normally seen by the original program. In addition, the address traces must be written somewhere, whether to a UNIX^{TM} pipe or a file, and are bound to cause page faulting and TLB displacement. Reducing most of these side-effects and abnormal behavior is another concern in selecting a good trace generation method.

Closely related to the side-effect issue is the performance degradation of the code that is traced. If additional code is added to the original program in order to trace the address references, there is little chance that this added code will not degrade program performance. Performance degradation can cause several unfortunate by-products. First, system clocks and timers appear to run faster than as seen by the original program. Since fewer instructions of the original program are executing between timed events it appears to the executing program that clocks and timers run faster. Furthermore, I/O will appear faster, the program will appear to have a smaller time-slice before preemption, and kernel interactions will appear to execute faster if kernel code is not traced. For example, the Titan address generation scheme [5] slows down the execution of a program by as much as 12 times. ATUM [9] increases the time of execution by a factor of 10 and AE [11] induces a factor of 4 increase in execution time.

Finally, an enormous amount of data is created when generating address traces for large runs. Manipulating this data into a manageable form is our last consideration in tracing data. Two approaches are available to solve this problem. The first and most straightforward approach [5, 12] pipes the traces from the traced file directly into the program that analyzes them. This saves all the overhead of storing the traces into a file and, depending upon the disk cacheing method, could save time. In addition, disk space is no longer an issue when using pipes. The primary drawback with this method is that not all experiments are repeatable with the same set of traces, especially those involving kernel interaction. Each run will produce a slightly different behavior which could skew results when comparing different cache configurations to the same programs. The second approach is to save the traces in compressed form [13], or to save a smaller set of events that can be used to extract the real traces [11]. These approaches allow different experiments to run on the same set of data but suffer from the extra file system overhead that the piped version eliminated. They also require a great deal of file space.

The Mache compaction scheme used with UNIX^{TM} compress has been shown to reduce the traced data to approximately 2.5 bits per reference [13]. The AE method of saving compressed significant events have been shown to reduce the traced data close to 0.5 bits per reference [11].

TOOLS

For this study, an address tracing tool was employed which annotates the object code of the executable program. This choice was made because it could generate addresses from the original program as well as the library routines that were called (since the annotation is performed after linking). The address tracer also allowed the address stream to be sent to a UNIX^{TM} file descriptor which simplified piping multiple streams into the cache simulator.

The cache simulator reads in the address streams from the various executing programs via the UNIX^{TM} file descriptors. In addition, the simulator can sequence the reading of the file descriptors according to any particular process scheduling algorithm. As the addresses were read, the cache arrays were examined and updated in accordance with the cache consistency algorithms. In this study, only snoopy bus algorithms were examined. Both update and invalidate protocols were modeled to study their respective effects on cache behavior in the presence of process migration.

The caches in the simulator are direct-mapped with variable index and line sizes. Tag matches are based upon the non-index and non-line portion of the physical address and the pid (process identifier) of the process. Cache lines are allocated on read, as well as write, misses. Context switching is modeled by scheduling a process to execute for 3000 instructions on average[14]. A Poisson distribution with an expected value of 3000 is generated when a process is scheduled to execute. This value is set as the limit to how long the context of the current process will run. Context switch times thereby distribute around a Poisson mean of 3000 instructions.

The pid of each process is included in each address tag. This allows the disambiguation of virtual addresses of different processes. Since no sharing between processes exist this modified tag causes no unwanted mismatches between different process' addresses. Since only virtual address traces were available, special care was required to distribute the references in the cache. In a physical cache, virtual pages are translated into physical pages which create a random distribution over each process' address space. A method to emulate this behavior is highly desirable. Sites and Agarwal proposed a method to hash the virtual addresses based on the pid of the process[15]. They found that caches fed with hashed virtual addresses provided similar performance to physically addressed caches. Virtual address hashing gives a pseudo-random distribution of each process' virtual address space inside the physical cache. If no adjustment to the virtual addresses were made the miss rate would be unrealistically high because many programs reside in the same range of virtual space. Physical page allocation tends to randomize pages in this space thus causing fewer cache line conflicts between processes.

A piping program linked the address trace generation program to the cache simulator in such a way that the cache simulator could read off each trace from a unique file descriptor. The piping program created a UNIX^{TM} pipe for each executing program and sequenced the file descriptor for each pipe starting at a predetermined base.

Scheduling Details

Two types of scheduling are examined, one that schedules globally and one that schedules locally. The global scheduler takes the processor which has been idle the longest, or if none, the first to become available, and schedules the process that has been waiting the longest to execute. Jobs are maintained in queues that hold processes which are waiting for execution. As a process' time-slice expires, it is placed at the rear of the queue and the process at the head is then chosen to run on the first available processor. Process priorities are not considered in the scheduling mechanism, so all processes have equal priority and equal access to each processor. In contrast, the local scheduler assigns each process to a unique processor corresponding to its initial context of execution. From then on that process only executes on its assigned processor. While this local scheduler is highly unrealistic, it does show how complete process affinity can affect cacheing behavior. For this reason it was chosen for this study. Realistic schedulers usually schedule globally or provide a mixture of global and local scheduling. Local scheduling by itself does not allow for fair load sharing among the processors in the system. Refer to Figure 1 for details concerning the flow of the scheduler.

Particular attention must be paid to how each process stream interacts with the others. How much processing should be allowed on one stream before work begins on the others? How do the separate address streams synchronize with each other given the states of the caches of the concurrently executing processors?

A logical separation of address stream execution allows one processor to work on an address stream from the beginning of the context switch to the end. This works in all cases where no data sharing occurs between separate processes and when processes run sequentially in the system. When a process exits a processor and is later rescheduled, the cache coherency transactions for its address space are guaranteed to be resolved for any memory reference occurring before the process starts. Thus every processor can run an address stream for a current process until it the stream switches to a new context. During execution of each context the address references are made consistent in the other caches such that when a process begins execution in another cache, its cache is guaranteed consistent.

One problem with this approach is that even unrelated processes share some amount of data in the kernel. Therefore, since coherency is not maintained on a cycle-by-cycle basis between all caches, some degree of error is introduced into the results. This problem is difficult to overcome without expanding the simulator to provide cycle-by-cycle simulation. This would run a great deal slower due to the added overhead of the more detailed model. In addition, a method is not available to produce kernel traces. As noted, in this study the targeted user programs contain no parallelism or data sharing. Thus, a process can only invalidate or update cache lines in other caches that were allocated on previous contexts of that process. In other words, process A cannot invalidate or update cache lines that were allocated to process B since they do not share data (address tags and pids will not match during snoopy look-up). The only way for process A to affect the cache lines of process B is to displace

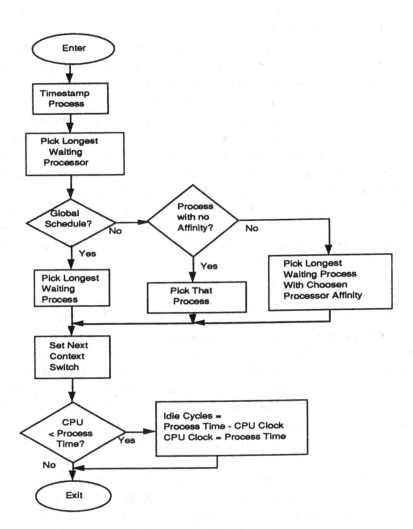

Figure 1: The Scheduler

them in the cache in which process A is currently executing.

Since a process is simulated in sequential order as dictated by the scheduling algorithm, we can guarantee that no execution of a process will precede (in the simulated context) a previous execution of that process. This is accomplished by time stamping a process when it is context switched out of a processor. Then if that process is scheduled to a processor whose clock (cycle count) is less than the time stamp, the processor's clock is set to the time stamp. This guarantees the sequential (with respect to cycle count) execution of the process. This argument when combined with the one from the paragraph above guarantees that misses due to invalidations can only occur when a previous instantiation of the process on another processor caused those invalidations.

Furthermore, we can detect when a miss was due to invalidation or displacement. This is accomplished by noting that even though simulation is not accomplished cycle by cycle, a processor's cache is consistent at the time a process is scheduled on it. Since a process cannot schedule itself on two processors at the same time there are no race conditions with respect to coherency. The question must be asked: Is there a race condition between invalidation of a line and another process' displacement of that line? This reduces to a don't care situation because upon completion of the time-slice the line will be displaced to the new value and pid whether the invalidation or displacement occurs first. The next process using the cache only knows that it missed due to displacement and not invalidation. For example, a cache line in processor 1 is valid from a previous instantiation of process A (tag = "pid + tag"). Now process B is executing on processor 1 and process A is executing on processor 2. If process A invalidates X and then process B allocates that line, the resulting state of the cache line is that of the allocation of process B. Conversely, if process B displaced X first then the invalidation from process A occurred, the invalidation would not match the new tag so the cache line would still contain the valid reference of process B. In either case the result is the same, a valid cache line for the reference of process B. For these reasons we can justify processes executing for their entire time-slice without cycle by cycle synchronization.

Coherency Details

This study examines snoopy based coherency algorithms since they are more flexible and are more prevalent in today's computers. The two basic types of snoopy protocols are invalidation and update protocols. We chose to simulate both and compare their effects on cache migration. The invalidation protocol is represented with a "Berkeley" type of coherency while the update protocol is represented with a "Firefly" type of protocol [8]. The Berkeley approach is a write-back protocol that maintains coherency on writes by invalidating matching lines in other caches. Digital Equipment Corporation's "Firefly" approach is also a write-back protocol but maintains coherency on writes by updating the matching cache lines in the other caches.

BENCHMARK PROGRAMS

Four benchmarks were chosen for simulation. Each of these was compiled and the object code annotated to generate address traces. The address traces of each program were fed into the simulator via a UNIX^{TM} pipe. The simulator then interleaved the traces corresponding to the type of scheduling selected. All programs ran in a UNIX^{TM} environment on a DECstation 3100^{TM}. Below is a description of each program; Table 2 provides characteristic data for each.

awk A UNIX^{TM} pattern scanning and processing language which scans a file for matching patterns and executes associated actions upon a match.

diff The UNIX^{TM} differential file comparator utility. This command compares the contents of two files and lists their differences.

dry2 The Drystone benchmark written in C. 50,000 iterations of this program were executed.

nroff A UNIX^{TM} text formatter. This command formats the text of a given file.

Benchmark	I-references	D-reads	D-writes
awk	32388725	4871777	3158560
diff	30939027	5870564	2582993
dry2	30254676	7060852	2858599
nroff	32036008	5983441	2701127
total	125618436	23786634	11301279

Table 2: Benchmark Programs

RESULTS

This section discusses the results of three experiments. In each experiment, simulations were conducted on a unified, direct-mapped cache with a line size of four words. Four pairs of scheduling and coherency combinations were modeled in each experiment: Global Berkeley, Local Berkeley, Global Firefly, and Local Firefly. As previously described, local scheduling refers to adding a processor affinity to each process and only allowing it to run on that processor. Global scheduling sends each process to the first available processor in a round-robin fashion. The cache coherency algorithms are modeled after the Berkeley and Firefly approaches described in a prior section. Each experiment was performed on models containing one to four processors. The measurements focused on three areas: total cache misses, transient cache misses, and misses due to invalidations. In addition, read and write miss measurements were recorded for the last two experiments.

The first experiment set the cache size to 32K words and applied the hashed virtual address traces of the four benchmarks to the simulator. Figures 2 through 4 illustrate these results. The second experiment increased the cache size to 128K words with everything else remaining the same. Figures 5 through 9 illustrate the cache performance resulting from the simulations of this larger cache. Finally, an experiment modeling a virtual 128K word cache was performed by applying the unhashed traces to the cache configuration of the second experiment. Its results are presented in Figures 10 through 14.

Cache Sizes

As expected, larger caches reduce the amount of cache misses across all scheduling and coherency algorithms. Larger reductions are seen with respect to the global scheduling and Firefly algorithms. As seen from Figure 5, the three processor 128K word cache used with the Global Firefly algorithm reduced cache misses by 46 percent over the same configuration with a 32K word cache (Figure 2). Large caches are effective in reducing miss rates in global schedulers since they greatly decrease the amount of transient misses. Recall that the causes of transient misses are interference by processes displacing each other's cache lines or initial cold start misses. Since larger caches tend to spread out the processes in the cache, less interference is seen. As the cache size grows, the number of transient misses due to global scheduling approaches the number of misses generated by local schedulers thereby alleviating some of the global scheduling penalties. Compare Figure 3 and Figure 8 to see how the number of transient misses due to global scheduling approach the number of transient misses due to local scheduling.

The Berkeley approach, although also benefiting from the reduction of transient misses, does not reduce its miss rate as drastically in larger caches. This is due to the additional cache misses from invalidations. In fact, by increasing the cache size, more misses are generated from invalidations from other processors. This is seen by comparing Figures 4 and 9. Larger caches are more likely to contain cache lines which match during an invalidation cycle thereby creating a miss if referenced later. The update approach generates no miss in this case since the cache line is kept active by updating the data.

Both the amounts of invalidates and updates increase with the larger caches during process migration. Invalidate traffic increases a modest amount due to the increase of shared-dirty states in the caches as processes migrate from cache to cache. The larger caches retain more data thereby keeping cache data around for longer periods of time. Update traffic increases by a slightly larger amount as the cache size increases. This is primarily due to the larger caches having a greater likelyhood of retaining data. Since the data has a greater chance of surviving in larger caches, more updates are required to keep the data coherent. Only when

no other cache contains a copy of the cache line may updating stop for
that particular line.

Scheduling

Scheduling was shown to have the greatest impact on the total cache
miss rate. It should be noted that when the processor count reaches
four, even the global algorithms begin to schedule fairly locally. This
is due to each process having a processor all to itself. When a process'
context expires, no other process is waiting, so it gets scheduled back on
the same processor immediately. This is true until one of the programs
finishes execution, at which time two processors would be free upon each
context switch. The global scheduler then schedules the switched out
process to the "other" processor since it was waiting the longest (load
sharing).

As seen from Figures 2 and 5, local scheduling provides the greatest
reduction of total misses especially with larger numbers of processors
(discounting the four processor case). In many cases, local scheduling
reduces the number of misses by one-half or more compared to the corresponding global scheduler. As the number of processors increases, the
amounts of transient misses and misses due to invalidations increase for
global scheduling (discounting the one and four processor case). The
global scheduler sends a process to more and more processors between
successive visits to the same cache. This tends to increase the number
of transient misses resulting from processes interfering with each other
by displacing one another's data and by increasing the amount of cold
start misses (see Figures 3 and 8). It also increases the amount of invalidations to each process' footprint since each process spends a smaller
amount of time on each processor. This becomes more of a problem for
small caches since the contention for the smaller number of cache lines
increases. Local scheduling is beneficial in systems with large numbers
of processors since it prevents this type of behavior. This is encouraging
from a scheduler design perspective because there is the potential for a
large reduction in the number of cache misses.

The Berkeley protocol benefits from local scheduling the most. Since
the Berkeley protocol uses invalidations to keep the multiple caches

coherent, reducing the amount of invalidations will help increase the amount of data retained in each cache for each process. Local scheduling eliminates invalidation of cache lines (not invalidate traffic) by keeping the process on one processor as shown by Figures 4 and 9. A data line only gets invalidated if another process writes to that address. Since sharing was not examined in this study, no other process would generate writes to that address. Therefore, the Berkeley protocol benefits from local scheduling by a reduction of transient misses and by an elimination of misses due to invalidations.

Local scheduling greatly reduces the invalidate traffic, sometimes by as much as 90 percent over global scheduling. This difference grows as the numbers of processors increase. In fact, as the number of processors increase, the number of invalidates will increase for global scheduling while they decrease for local scheduling. This is explained by the amount of hits to dirty data lines in the caches. While a process runs out of a particular cache, writes to dirty data lines require no invalidations. Once a process migrates to a new cache, writes to what were once dirty cache lines now require invalidations to purge the other caches of matching lines. Local schedulers, on the other hand, do not generate this added invalidation traffic due to migrating dirty lines. They do generate extra traffic when dirty lines are displaced by other processes if future writes are made to the displaced address. Even so, local schedulers were also seen to reduce displacement of data over their global counterparts.

Updates are completely eliminated in a local scheduler since no process ever migrates to another cache. Global scheduling does generate update traffic which increases as the processor count increases. As processors are added, there is a greater likelihood that a migrating process has left an active line in one of the caches since the only way to purge lines from past caches is for other processes to displace them. An update is only required if another cache contains the data line the current cache is writing. Since increasing the number of processors increases the likelihood of a process' lines existing in other caches, the number of overall updates must increase.

Cache Coherency

The Firefly coherency protocol does the best with respect to reducing cache misses in the global scheduling approach. As seen from Figures 2 and 5, the Global Firefly approach reduces the amount of misses up to 54 percent over the Berkeley method. This is primarily due to Firefly generating no invalidations. Thus no cache misses are due to invalidates in the Firefly approach, while the Berkeley approach generates a sizable amount of misses due to invalidates. The amount of transient misses between the two approaches are practically identical as would be expected since transient misses are a function of the scheduling algorithm.

Local scheduling evened the differences between the miss rates of the Berkeley and Firefly protocols. Since the transient miss behavior is the same between the two (Figures 3 and 8), the only difference lies in misses due to invalidations. While Firefly never generates invalidations, local scheduling reduces misses due to invalidations in the Berkeley approach to zero. Therefore local scheduling causes both Berkeley and Firefly to generate the same amount of transient and invalidation misses resulting in the same overall miss behavior.

The miss rate of Firefly verses Berkeley is misleading since Firefly pays a large overhead to prevent invalidations. On every write to a word that is in multiple caches, an update must be performed. As a process migrates from processor to processor, the amount of duplicate cache lines increases between the multiple caches. Since multiple caches will retain each process' cache lines until they are displaced, updates will have to be performed while multiple copies exist. As the number of processors increases the probability that a cache line does not exist in multiple caches decreases. This gives rise to an abundance of update cycles to keep all the caches coherent. The Berkeley protocol, on the other hand, invalidates all the other duplicate cache lines after the first write of a process to the duplicate line. From then on, the cache line is dirty and resides only in the current processor. From a process migration point of view, this smaller number of invalidations verses updates gives the Berkeley protocol the advantage with respect to the number of bus transactions required to keep the caches coherent.

Local scheduling greatly reduces the amount of invalidations performed in the Berkeley protocol as the number of processors increase. This is primarily due to fewer processes executing on each processor. This reduction produces fewer displacements in each cache. This will increase the amount of write hits to dirty data lines and thereby reduce the amount of invalidate traffic. Local scheduling eliminates all the update traffic generated by Firefly since there is no way for duplicate lines to exist in multiple caches. Therefore, in a local scheduler, the Firefly approach would generate fewer bus consistency cycles compared with the Berkeley approach.

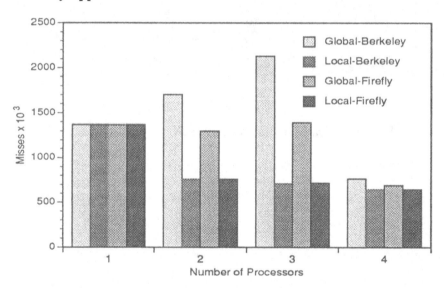

Figure 2: Total misses in a 32K physical cache.

Virtual Verses Physical Cacheing

A virtual cacheing strategy produced consistently more cache misses over the physical caches in every instance except for the four processor cases. This occurs because virtual addresses between processes conflict more than physical addresses. Physical addresses are spread out by the paging algorithm while virtual addresses tend to occupy the same page space between processes. This is especially true within the instruction space

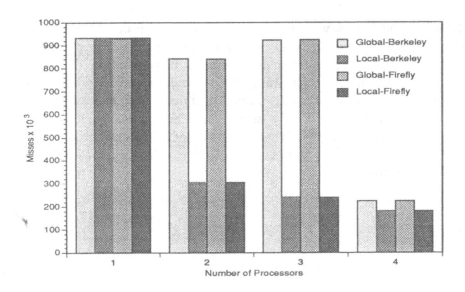

Figure 3: Transient misses in a 32K physical cache.

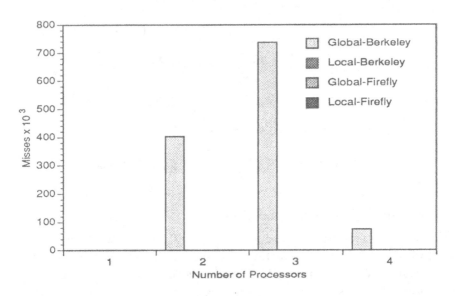

Figure 4: Invalidate misses in a 32K physical cache.

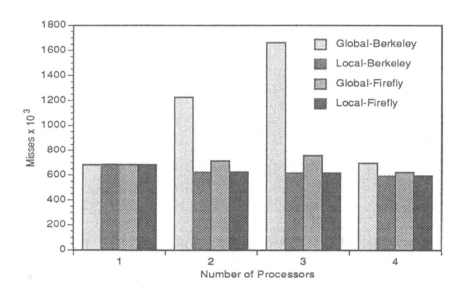

Figure 5: Total misses in a 128K physical cache.

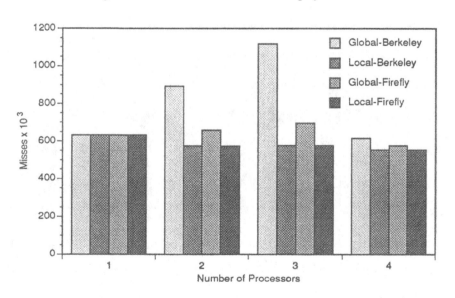

Figure 6: Read misses in a 128K physical cache.

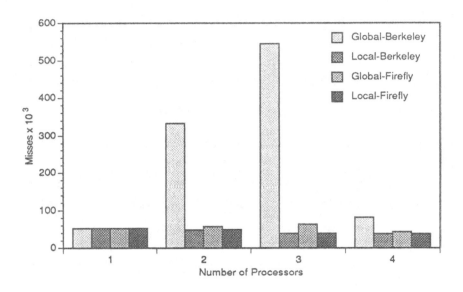

Figure 7: Write misses in a 128K physical cache.

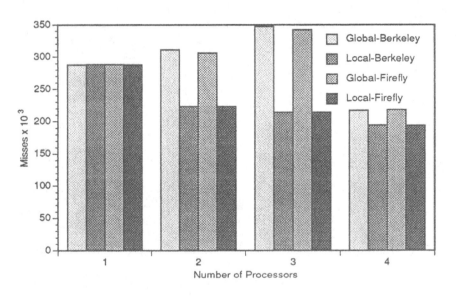

Figure 8: Transient misses in a 128K physical cache.

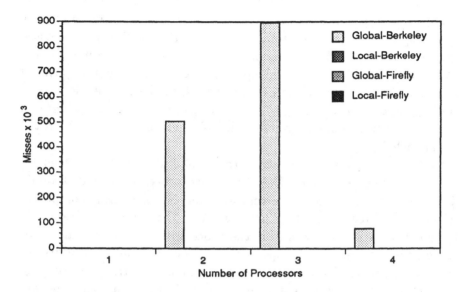

Figure 9: Invalidate misses in a 128K physical cache.

since most code is condensed at the beginning of each virtual address space. The read case in Figure 11 illustrates this well when compared to the write case in Figure 12 and the corresponding graphs in the physically addressed 128K word cache (Figures 6 and 7). The read case produced many more misses relative to the physically addressed cache while the write case produced a modest increase over its physical counterpart. This is primarily due to the interference of the virtual I-streams and the virtual stack regions of the processes. The virtual stack regions also start at the same location in virtual address space. The interference of virtual address spaces can clearly be seen by examining the transient misses of the virtual cache in Figure 13 and comparing them with the misses of the physical cache in Figure 8. The transient misses are much higher in the virtual cache with the exception of the four processor simulation.

One should expect that the global scheduling of a large number of processors would aggravate the difference between physical and virtual caches even more because virtual caches suffer from greater process interference than physical caches. This is indeed true and can be seen by comparing the two graphs of total misses for virtual and physical caches, Figures 5 and 10. With three processors the global scheduler for the virtual cache produces twenty-five percent more misses than its physical counterpart while only five percent more with the local scheduler. Since Firefly generates no misses due to invalidates, its percentage difference is greater when compared with Berkeley (63 percent more misses in the virtual cache).

In the four processor case, each process had a processor to itself for most of its execution time. Only when one process terminated would migration start up again. Since very little displacement from competing processes occurred in the four processor case, the only significant displacement of cache lines was from the process itself. The virtual caches reduced the amount of self displacement by keeping the page addresses contiguous. Physical caches tend have a random distribution of page addresses and can cause greater amounts of displacements as pages are mapped so that they compete for the same cache line. While this is detrimental when there is little interference between processes, this miss rate penalty is more than offset when there is significant interference between competing processes as seen above.

Physical caches generate more update traffic than the corresponding virtual caches in multiprocessor environments. This can probably be attributed to the higher interference of virtual caches. Since it is less likely for data to remain in a cache (higher interference), it is less likely that an update is required.

CONCLUSIONS

This study examined process migration effects with respect to two scheduling algorithms and two cache coherency algorithms. Local and global scheduling were used to illustrate the extremes of scheduling algorithms and update (Firefly) and invalidate (Berkeley) based cache coherency schemes were chosen as the extremes of bus-based coherency.

The results illustrated that scheduling algorithms have a significant impact on the amount of cache misses in a multiprocessor system. As processes migrate they interfere with one another and increase the amount

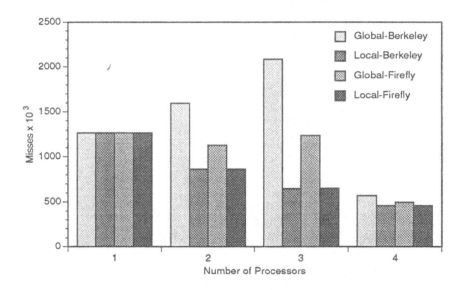

Figure 10: Total misses in a 128K virtual cache.

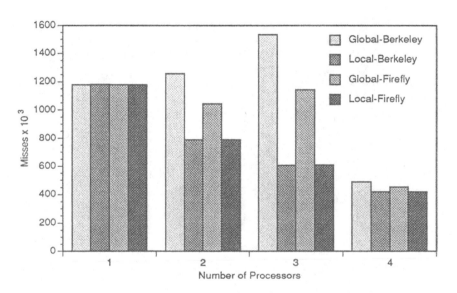

Figure 11: Read misses in 128K virtual cache.

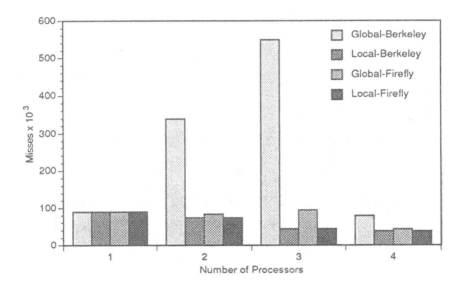

Figure 12: Write misses in 128K virtual cache.

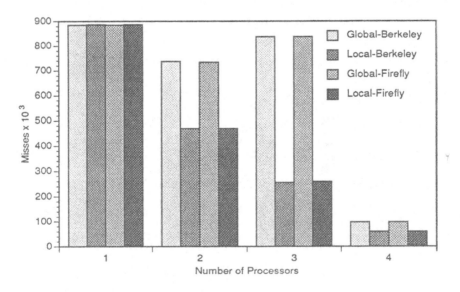

Figure 13: Transient misses in 128K virtual cache.

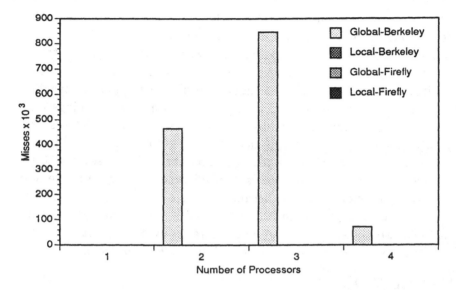

Figure 14: Invalidate misses in 128K virtual cache.

of transient misses per process. Local schedulers reduce these transient misses and eliminate the misses due to invalidations in write invalidate protocols. However, as cache sizes grow, the advantages of local scheduling are diminished because process interference is reduced as each process' addresses are spread across the larger caches. Since local scheduling eliminates misses due to invalidates, the advantages of update protocols over invalidate protocols are eliminated with respect to miss rates. On the other hand, local scheduling eliminates the update bus traffic while only reducing the invalidate traffic (the Berkeley algorithm does not determine when data is exclusively held by a cache).

Firefly provided the best miss rates for the global scheduling approaches since it generates no invalidations that could later force a miss. This is misleading though, since the elimination of invalidates requires update cycles to keep the cache lines consistent with each other. As seen from the global scheduling simulations, the amount of update cycles greatly exceeded the amount of invalidation cycles. With respect to local schedulers, both the Firefly and Berkeley protocols produced equal miss rates. In this scenario, Firefly performed better since it generated no extra bus traffic to maintain bus coherency.

Virtual caches performed significantly worse when compared to the physical mapped (hashed) caches. Increased process interference was responsible for this and can be explained by the overlapping instruction and stack regions in the virtual address space. Physical mappings tend to randomly distribute page addresses in the caches which reduces process interference. Relative to physically addressed caches, virtual caches increase processor interference yet show no increase in misses due to invalidates. This tends to decreases the difference between update and invalidate coherency protocols because misses due to invalidations were responsible for this difference in the first place. Increased processor interference also makes local scheduling strategies even more attractive for virtual caches by providing processor affinity to each process.

FUTURE WORK

No tools were available to generate kernel traces in this study. Since many kernel routines execute during each benchmark execution, the address references made by these routines are likely to remain in each processor's cache, especially if the kernel address space is shared. A study of the multiprocessing behavior of programs with their corresponding kernel calls could provide a much greater understanding of the complete process migration effects on cacheing. Lower cache miss rates should be seen because more data in each cache is likely to be reused by each process.

Also, context switching was approximated using a Poisson distribution. In reality, context switches are produced by a combination of system calls and time-slice expirations. A more accurate model of context switch behavior could identify which system calls generate a context switch. This model could isolate which addresses in the trace correspond to these system calls and generate a context switch when such an address is encountered. The model would still implement a context switch due to time-slice expiration for the case when no change of context occurs before the time-slice expires.

Another path of investigation corresponds to Stone's [1] assertion that cache misses can be reduced if the processor stops allocating cache lines when a process is close to the end of its time-slice. This type of behavior would be fairly easy to investigate with the tools developed for this study.

Finally, the simulator used here could easily be modified to a particular instance of a scheduling algorithm. Operating system designers then can create their favorite scheduler and simulate it with these tools. The benefits or limitations of such an new algorithm can be compared with the more conventional algorithms.

ACKNOWLEDGEMENTS

The authors wish to thank Maureen Ladd for her help in preparing this chapter and the Digital Equipment Corporation, who supported Andrew Ladd on a GEEP scholarship.

References

[1] H. Stone. Cache allocation strategies for competing processes, February 1990. Presentation in Distinguished Lecture Series at University of Michigan.

[2] S. Thakkar and M. Sweiger. Performance of an OLTP application on the Symmetry multiprocessor system. In *Proceedings of the 17th International Symposium on Computer Architecture*, volume 1, pages 228–238. IEEE, 1990.

[3] A. J. Smith. Cache memories. *ACM Computing Surveys*, 14(3), Sepetember 1982.

[4] M. Kobayashi and M. MacDougall. The stack growth function: Cache line reference models. *IEEE Transactions on Computers*, 38(6), June 1989.

[5] A. Borg, R. Kessler, G. Lazana, and D. Wall. Long address traces from RISC machines: Generation and analysis. WRL research report 89/14, Digital Equipment Western Research Laboratory, Palo Alto, California, September 1989.

[6] M. Papamarcos and J. Patel. A low-overhead coherence solution for multiprocessors with private cache memories. In *Proceedings of the 11th International Symposium on Computer Architecture*, volume 1, pages 348–354. IEEE, 1984.

[7] J. Archibald and J.-L. Baer. An economical solution to the cache coherence problem. In *Proceedings of the 11th International Symposium on Computer Architecture*, volume 1, pages 355–362. IEEE, 1984.

[8] J. Archibald and J.-L. Baer. Cache coherence protocols: Evaluation using a multiprocessor simulation model. *ACM Transactions on Computer Systems*, 4(4):273–298, November 1986.

[9] A. Agarwal, R. Simoni, J. Hennessy, and M. Horowitz. An evaluation of directory schemes for cache coherence. In *Proceedings of the 15th International Symposium on Computer Architecture*, volume 1, pages 280–289. IEEE, 1988.

[10] R. Clapp, T. Mudge, and J. Smith. Performance of parallel loops using alternative cache consistency protocols on a non-bus multiprocessor. In M. Dubois and S. Thakkar, editors, *Cache and Interconnect Architectures in Multiprocessors*, pages 131–152. Kluwer, 1990.

[11] J. Larus. Abstract execution: A technique for efficiently tracing programs. Technical report, University of Wisconsin-Madison, February 1990.

[12] MIPS. *System Programmer's Package (SPP) Reference*. MIPS Corp., Boston, 1988.

[13] D. Samples. Mache: No-loss trace compaction. In *Proceedings of the International Conference on Measurement and Modeling of Computer Systems*, volume 1, pages 89–97. IEEE, 1989.

[14] S. Laha, J. Patel, and R. Iyer. Accurate low-cost methods for performance evaluation of cache memory systems. *IEEE Transactions on Computers*, 37(11), November 1988.

[15] R. Sites and A. Agarwal. Multiprocessor cache analysis using ATUM. In *Proceedings of the 15th International Symposium on Computer Architecture*, volume 1, pages 186–195. IEEE, 1988.

Design and Analysis of a Scalable, Shared-memory System with Support for Burst Traffic *

Elana D. Granston   Stephen W. Turner
Alexander V. Veidenbaum
Center for Supercomputing Research and Development
University of Illinois at Urbana-Champaign
Urbana, Illinois, 61801

Abstract

This simulation-based study examines the behavior of a *realistic* shared-memory multiprocessor system that utilizes Omega networks. A unique aspect is the presence of bursts of requests, such as processors with associated vector units or caches would generate. It is demonstrated that the forward network, the memory modules, and the reverse network of such a system interact and affect each other's performance such that good performance depends less on the speed of any one component than on the interaction between them. Cost-effective modifications for improving this balance are evaluated. Within the range of system sizes studied (32 to 512 processors), results show that MIN-based systems that operate close to their peak memory bandwidth can indeed be constructed.

1 Introduction

The shared-memory access bottleneck is key to harnessing the power of large-scale, shared-memory multiprocessors. Interleaved memory systems connected via multistage interconnection networks (MINs) have can potentially alleviate this bottleneck by providing throughput proportional to the number of input/output pairs (P), with a hardware cost that grows only as O(P log P).

---

*This work was supported by the Department of Energy under Grant No. DE-FG02-85ER25001, the National Science Foundation under Grant No. NSF 89-20891, the NASA Ames Research Center under Grant No. NASA NCC 2-559, Cray Research Inc. and Alliant Computer Systems.

Several multiprocessors based on MINs are currently in existence or under construction [Hiraki *et al.*, 1984, Gottlieb *et al.*, 1983, Gajski *et al.*, 1983, Pfister *et al.*, 1985]. The performance of the memory system of such a multiprocessor depends not only on the behavior of its individual components, but also on the request issue rate of the processors, that in turn is affected by the memory system performance. This interdependence creates a feedback loop that profoundly affects the performance of the total system. Although some theoretical results have been previously obtained regarding the behavior of the components of the shared memory system, such as the behavior of MINs in isolation [Barnes and Lundstrom., 1981, Dias and Jump, 1981, Kruskal and Snir, 1983, Kruskal *et al.*, 1988, Lawrie, 1975, Patel, 1981], these do not reflect the performance of an entire system. A primary goals of this study is to evaluate the performance of MIN-based memory systems in the context of closed processor-memory-processor loops.

In this study, performance estimates obtained through simulation of such systems are used to develop a cost-effective, scalable, shared-memory system. The term *scalable* is used to describe systems whose per-processor performance is roughly constant across the range of system sizes examined. In particular, our goal is to design a system that both allows the processors to utilize virtually all of the available memory bandwidth, across this range. For our experiments, a range of system sizes between 32 to 512 processors is used.

Realistic models of both the target architecture and associated traffic patterns are essential. Accordingly, relative timings based on existing hardware are used to define system behavior. Furthermore, we strive to keep the memory system hardware cost from dominating the entire system cost. This eliminates such options as over-interleaving or multiple network ports per processor, as these become prohibitively expensive for large systems.

To realistically represent the highly non-uniform memory traffic that results from loads and stores of vector registers, cache lines and page frames, a *burst traffic* model is used. In this model, memory requests consist of bursts of individual messages, where each message is associated with a single memory address. Bursts are characterized by three traits: (1) memory locations referenced in a burst are addressed to consecutive blocks of data, (2) all the messages within a burst are issued in a continuous stream, and (3) all messages in a burst must complete before the next burst can be issued.

Other studies [McAuliffe, 1986, Brooks III, 1987, Pfister *et al.*, 1985] have addressed the performance of complete systems based on MINs, but each has a serious limitation. McAuliffe's work concentrates on the behavior of caches connected to the shared-memory system; he gives little information about network or shared-memory behavior. Brooks' work does detail network behavior, and also addresses burst traffic, but relies on an expensive switch design and assumes each network port can generate and absorb individual messages in a single cycle. The RP3 project has conducted several studies of a MIN-based system, but their work concentrates on the effects of "hot-spot" traffic, and the use of a separate combining network.

The remainder of this paper is organized as follows. Section 2 outlines the class of multiprocessor architectures under study. Section 3 describes the traffic models that load them. Section 4 details the metrics used to evaluate system performance. Sections 5 and 6 examine the behavior of the initial system configuration and the effects of varying traffic loads. Sections 7, 8 and 9 evaluate the cost/performance benefits of various configuration modifications. Section 10 draws conclusions as to the relative efficacy of the various modifications and the implications for MIN-based memory system design.

2 System Configuration

The class of systems under study is a family of generalized Cedar-like multiprocessors [Gajski et al., 1983], based on a pair of Omega networks [Lawrie, 1975] that interconnect the processors with a number of interleaved memory modules. Shared-memory burst requests are initiated by the processors, sent through the forward network to the memory modules, and returned to the processors via the reverse network. Network data paths are one word wide. Processors and memories have separate connections to the forward and reverse networks. A processor can both issue and receive a single word on each clock cycle. Each processor is restricted to at most one outstanding burst request, as is characteristic of most processors that do not issue new memory requests until their current request has completed.

A shared-memory burst request is issued by a processor as a series of up to ν messages to consecutive memory modules, where ν is the burst length supported by the target architecture. One message is required to read (write) a block of τ consecutive words from (to) a single memory module, where τ is the transfer unit size. A message consists of a single address/control word together with τ data words, as needed. Hence, a processor write message contains $\tau + 1$ words in the forward network, and a single word for acknowledgment in the reverse. A processor read message requires the opposite.

The switches are capable of transferring a word from any input port into any output port during a single cycle. Each switch is equipped with a finite length first-in first-out (FIFO) buffer on each of its input ports and a single-word buffer on each of its output ports. A contention resolution scheme is employed to ensure fair and bounded waiting: when two or more messages contend for the same output port, priority is given to the message that reached the front of its respective input buffer first.

Memory modules are interleaved on τ consecutive word addresses and have FIFO buffers on both their inputs and outputs. Upon completion of a memory access, a memory module first places the response message in its output buffer (one word at a time) and then accepts the next message into its input buffer.

134

To reflect realistic hardware design parameters, the memory modules require $T_m(\tau) > 1$ cycles to service a message of length τ.

The entire memory system is pipelined and all components attempt to move a word onward as soon as possible. Handshaking between components causes one to hold a word in its output buffer when the associated input buffer in the next component is full.

A modestly-configured system is used as a base against which modified configurations are compared. This configuration and its timings are based on those of the Cedar multiprocessor at the time this study was started, as this facilitated verification of the simulator against a real system. The base configuration is composed of an equal number of processors and memory modules, with minimal switch and memory buffering (two buffers on each input and one on each output). The memory modules service a message in five processor (alternatively, network) cycles. The networks utilize 8x8 switches. The transfer unit size is one.

We strive to model the systems realistically. Simplifying assumptions such as uniform traffic behavior or independence of successive network stages are avoided. Due to the level of detail required to accomplish this, and to gather the desired statistics on packet behavior in each of the individual system components, queuing theory arguments do not suffice. Hence, systems are simulated at the register-transfer level. The experiments for which values are presented are the result of at least 160,000 data words traveling the system so that steady state behavior is achieved.

3 Traffic Model

The traffic model is designed to capture the important aspects of vector register, cache line and page accesses. The bursty nature of this traffic is not accurately modeled by the standard, uniformly-distributed request model; yet a simple stochastic model is still useful because of its implementation efficiency. Accordingly, a hybrid model is used: the base address for each burst is generated through a uniform random distribution, and the remainder of the burst is addressed to consecutive blocks. Recall from the previous section that each block contains τ data words.

Each burst issued by a processor has a 0.67 probability of being a read request as opposed to a write, as is expected to characterize real programs [Granston et al., 1991].[1] On a given clock cycle, there is a burst issue probability β, $0 < \beta \leq 1$, that a processor without an outstanding burst request will initiate a new one. After issuing a request, the processor waits for all the messages associated with that request to return, before repeating the

---

[1] A study on the effects of varying the probability of a request being a read (versus a write) can be found in [Granston et al., 1991].

process. Note that even at a burst issue probability of one, a processor is not issuing on every clock cycle. Specifically, after a processor issues ν messages into the network, it must wait at least T_b^{min} cycles (where $T_b^{min} > \nu$) for the burst to complete before beginning the next request. Therefore, the maximum effective message-issue probability is $P^{max}(msg) = \nu/T_b^{min}$. Note that this probability is always less than one, even if the burst issue probability is one and messages encounter no conflicts in the network.

For each configuration a minimum burst completion time T_b^{min} can be determined as:

$$T_b^{min} = T_l^{min} + (\nu - 1) * T_i^{min},$$

where T_l^{min} is the minimum latency for the first message of a burst and T_i^{min} is the minimum message-interarrival time. Under the assumptions stated in the previous section,

$$T_l^{min} = 2 \times \lceil LOG_s(MAX(p, m)) \rceil + T_m(\tau) + 1,$$

where p is the number of processors, m is the number of memories, s is the basic switch size and $\lceil LOG_s(MAX(p, m)) \rceil$ is the number of stages in either the forward or reverse network.

$$T_i^{min} = \tau + 1,$$

where $\tau + 1$ is the maximum number of words required per message in either the forward or reverse network. This arises from the assumption that data paths are one word wide, so at most one word can be issued (or absorbed) by a processor in a single network cycle.

For example, consider a sixty-four processor system with an equal number of memories that utilizes 8x8 switches. Assume the transfer unit size (τ) is one, the memory cycle time $T_m(\tau)$ is five, and the burst length ν is thirty-two. Under the above assumptions, $T_l^{min} = 10$ and $T_i^{min} = 2$, so $T_b^{min} = 72$ and $P^{max}(msg) = 32/72 = 0.44$.

4 Performance metrics

System performance is measured primarily by the metric *burst throughput per processor* (B). This metric is derived from burst latency (T_l) and message interarrival time (T_i), that describe the burst completion rate (Table 1). T_l and T_i are determined by directly measuring individual latency and interarrival times, and then calculating the arithmetic mean over these values. Individual variances for these directly measured metrics are typically large, roughly one to four times the mean. Since the averages are much closer to the minima than the maxima, the distribution is undoubtably skewed towards the low end. Consequently, the arithmetic average represents a higher value than the median. In this study, the arithmetic average is used to measure overall performance, since

Burst Latency (T_l): The number of clock cycles that has elapsed between the time a processor begins issuing a burst and the time that first message is absorbed by the processor.

Message Interarrival Time (T_i): The time between the return of successive messages to the processor that issued them.

Burst Throughput per Processor (B): Measurement in data words per cycle of the throughput seen by *each* processor *only* during those times that it is accessing memory.

Table 1: Metric definitions.

it better represents the relative performance impact of the large but infrequent values.

Burst throughput per processor (B) describes overall memory system performance with a single number that measures throughput (1) *as seen by each processor* (in contrast to system-wide throughput), and (2) *only during those times that the processor has a pending memory access request*. B factors out the direct effect of processor workload on per-processor throughput by ignoring cycles spent doing local computations. Aggregate achieved memory bandwidth can be approximated as $p * B * \beta$.

B is measured in data words per cycle. It can be derived from the latency and interarrival time measures by dividing the total number of data words in a burst by the average time for a processor to complete a memory access instruction, as follows:

$$B = \frac{\nu \times \tau}{T_b^{avg}} = \frac{\nu \times \tau}{T_l^{avg} + [(\nu - 1) \times T_i^{avg}]}$$

where T_b^{avg} is the average turnaround time for a burst request, and T_l^{avg} and T_i^{avg} are the average burst latency and message interarrival time, respectively.

This measure is subject to two different limiting factors. The first of these is due to the hardware-imposed lower bound of T_b^{min} on burst completion time of:

$$B^{max} \le \frac{\nu \times \tau}{T_b^{min}}. \tag{1}$$

The second factor limiting B is the system's peak memory bandwidth. Even in the absence of network conflicts, a system with m memory modules and a memory service rate of $T_m(\tau)$, has maximum memory bandwidth of $m \times \tau / T_m(\tau)$

data words per cycle. The memory bandwidth available to an individual processor on average is inversely proportional to the number of processors actively accessing memory. More specifically, for a system with p_a active processors, an effective upper limit on average burst throughput per-processor is:

$$B^{max} \leq \frac{m \times \tau}{p_a \times T_m(\tau)}. \tag{2}$$

If $p_a = m$, the above simplifies to $B^{max} \leq \tau/T_m(\tau)$. In essence, this limit reflects the amount of pipelining employed by the memory modules. The upper bound on burst throughput is the minimum of the above two limiting factors, specifically:

$$B^{max} = \text{MIN}\left(\frac{\nu \times \tau}{T_b^{min}}, \frac{m \times \tau}{p_a \times T_m(\tau)}\right) \tag{3}$$

At very low burst issue probabilities, $p_a \leq 1$, so each processor is likely to accesses the memories without contention from other processors. Therefore, the memory system performs well from an individual processor's point of view, even though total utilized memory bandwidth may be low. In this case, the constraint on B^{max} is the rate at which the processor can issue requests, given by Equation (1). As the burst issue rate increases, the number of simultaneously active processors also increases, causing the per-processor memory bandwidth to decrease. Under heavy traffic loads, particularly in systems with relatively slow memories, the constraint specified in Equation (2) is likely to be the limiting factor.

Note that $p_a \leq p$, where p the number of processors in the system. As the burst issue probability increases, $p_a \longrightarrow p$. Since the upper bound designated by Equation (2) generally limits burst throughput under high burst issue probability only, p can reasonably approximate p_a in Equation 3 to obtain the following approximation:

$$B^{max} \approx \text{MIN}\left(\frac{\nu \times \tau}{T_b^{min}}, \frac{m \times \tau}{p \times T_m(\tau)}\right) \tag{4}$$

Since $p \geq p_a$, Equation (4) yields an approximate limit rather than a strict upper bound. In practice, however, this approximation works well for the range of systems under study. So, in the remainder of this paper, calculations of B^{max} are based on Equation (4).

For example, consider a 64 processor system connected to 64 memories, which supports a transfer unit of one data word and has a memory service rate of of five clock cycles per message. Recall from Section 3 that, for this configuration, T_l^{min} and T_i^{min} are 10 and 2, respectively. Consequently, if $\nu = 32$ and burst issue rate is at a maximum, the resulting limit on burst throughput is:

$$B^{max} = \text{MIN}\left(\frac{32}{10 + (31 \times 2)}, \frac{64 \times 1}{64 \times 5}\right) = \text{MIN}(0.44, 0.20) = 0.20.$$

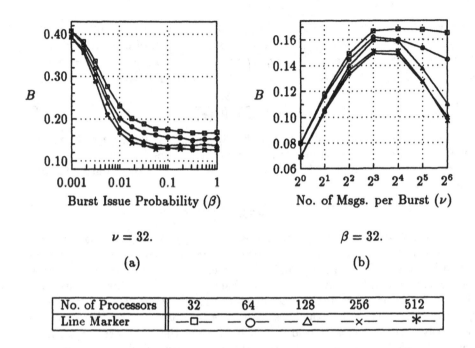

Figure 1: Varying burst issue probability and burst length.

Hence, B is constrained by Equation (2). In contrast, with a very low burst issue probability, the burst throughput of this same configuration is constrained to $B = 0.44$ by Equation (1). Therefore, if this system is not heavily loaded, each processor can realize burst throughput of over twice that potentially achieved in a fully utilized system.

5   Burst Issue Probability

In this section and the next, the behavior of the inexpensively configured base system described in Section 2 is analyzed. A more complete presentation can be found in [Granston et al., 1991].

Consider the effects of varying the probability of a memory access request being issued. As traffic loads increase, per-processor throughput initially tails off. However, due to feedback effects between the memory system and the processors this performance degradation is limited. This can be clearly seen in Figure 1(a), that shows how burst throughput varies with burst issue probability, for thirty-two word bursts of requests. The lower bound for burst throughput is at least partially attributable to the method by which input is introduced into the network. As mentioned in Section 3, even with a β of 1.0, a word is not injected into the network every clock, because a processor does not generate a new burst request until the previous one has been satisfied. This creates a negative feedback effect. As more new requests are generated, each request takes longer to complete, thereby delaying the generation of further burst requests by participating processors, accordingly. The flattening of the graph when the burst issue probability β increases beyond 0.1 is due to this feedback effect.

Note that three distinct areas can be observed. In the first area, with the burst issue probability well below 0.01, the burst throughput per processor is close to the hardware maximum. This is followed by another rather narrow range of burst issue probabilities in which throughput decreases linearly. Finally, a wide range of burst issue probabilities up to 1.0 follows, in which the throughput has reached its minimum and stays constant. As the burst issue probability β increases, the average time between the completion of one burst and the initiation of another decreases. As such, memory system performance remains constant after a point, but the processors spend a proportionately greater amount of time accessing the shared memory, as opposed to performing local processor operations. The actual range of burst issue probabilities for each area depends on the system configuration and burst length, but the shape of the curves is consistent across all experiments run by the authors.

Most programs are expected to fall within the wide range of burst issue probabilities with performance equal to that achieved with $\beta = 1.0$. For example, the benchmark kernels studied in [Turner and Veidenbaum, 1988] have equivalent burst issue probabilities in the range of 0.02 to 0.04. With compile-time memory management optimization, these programs may have even higher burst issue probabilities [Gornish et al., 1990]. Therefore, a burst issue probability of $\beta = 1.0$ will be used for the remainder of this study.

6 Burst Length

Burst length (ν) can also have a significant effect on system performance. When a processor issues a burst, there are three stages of activity: an initial stage when relatively few of the messages have entered the network, a steady-state stage of messages moving through the network, and a tailing-off stage, as the last few messages are absorbed by the processor. Therefore, even at a burst issue probability of one, the traffic generated by a processor is not steady.

When the burst lengths are small, the initial and tailing-off stages dominate over the middle (steady-state) stage. As such, small bursts do not allow the pipelining effect of the system to offset the initial latency. As can be seen in Figure 1(b), where burst throughput is plotted for varying burst lengths, initially performance improves with increasing burst length. As the burst length is increased further, the greater number of messages in the network begin to conflict with each other, causing the performance to peak and possibly drop. This peak occurs at roughly eight messages per burst. The amount of the drop, if any, depends on the number of network stages. In these base configurations,

Network Stage	Switch Sizes	
	32 Memories	64 Memories
Fwd 1	8x8	8x8
2	4x4	4x8
Rev 1	4x4	8x4
2	8x8	8x8

Table 2: Network configurations for thirty-two processor systems.

m/p	$T_m(1)$	B^{max}
1	5	0.20
1	2	≈ 0.45
2	5	0.40
2	2	≈ 0.45

Table 3: Maximum burst throughput for various system configurations.

the systems with the extra network stages (the larger systems) are much more sensitive to changes in burst length.

Bursts of length thirty-two will be used from now on, as they appear to be median in performance. Moreover, the vector processing units often operate on arrays in groups thirty-two or sixty-four elements. For example, Cedar supports a vector length of thirty-two.

7 Memory Bandwidth

In the remainder of this paper, we attempt to the performance and scalability of this class of systems by varying individual architectural parameters. Given that the processor and switch ports can send (receive) one word per clock, a five-clock memory may seem too slow, even though it is a realistic ratio for modern components. Are the memory modules themselves the primary bottleneck? As a first experiment, the memory access time $T_m(1)$ is decreased from five to two cycles per message, thereby increasing the system's memory bandwidth $2\frac{1}{2}$ times. The reason for selecting two clocks rather than one is that two words need to be sent (received) by a memory module for each read (write) operation. As a second experiment, the degree of memory interleaving is increased by connecting a given number of processors to double the number of memories. For thirty-two processor systems, the switch configurations for the thirty-two and sixty-four memory systems are depicted in Table 2. Similar changes in the switch dimensions allow twice the number memories to be connected to any given number of processors. This doubles the system's memory bandwidth. In the last experiment, both strategies for increasing memory bandwidth are applied simultaneously. As a result, the memory bandwidth is increased five-fold.

The theoretical maximum burst throughputs for these four cases are listed in Table 3. For the configurations with $T_m(1) = 5$, the bound on B^{max} arises from Equation 2. For the remaining configurations, system performance con-

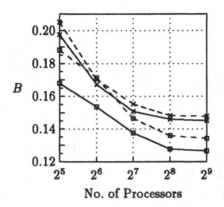

m/p	1	1	2	2
$T_m(1)$	5	2	5	2
Line Marker	—□—	- -□- -	—×—	- -×- -

Figure 2: Varying memory bandwidth.

strained by 1. The experimental burst throughputs for these same cases are displayed in Figure 2. Despite modest improvements in average throughput, the performance of the memory system drops off with increasing system size. Furthermore, requests are still being processed at a rate much less than the aggregate bandwidth of the memory modules. In the latter experiment, the memory bandwidth now exceeds the rate at which requests are generated and absorbed by the processors, so contention in the networks must be to blame.

8 Buffer Length

In this next set of experiments, switch and memory buffers are extended to alleviate tree-saturation by preventing blockage at one stage in the memory system from spreading backwards into earlier stages. To determine the most cost-effective method for extending buffering, several strategies are investigated. To prevent tree-saturation in the forward network, the length of input buffers on forward network switches and memory modules is increased (Figure 3(a)). This modification is relatively inexpensive compared to doubling the number of memories, yet with sixteen-word buffers on input to forward network switchs and memory modules, yields the same improvement. Similar performance improvements can be obtained by extending memory input buffers only (Figure 3(b)). In both cases, for thirty-two processor systems, the maximum

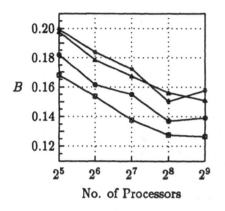

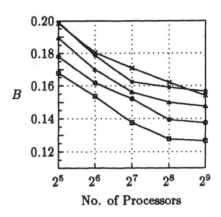

Input buffer lengths: fwd. net. switches: ℓ, memory modules: ℓ, rev. net. switches: 2.

(a)

Input buffer lengths: fwd. net. switches: 2, memory modules: ℓ, rev. net. switches: 2.

(b)

Input buffer lengths: fwd. net. switches: 2, memory modules: ℓ, rev. net. switches: ℓ.

(c)

Buffer Length (ℓ)	2	8	16	32
Line Marker	—□—	—○—	—△—	—×—

Figure 3: Varying buffer lengths.

burst throughput (0.20 data words/cycle for these configurations) is achieved. Unfortunately, burst throughput still decreases as system size increases. Therefore, there must still be congestion in the reverse networks of the larger systems.

The heavy concentration of read traffic loads the reverse network more heavily than the forward network. As discussed in [McAuliffe, 1986], the main problem is the fan-in of read bursts to the processors that issued them. To alleviate this congestion, the buffer length at each reverse network switch input is also extended. The results of varying these buffer lengths in combination with memory input buffer lengths are presented in Figure 3(c). When the additional buffering is sufficient, the burst throughput remains around 0.20 data words/cycle. Thus, the system is not only *scalable*, but the memory is operating *close to its peak bandwidth* throughout this range, returning a message to each processor every five clock cycles. While extending buffers helps decouple system components, this decoupling effect is not complete. Hence, the importance of studying the effects of individual system components in the context of a complete system must still be stressed.

9   Transfer Unit Size

Under high burst-issue rates, can burst throughput be increased beyond the range of 0.19 to 0.20 data words/cycle achieved in the previous section? Recall from Section 4 that the ceiling on burst throughput of 0.20 data words/cycle is due to the memory bandwidth limit. Since these systems are already performing at their peak memory bandwidth, this peak must be increased to allow further performance improvement.

One method would be to increase memory bandwidth as was done in Section 7, this time using longer buffers. Figure 4(a) displays the results for the same experiments described in Section 7 except that the memory and reverse-network switch input buffers are extended to sixteen words. While an additional performance improvement of twenty-five to fifty percent is achieved, the cost of this enhancement is very high. Even with the extra hardware, these systems are all performing well below their maximum theoretical burst throughput. Once again, the network is a bottleneck. This time, even if all switch and memory input buffers are extended infinitely (Figure 4(b)), burst throughput is not increased much further.

Alternatively, memory system bandwidth can be increased by increasing the transfer unit size. During each memory access, a percentage of the memory service rate is overhead for absorbing and retransmitting the address word associated with each data word. If multiple data words are accessed at one time, then only one address word is required for the lot. Assuming that consecutive words in a block can be fetched at a cost of one additional word per cycle (by using DRAM page mode, for example), $T_m(\tau) = T_m(1) + \tau - 1$. Hence, system

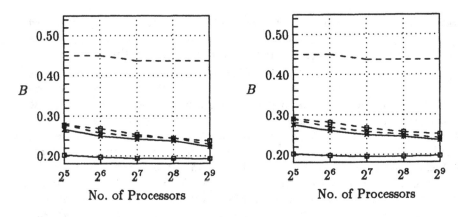

No. of Processors   No. of Processors

Input buffer lengths: fwd. net. switches: 2, memory modules: 16, rev. net. switches: 16.

Input buffer lengths: fwd. net. switches: ∞, memory modules: ∞, rev. net. switches: ∞.

(a)   (b)

m/p	1	1	2	2	B^{max} when
$T_m(1)$	5	2	5	2	$T_m(1) = 2$
Line Marker	—□—	- -□- -	—×—	- -×- -	- - - - -

Figure 4: Varying memory bandwidth in heavily buffered systems.

bandwidth can be increased from $m/T_m(1)$ to:

$$\frac{m \times \tau}{T_m(\tau)} = \frac{m \times \tau}{T_m(1) + \tau - 1}.$$

Employing transfer units larger than one has several other advantages and disadvantages. Increasing the transfer unit size reduces the total number of words that must travel through the memory system by reducing the number of address words required per data word. As a result, the likelihood of any two messages colliding in the network or vying for the same memory module is decreased. However, the network backup and consequential delays resulting from collisions that do still occur are likely to be more detrimental, as mentioned in [Siegel et al., 1989].

Figure 5 displays the resulting burst throughput when the transfer unit size is increased beyond one. In Figure 5(a), the number of messages in a burst is maintained at a constant thirty-two. In Figure 5(b), the number of data words in a burst is maintained at a constant thirty-two: as the transfer unit size doubles, the number of messages per burst is halved. For both these experiments, the systems have been configured with sixteen-word buffers at input to each memory module and reverse network switch.

In both cases, performance peaks at eight to sixteen words per message. If the number of messages is not decreased proportionately to the transfer unit size (Figure 5(a)), then the number of words per burst and, hence, the traffic level in the memory system increase proportionately. This higher traffic level increases contention, thereby degrading system performance. Therefore, in all but the thirty-two processor case, per-processor throughput is higher when the number of messages per burst is decreased proportionately to the increase in transfer unit size (Figure 5(b)). Compare the throughputs obtained from increasing transfer unit size to those obtained previously by doubling the number of memory modules and/or reducing the clock cycle rate (Figure 4). Increases in transfer unit size lead to much greater performance increases and are likely to be a much less expensive improvement.

For theoretical purposes, the above two experiments have been repeated with infinitely extended buffers on input to memory modules and reverse network switches. When the number of messages per burst is held constant (Figure 5(c)), the additional buffering allows higher traffic levels to be sustained so that performance does not level off until the transfer unit size reaches approximately thirty-two data words. The situation is slightly different when the number of data words per burst is held constant. In this case (Figure 5(d)), the performance is virtually the same as before. There is no additional gain from the added buffers. Again, in all but the smallest systems, performance is higher when the number of data words per burst is constant. Consequently, even if the infinitely extended buffers could be employed, burst length should be decreased as message length is increased, especially for large systems.

When considering the benefits of using larger transfer units, raw performance numbers are insufficient for analyzing the advantages and disadvantages. If only a fraction of the accessed data is actually used, then the effective throughput is proportionally lower. While it is beyond the scope of this study to determine the fraction of accessed data that is actually used on average, the fraction of data that must be used for a larger transfer unit size to be more efficient can be calculated. Burst throughput per processor (B) is calculated in data words per cycle. If only a fraction f, $0.0 \leq f \leq 1.0$, of these accessed data words are actually used, then the effective burst throughput per processor is:

$$B^{eff} = f \times B.$$

When is it worth using a transfer unit of size $\tau_1 > \tau_0$ rather than a transfer unit of size τ_0? If a transfer of τ_1 is used, the fraction f_1 of data words that are actually used is likely to be lower. If the resulting burst throughput B_1 is also lower, then the effective burst throughput B_1^{eff} will also be lower. For example,

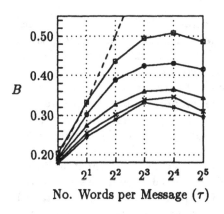

No. Words per Message (τ)

$\nu = 32$, Input buffer lengths: fwd. net. switches: 2, memory modules: 16, rev. net. switches: 16.

(a)

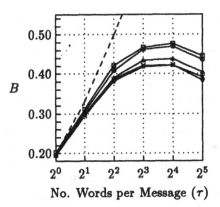

No. Words per Message (τ)

$\nu = 32/\tau$, Input buffer lengths: fwd. net. switches: 2, memory modules: 16, rev. net. switches: 16.

(b)

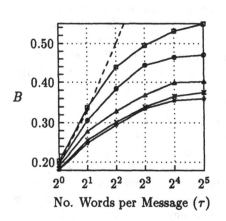

No. Words per Message (τ)

$\nu = 32$, Input buffer lengths: fwd. net. switches: 2, memory modules: ∞, rev. net. switches: ∞.

(c)

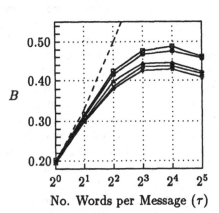

No. Words per Message (τ)

$\nu = 32/\tau$, Input buffer lengths: fwd. net. switches: 2, memory modules: ∞, rev. net. switches: ∞.

(d)

p	32	64	128	256	512	B^{max}
Line Marker	—□—	—○—	—△—	—×—	—*—	- - - -

Figure 5: Varying transfer unit size.

consider the burst throughputs displayed in Figure 5(b). When a transfer unit of thirty-two data words is used in any size system under study, the resulting burst throughput is always lower than when a transfer unit of sixteen data words is used. Since the fraction of data accessed will generally be lower, there is no performance benefit to using a transfer unit of thirty-two over a transfer unit of sixteen.

What if the burst throughput resulting from a transfer unit of $\tau_1 > \tau_0$ is higher than the burst throughput resulting from a transfer unit of τ_0? Then, a transfer unit of size τ_1 leads to higher effective burst throughput if $B_1^{eff} > B_0^{eff}$ or

$$\frac{f_1}{f_0} > \frac{B_0}{B_1}.$$

For example, consider the burst throughput results from Figure 5(b), again. What is the fraction f_1 of accessed data that must be used for a transfer unit of size $\tau_1 = 2$ to lead to higher effective throughput than a transfer unit of $\tau_0 = 1$? For all system sizes, when the transfer units are one and two, the corresponding burst throughputs are approximately 0.20 and 0.31 data words/cycle, respectively. Note that when a transfer unit of one data word is used, all the accessed data is actually used. So, $f_0 = 1$. Suppose that f_1 is the fraction of data words that is actually used when the transfer unit size is τ_1. Then, a transfer unit of size $\tau_1 = 2$ leads to higher effective burst throughput if:

$$\frac{f_1}{1} > \frac{.20}{.31} = .645.$$

So, a transfer unit of two data words is better than a transfer unit of one if at least sixty-five percent of the data is being used or, equivalently, if the second data word in the message is used more than 28% of the time.

f_1/f_0 is referred to as the *minimum data utilization ratio*. When the minimum utilization ratio is greater than one, there is no performance benefit to utilizing a transfer unit of size τ_1 over a transfer unit of size τ_0. For this same set of burst throughputs as before, Table 4 displays the minimum data utilization ratio for a transfer unit of size $\tau_1 = 2 \times \tau_0$ to yield better performance than a transfer unit of size τ_0. Note that these minimum data utilization ratios are almost constant across system sizes.

Thus far, a *fixed size transfer unit* has been assumed: τ consecutive data words are accessed whether or not they are all used. Alternatively, *variable size transfer units* can be used so that only necessary data are accessed. In this case, each message header (the address/control word) carries not only the starting address but also a bit vector of length τ. The ith bit of the vector specifies whether the ith data word should be read (written). Thus, each message has a variable size and contains up to τ data words, as needed. The advantage of this latter method is that data that are not needed are not accessed, thus decreasing the total number of data words that must travel through the network. When variable size transfer units are used, $B = B^{eff}$.

Transfer Unit		No. of Processors				
τ_0	τ_1	32	64	128	256	512
1	2	0.645	0.657	0.657	0.661	0.655
2	4	0.738	0.748	0.770	0.764	0.777
4	8	0.894	0.883	0.900	0.916	0.911
8	16	0.980	0.985	0.991	0.997	0.988
16	32	> 1	> 1	> 1	> 1	> 1

Table 4: Minimum data utilization ratio (f_1/f_0) necessary for transfer unit of fixed size $\tau_1 = 2 \times \tau_0$ to be more effective than transfer unit of size τ_0 (based on results in Figure 5(b)).

For a fixed size transfer unit, the memory service rate is $T_m(\tau) = T_m(1) + \tau - 1$ cycles per message, $T_m(\tau)$ cycles to access the first data word and one clock cycle for each additional data word. When variable-size transfer units are employed, the memory controller must still check each of the τ bits to determine whether to access each individual data word. Assuming that one clock cycle is required to check a bit and optionally access a data word, the memory access time is still $T_m(\tau)$ regardless of whether all τ data words are accessed. Therefore, the memory bandwidth is the same as for fixed-size transfer units. If locality of reference is low, the overhead for permitting larger transfer units may still be prohibitive. Alternatively, more complex hardware can be employed to check the vector bits in parallel, but this adds to the expense of the memory module controllers. Therefore, larger transfer units (fixed or variable) have potential to increase system performance, but only if a good data placement strategy is enlisted and locality of reference is high.

10   Conclusions

In this paper, the performance of the shared memory system and the behavior of its components have been studied. This study has several unique aspects, in particular its attention to feedback effects on network loading and to scalability. It has been shown that even under heavy burst traffic the request service rate of the memory system has a rather small upper bound. The system regulates itself by reducing the input rate with more processors requesting memory, thereby bounding performance. Performance drops very fast starting at very low probabilities of memory access instructions (around 0.01), and then stays constant for any issue probability above that. Thus, the results hold for real programs, that are expected to have burst issue probabilities in this range.

Not unexpectedly, these results demonstrate that the components of a system form a complex circular pipeline with forward network, memory modules, and reverse network all affecting each other's performance. Network contention, the primary cause of performance degradation, is extremely sensitive to traffic composition and the interaction between the networks, memories and processors. This results in under-utilization of available memory bandwidth in the base "inexpensive" systems and performance that does not scale well with increases in the number of processors. However, changes that appear obviously desirable do not result in any noticeable performance improvement, for the above-mentioned reasons. For example, a drastic increase in the memory module service rate buys almost nothing by itself.

Overall, extending input buffers is the most cost effective method studied for increasing processor performance. Properly deployed buffering can be used to partially decouple the memory from the networks. Since a processor does not issue a new request until its current one completes, there is a finite limit to the traffic in the system and hence a finite limit to the length of buffers necessary to affect this decoupling. The exact amount of buffering is a function system size, traffic rate, traffic composition and memory service rate. Extending memory input buffers allows the memories to be more highly utilized and causes the reverse network to become an acute problem. In an interleaved memory system servicing predominantly read traffic, the memory modules generate traffic more rapidly than a processor can absorb it. Extending reverse network buffers helps solve the problem, especially for larger system sizes. However, the extended buffers only partially decouple the system's components. Hence, it is still important to study the the performance of the MINs and memory modules in the context of a complete system.

Most importantly, a strategy has been presented for constructing a system that achieves a flat per-processor throughput of greater than 0.19 data words/cycle for a range of system sizes with five-clock memories. At this performance level, the memory system is operating at its maximum possible bandwidth, given the speed and the number of memory modules. Memory bandwidth can now be increased by increasing interleaving or decreasing memory cycle time. However, the fan-in problem at the processors again becomes dominant, and cannot be eliminated by the above techniques. Therefore, even with the additional buffering, full scalability is only achievable for slow memory modules. Fortunately, another method potentially offers good cost/performance benefits. A larger transfer unit can be employed and a consecutive block of data words (rather than an individual data word) can be accessed via a single message to a single memory module. Using larger transfer units can potentially reduce the effective service time per data word accessed, thereby increasing the memory module bandwidth. This method can also reduce address traffic in the network, since one address word is now required for a block of data words rather than for each individual data word.

Even without attempting to increase memory bandwidth, a burst throughput level of 0.19 data words/cycle is quite high for a 512-processor system under very heavy burst traffic. For a conservative clock rate of 50ns and a slow five-clock memory, this gives $0.19 * 512 * 20$ MW/s or almost 2 GW/s of *sustained* memory system bandwidth! If larger transfer units are utilized, a sustained memory system bandwidth of up to $0.46 * 512 * 20$ MW/s or almost 5 GW/s is achievable.

References

[Barnes and Lundstrom., 1981] G. H. Barnes and S. F. Lundstrom. Design and Validation of a Connection Network for Multiprocessor Systems. *IEEE Computer*, pages 31–41, Dec 1981.

[Brooks III, 1987] Eugene D. Brooks III. A butterfly processor-memory interconnection for a vector processing environment. *Parallel Computing*, 4:103–110, 1987.

[Dias and Jump, 1981] Daniel M. Dias and J. Robert Jump. Analysis and Simulation of Buffered Delta Networks. *IEEE Transactions on Computers*, C-30(4):273–282, April 1981.

[Gajski et al., 1983] Daniel Gajski, David Kuck, Duncan Lawrie, and Ahmed Sameh. Cedar – a Large Scale Multiprocessor. In *Proceedings of the International Conference on Parallel Processing*, pages 524–529, Aug 1983.

[Gornish et al., 1990] Edward H. Gornish, Elana D. Granston, and Alexander V. Veidenbaum. Compiler-directed Data Prefetching in Multiprocessors with Memory Hierarchies. In *Proceedings of the International Conference on Supercomputing*, pages 354–368, June 1990.

[Gottlieb et al., 1983] Allan Gottlieb, Ralph Grishman, Clyde P. Kruskal, Kevin P. McAuliffe, Larry Rudolph, and Marc Snir. The NYU Ultracomputer – Designing an MIMD Shared Memory Parallel Computer. *IEEE Transactions on Computers*, C-32(2):176–189, February 1983.

[Granston et al., 1991] Elana D. Granston, Stephen W. Turner, and Alexander V. Veidenbaum. Designing a Scalable Shared-memory System with Support for Burst Traffic. Technical Report 1084, Center for Supercomputing Research and Development, University of Illinois at Urbana-Champaign, 1991.

[Hiraki et al., 1984] Kei Hiraki, Toshio Shimada, and Kenji Nishida. A Hardware Design of the Sigma-1, A Data Flow Computer for Scientific Computations. In *Proceedings of the International Conference on Parallel Processing*, pages 61–68, August 1984.

[Kruskal and Snir, 1983] Clyde P. Kruskal and Marc Snir. The Performance of Multistage Interconnection Networks for Multiprocessors. *IEEE Transactions on Computers*, C-32(12):1091–98, December 1983.

[Kruskal *et al.*, 1988] Clyde P. Kruskal, Marc Snir, and Alan Weiss. The Distribution of Waiting Times in Clocked Multistage Interconnection Networks. *IEEE Transactions on Computers*, 37(11):1337–52, November 1988.

[Lawrie, 1975] Duncan H. Lawrie. Access and Alignment of Data in an Array Processor. *IEEE Transactions on Computers*, C-24(12):173–183, December 1975.

[McAuliffe, 1986] Kevin McAuliffe. *Analysis of Cache Memories in Highly Parallel Systems*. PhD thesis, Dept. of Computer Science, New York University, May 1986.

[Patel, 1981] Janak H. Patel. Performance of Processor-Memory Interconnections for Multiprocessors. *IEEE Transactions on Computers*, C-30(10):771–780, October 1981.

[Pfister *et al.*, 1985] Gregory F. Pfister, W. C. Brantley, D. A. George, S. L. Harvey, W. J. Kleinfeider, K. P. McAuliffe, E. A. Melton, V. A. Norton, and J. Weiss. The IBM Research Parallel Processor Prototype (RP3): Introduction and Architecture. In *Proceedings of the International Conference on Parallel Processing*, pages 764–771, August 1985.

[Siegel *et al.*, 1989] Howard Jay Siegel, Wayne G. Nation, Clyde P. Kruskal, and Jr. Leonard M. Napolitano. Using the Multistage Cube Network Topology in Parallel Supercomputers. *Proceedings of the IEEE*, 77(12):1932–1953, December 1989.

[Turner and Veidenbaum, 1988] Stephen W. Turner and Alexander V. Veidenbaum. Performance of a Shared Memory System for Vector Multiprocessrs. In *Proceedings of the International Conference on Supercomputing*, pages 315–325, July 1988.

Scalable Cache Coherence Analysis for Shared Memory Multiprocessors[*]

Manu Thapar and Bruce Delagi
Digital Equipment Corporation
Stanford University
701 Welch Road, Building C, Palo Alto, California 94304
manu@ksl.stanford.edu

Abstract

This paper analyzes a new hardware solution for the cache coherence problem in large scale shared memory multiprocessors. The protocol is based on a linked list of caches – forming a *distributed directory* and does not require a global broadcast mechanism. Fully-mapped directory-based solutions proposed earlier also do not require a global broadcast mechanism. However, our solution is more scalable and provides potentially better performance than the fully-mapped directory-based protocol. We provide simulation results to show that the performance of the distributed directory protocol is more robust when there is contention for the data and for variations in memory technology. Further, we do not assume that the network preserves the order of messages. Thus we do not preclude adaptive routing.

1 Introduction

Cache coherence protocols are well understood for bus-based shared memory architectures [2]. These protocols, called "snoopy" cache coherence protocols, require that each cache watch all traffic on the bus and take appropriate action for addresses that are present in that cache. Addresses are, in effect, transmitted to each cache by global broadcast. The shared bus limits the number of processors to the number that can

---

[*]This work was supported by equipment provided by the Knowledge Systems Laboratory, Department of Computer Science, Stanford University.

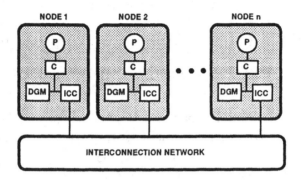

Figure 1: The basic architecture

be connected to the bus without saturating it. To support *scalable* shared memory architectures, the cache coherence protocol needs to be able to work in the absence of a global broadcast mechanism. Centralized directory based schemes [1, 7] are a possible solution in this environment. We present some drawbacks of these schemes in section 2.

Based on a linked list of caches [5], this paper describes a new distributed directory cache coherence protocol. The information about which caches have copies of the data is decentralized and distributed among the cache lines. Our implementation, like the fully mapped centralized directory scheme [7], tracks any number of cache copies and never requires invalidates to be sent to all caches in the system. It has a lower cost and better performance than the fully mapped directory based coherence scheme for expected memory and cache sizes in high performance systems. In the fully mapped scheme, the size of the memory required to hold the state information is $O(MN)$, where M is the size of main memory and N is the number of caches. In our scheme, on the other hand, the size of the memory required to hold the state information is only $O(M \log N)$. We allow adaptive routing (so that network performance may be more robust) and thus do not assume that the interconnection network preserves the order of messages. An important feature of the protocol is that locks can be supported efficiently with minimal extra cost [15].

2 Centralized Directory Protocols

We will assume a very general computing system structure in our discussions. Figure 1 describes this basic architecture. Each node consists of a processing element (P), a cache (C), an interconnect controller (ICC) and part of the distributed global memory (DGM). The DGM includes the directory. For the distributed directory protocol we do not assume that the interconnection network preserves the order of messages. This allows adaptive routing (making network performance more robust).

In the directory based protocols there is a directory "tag" associated with each line in main memory. This directory is used to hold information about which caches have copies of the line. In the fully mapped centralized[1] directory scheme [7], the directory has N valid (or "present") bits per line, where N is the number of caches. The amount of storage needed for the directory in the fully mapped scheme is thus $O(MN)$, where M is the size of main memory. If a cache has a copy of the line, the present bit corresponding to that cache is set. The directory also has a dirty bit. If the dirty bit is set, only one of the caches can have a copy of the line.

On a read miss, the directory is checked to see if the block is dirty in another cache. If so, consistency is maintained by copying the dirty block back to the memory before supplying the data. The reply is thus serialized through the directory. To ensure correct operation, the memory line has to be "locked" by the directory controller until the write-back signal is received from the cache with the dirty block. No other coherency related operations on this line may be undertaken while a line is locked. If the line is not dirty in another cache, then data is supplied from the main memory and the corresponding present bit is set in the directory.

On a write miss, the central directory is checked to determine the state of the line. If the line is dirty in another cache, then the line is first flushed from the cache before supplying the data. Again, the reply is serialized through the directory. The memory line is locked while this is being done. If the line is clean in other caches, invalidate signals are sent to the caches. The memory line is locked until acknowledgements are received from the caches. The data can then be supplied to the

---

[1]We use the term *centralized* since the information about caches that have copies of the data is located at one place. The directory tags are an extension of the lines in the DGM and are located on the same node as the corresponding lines in main memory.

requesting cache.

The serialization of responses through the directory and the locking of lines by the directory controller impacts the performance of the cache coherence scheme. Requests that arrive while a line is locked have to be either buffered at the directory, or else bounced back to the source to be reissued at a later time. If the requests are buffered at the directory, the network traffic is lower. However, if the buffer overflows, the requests still have to be bounced back. Requiring transactions to be serialized through the centralized directory (and the locking of lines while servicing a request that requires a coherency–related transaction) could make the directory a bottleneck. Some optimizations to improve the performance of the fully mapped centralized directory protocol are possible [12].

To reduce the amount of storage required, a number of modifications to the above scheme may be made. However, these modifications either require the implementation of an efficient broadcast mechanism contradicting our assumption about scalable systems, or may generate excess network traffic along with performance penalties. For example, one simple modification is to have i pointers per line in the directory. Each pointer may point to a cache that has a copy of the line. If more that i caches have copies of the line, a broadcast has to be done to *all* caches to service a write miss. The memory line has to be locked until all caches acknowledge the invalidation. This is classified as a $Dir_i B$ scheme [1], where i is the number of indices kept in the directory and B stands for broadcast. A $Dir_i NB$ scheme, where i is less than the number of caches and NB stands for no broadcast, is possible also. In such a scheme, at most i caches can have copies of a line at the same time. In the case where a read miss occurs when i caches have copies of the line, the directory has to invalidate one of the copies before the data can be supplied to the requesting cache. This might result in "thrashing" the line between caches.

3 The Distributed Directory Protocol

In our distributed directory protocol, caches that share data are linked together in a list. Each line in the main memory and the cache has a cache-pointer field associated with it. This pointer can specify any cache in the system. The directory services a read or write miss request by changing the cache-pointer in the directory entry associated with the line to point to the requesting cache. If the old value of the cache-pointer is nil, a reply is sent directly to the requesting cache. If the old value of the cache-pointer points to a cache, the request is forwarded to that cache. In case of read misses, that cache replies to the requesting cache, and the distributed list now includes the requesting cache. In case of write misses, the distributed list has to be invalidated before a reply can be sent to the requesting cache.

3.1 The Protocol Has Lower Cost

The amount of memory required for the pointer is $\log N$ where N is the number of caches. The total amount of memory needed is thus $O(M \log N + Nc \log N)$ where M is the total size of main memory, N is the number of caches and c is the size of each cache. The above expression can be written as $O(M(1 + k) \log N)$ where k is Nc/Nm (m being the amount of memory per node). We interpret k as the ratio of the size of cache memory per node to the size of main memory per node.

Assuming a constant value of k for the machine, the amount of memory required for the distributed directory scheme is $O(M \log N)$. We can expect then that, using the same technology, the cost of implementing the distributed directory scheme is significantly less than the fully mapped scheme—which requires $O(MN)$ amount of memory.

3.2 Resource Utilization is Distributed

In the distributed directory protocol, the information about which caches have copies of the data is distributed among the cache lines. The servicing of requests does not require any locking of lines as in the case of the centralized directory protocol. Direct cache-to-cache operations are used to send the replies and none of the replies have to be serialized through the main memory. The centralized bottleneck which is present in the centralized directory protocols is thus eliminated.

A line in main memory is originally in state "absent" from all caches. Each request causes the value of the cache-pointer to be updated to point to the requesting cache. If the line is absent from all the caches, the main memory sends a reply. Otherwise the request is forwarded to the last cache to make a request for the same line.

A line in cache memory is originally in state "invalid". A read or a write request from the processor causes the state to change to "writing-or-reading" and a read-miss or write-miss signal to be sent to the ap-

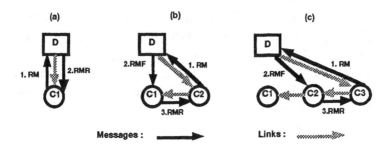

Figure 2: Linking of caches due to read misses

propriate main memory module. On a read-miss-reply, the value of the
cache-pointer is set to be the address of the object sending the reply.
This causes a linked list of caches that contain the data in shared state
to be formed. Figure 2 illustrates the process followed to set up the
linked list. Consider the case where cache C1 has a read miss for a line
followed by caches C2 and C3. As show in fig. 2(a), cache C1 sends a
read-miss signal to the directory. The cache-pointer of the line in the
directory is made to point to C1. Since no other cache has a copy of the
line, the main memory sends a read-miss-reply to C1. When C1 receives
the reply, the line is loaded into the cache in state "exclusive". Now,
when cache C2 sends a read-miss to the directory, a read-miss-forward
signal is sent to C1 as shown in fig. 2(b). The directory does not send a
reply directly to C2 since C1 may have written to the line locally. The
cache-pointer in the directory now points to C2. When C1 receives the
forwarded signal, it changes its state to "shared" and sends a read-miss-
reply to C2. The reply includes the data and the address of C1. When
C2 receives the reply, it sets its cache-pointer to point to C1. Thus a
linked list is formed. Fig. 2(c) shows how C3 gets linked into the list.

Write misses cause a write-miss signal to be sent to the directory. A
line is allocated in the cache before the miss signal is sent. This line is
used to buffer the write. Write buffering along with weak ordering [8, 13]
allows the processor to proceed immediately without stalling. A write is
considered to be *issued* when a write-miss is sent by the cache. A write
is considered to be *performed* when a write-miss-reply is received by the
cache. A write-miss-reply may consist of two signals as in the example
below. A *fence* [4] operation may be used to ensure that all writes that
have been issued by a processor are performed before that processor is

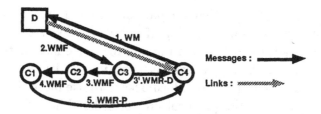

Figure 3: Invalidations due to write misses

allowed to proceed. If a copy of the line is not present in any other cache, the main memory directly sends a reply. Otherwise the copies of the line have to be invalidated before a reply can be sent.

Figure 3 shows the sequence of events that result when multiple caches have a copy of the line and C4 has a cache miss. The directory forwards the write miss signal to the old head (C3) pointed to by the cache-pointer and the cache-pointer is updated to point to C4. When C3 receives the write-miss-forward signal, it invalidates its copy and forwards the signal to C2. C3 also sends a write-miss-reply-data signal along with the requested data to the requesting cache C4. When C2 receives the write-miss-forward signal, it invalidates its copy and forwards the signal to C1. Since the cache-pointer of C1 points to the directory, it can be determined locally that C1 is the tail of the list and a write-miss-reply-performed signal is sent to C4 after the data in C1 is invalidated. C4 needs to receive both the write-miss-reply-data and the write-miss-reply-performed signals before the write can be considered to be performed.

A cache line would be in state "writing-or-reading" after a read-miss or a write-miss has been generated and before a read-miss-reply or a write-miss-reply has been received. If the line in the cache is in state "writing-or-reading" and a read-miss-forward or a write-miss-forward signal is received, the forwarded signal is stored in the cache-pointer field of the cache line. The state is changed to note that a forwarded signal has been stored. Such signals that are stored are called *pending signals* and are serviced when the reply to the local read or write miss is received. If multiple transactions for the same line are pending, the caches form a *distributed queue* of pending signals. The requests are thus serviced in a pipelined manner rather than causing contention at the directory as in the case of the centralized directory protocol.

Replacement of lines that are part of a shared list is done by invalidating the lower portion of the list. If care is not taken, the forwarding of signals may lead to deadlocks in the network since most network routing protocols assume that a message is *consumed* at its destination. One way of taking care of potential deadlocks is to use more than one logical network. Details of the protocol including handling of potential races may be found in [14].

As we have seen, when the directory controller receives a write or read miss request, and the data is present in some cache(s), the request is forwarded to the head of the list. We do not have the problem of locking lines at the main memory, buffering the signals and bouncing them to the sources as did the centralized directory protocols mentioned in section 2. Requests are serviced in a more decentralized fashion and the replies do not have to be serialized through the directory as in the case of the centralized directory protocol. This helps to prevent the directory from becoming a potential bottleneck.

An IEEE standards group is currently working towards defining a cache coherence protocol [11]. The proposed standard, called the scalable coherence interface (SCI) is also based on linked lists. Some comparison of our work with this proposed standard may be found in [15].

3.3 Performance Evaluation

The distributed directory protocol has good and robust performance. The latency of write misses may be a possible cause of concern since the invalidations of the caches linked in the list have to be done sequentially. However, if the writes to a line occur frequently, the number of caches that have to be invalidated between writes will be small. Thus the cases when the latency is large will be infrequent. Measurements on a range of applications [16] traced on upto 16 processor systems, support the assertion that the number of caches that have to be invalidated on writes is (on average) small. Additionally, we use write buffering to reduce the effect of sequential invalidation operations. Write buffering is frequently used in uniprocessor systems to prevent the processor from stalling on a write miss. The writes to memory are buffered in the cache and the processor is allowed to proceed. In multiprocessor systems, write buffering has to be done with care to avoid unexpected consistency violations. The problem of write buffering in multiprocessors has been studied in considerable detail [8, 13].

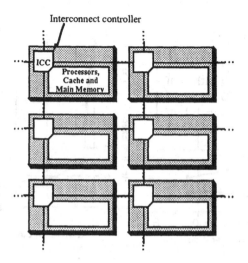

Figure 4: The interconnect topology

We studied the performance of the fully mapped centralized directory protocol and the distributed directory protocol by using a simple explicit partial differential equation (PDE) solver as a benchmark. A PDE algorithm was chosen since they are widely used in scientific and engineering communities in applications requiring high performance computation[2] [3]. Infinite caches were assumed for the simulation. The data was uniformly distributed and the computational threads were scheduled at random sites. Each node had one thread running on it. The same uniform distribution of the data and random placement of the threads was used for the comparisons. The simulation models were built upon an event driven simulation environment that has been used for other studies of multiprocessor operation [6].

A mesh topology with 32–bit bidirectional channels was used for the network. Figure 4 shows the topology used for the simulations. The memory line size was assumed to be 64 bytes and both the cache and the main memory were assumed to be 32 bits wide. The SRAM cache to DRAM main memory access ratio was assumed to be 1:10 based on current technology [9, 10]. The directories for both the protocols was assumed to be implemented in SRAM whose cycle time was taken to

---

[2]The explicit solver used has data access patterns similar to those found in SOR and conjugate gradient methods and so, while simple, is likely representative of a wide class.

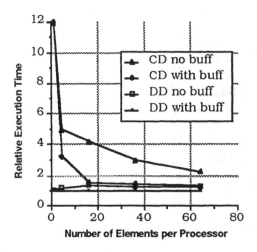
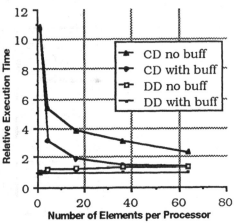

Figure 5: Performance comparison with and without write buffering – 16 processor model

Figure 6: Performance comparison with and without write buffering – 64 processor model

be 1 cycle. The network was assumed to be based on point-to-point interconnects between multichip units as used in the VAX9000 and thus transfer data between neighboring nodes in 1 cycle.

In the PDE algorithm used, for each element in the data array, two writes may be buffered at each time step before a fence operation is required. Figure 5 shows the relative execution time versus the number of elements per processor using a 16 processor model. The number of processors was kept constant and the number of elements per processor was varied by changing the size of the element array. When there are multiple elements whose values are being updated by a thread, writes for all the elements may be buffered at each time step before a fence operation. For example when we have one element per processor, two writes may be buffered before a fence operation. If the number of elements per processor is increased to four, eight writes may be buffered before a fence operation and so on. Thus an increase in the number of elements per processor implies an increase in the size of the data set as well as an increase in the number of writes that may be buffered.

The distributed directory protocol with write buffering had the best performance for the experiments that were performed. In the case of

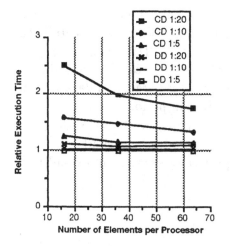
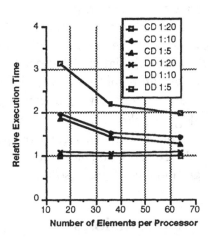

Figure 7: Effect of varying SRAM to DRAM access ratio – 16 processor model

Figure 8: Effect of varying SRAM to DRAM access ratio – 64 processor model

small data sets, the performance of the centralized directory protocol was exceptionally poor due to contention at the centralized directory. The effect of this contention was reduced in the distributed directory protocol due to the ability of the protocol to use the resources in a more distributed manner as explained in section 3.2. Write buffering improved the performance of both the protocols.

Figure 6 shows the relative execution time versus the number of elements per processor using a 64 processor model. The performance curves are very similar to those for the 16 processor model. We infer from the similarity of these figures that our results may be extended for even larger systems.

Figure 7 shows the effect of varying the SRAM cache to DRAM main memory access ratio using a 16 processor model. We focus on those cases with 16 or more elements per processor. Write buffering was used for all the curves in figure 7. In the case of the centralized directory protocol, slower DRAM memory causes read and write misses to be serviced more slowly since all replies have to be sent by the slower main memory. The slower DRAM also causes the contention at the main memory to increase in the case of the centralized directory protocol, resulting in further degradation in performance. In the distributed directory protocol, cache-to-cache transfers are used most of the time, and there is no centralized bottleneck at the main memory. Therefore, slower DRAM memory does not cause any significant degradation of performance. The distributed directory protocol thus allows the use of cheaper, larger and denser main memory without any significant degradation in performance.

Figure 8 shows the effect of varying the SRAM to DRAM ratio using a 64 processor model. Again, the performance curves are similar to those for the 16 processor model and we expect these results will extend to a larger number of processors.

4 Conclusions

We have presented a new protocol for providing cache coherence in large scale shared memory machines. Simulation results have shown that besides savings in cost, the protocol also provides good performance and is scalable to larger number of processors. The scalability and cost benefits of the implementation provides us with enough reasons to conclude that the distributed directory protocol may be considered to be a viable solution for the cache coherence problem in large scale shared memory multiprocessors.

The distributed directory protocol presented in this paper is an invalidate based protocol but update based and hybrid protocols are possible to implement also. Hybrid protocols could update a part of the list and invalidate the rest. It would be useful to determine the tradeoffs of such variations.

Acknowledgements: We are thankful to Mike Flynn, Greg Byrd and Max Hailperin for their comments and suggestions; and to the members of the DEC High Performance Systems Group, the Stanford Computer Systems Lab and Knowledge Systems Lab for their support.

References

[1] Anant Agarwal, Richard Simoni, John Hennessy, and Mark Horowitz. An evaluation of directory schemes for cache coherence. In *Proceedings of the 15th International Symposium on Computer Architecture*, pages 281–289, 1988.

[2] James Archibald and Jean-Loup Baer. Cache coherence protocols: Evaluation using a multiprocessor simulation model. *ACM Transactions on Computer Systems*, 4(4):274–298, November 1986.

[3] Sandra Johnson Baylor and Faye A. Briggs. The effects of cache coherence on the performance of parallel PDE algorithms in multiprocessors. In *Proceedings of the 1989 International Conference on Parallel Processing*, pages 233–236, 1989. Vol-I.

[4] W.C. Brantley, K.P. McAuliffe, and J. Weiss. RP3 processor-memory element. In *Proceedings of the 1985 International Conference on Parallel Processing*, pages 782–789, 1985.

[5] Greg Byrd. Personal communication regarding talk given by Tom Knight at a workshop on ultra large scale message passing computers, 1987.

[6] Gregory Byrd, Nakul Saraiya, and Bruce Delagi. Multicast communication in multiprocessor systems. In *Proceedings of the 1989 International Conference on Parallel Processing*, pages 196–200, 1989. Vol-I.

[7] Lucien M. Censier and Paul Feautrier. A new solution to coherence problems in multicache systems. *IEEE Transactions on Computers*, c-27(12):1112–1118, December 1978.

[8] Michel Dubois, Christoph Scheurich, and Faye Briggs. Memory access buffering in multiproceesors. In *Proceedings of the 13th International Symposium on Computer Architecture*, pages 434–442, 1986.

[9] M. Odaka et.al. A 512Kb/5ns BiCMOS RAM with 1KG/150ps logic gate array. In *Proceedings of the 1989 IEEE International Solid-State Circuits Conference*, pages 28–29, 1989.

[10] T. Takeshima et.al. A 55ns 16Mb DRAM. In *Proceedings of the 1989 IEEE International Solid-State Circuits Conference*, pages 246–247, 1989.

[11] David V. James, Anthony T. Laundrie, Stein Gjessing, and Gurinder S. Sohi. Scalable coherent interface. *IEEE Computer*, 23(6):74–77, June 1990.

[12] Daniel Lenoski, James Laudon, Kourosh Gharachorloo, Anoop Gupta, and John Hennessy. The directory-based cache coherence protocol for the DASH multiprocessor. Technical Report CSL-TR-89-404, Computer Systems Laboratory, Stanford University, 1989.

[13] Christoph Scheurich and Michel Dubois. Correct memory operation of cache-based multiprocessors. In *Proceedings of the 14th International Symposium on Computer Architecture*, pages 234–243, 1987.

[14] Manu Thapar and Bruce Delagi. Design and implementation of a distributed directory cache coherence protocol. Technical report KSL-89-72, Stanford University, 1989.

[15] Manu Thapar and Bruce Delagi. Stanford distributed-directory protocol. *IEEE Computer*, 23(6):78–80, June 1990.

[16] Wolf-Dietrich Weber and Anoop Gupta. Analysis of cache invalidation patterns in multiprocessors. In *Proceedings of the Third International Conference on Architectural Support for Programming Languages and Operating Systems*, pages 243–256, 1989.

Reducing Memory and Traffic Requirements for Scalable Directory-Based Cache Coherence Schemes[*]

Anoop Gupta, Wolf-Dietrich Weber, and Todd Mowry
Computer Systems Laboratory
Stanford University, CA 94305

Abstract

As multiprocessors are scaled beyond single bus systems, there is renewed interest in directory-based cache coherence schemes. These schemes rely on a directory to keep track of all processors caching a memory block. When a write to that block occurs, point-to-point invalidation messages are sent to keep the caches coherent. A straight-forward way of recording the identities of processors caching a memory block is to use a bit vector per memory block, with one bit per processor. Unfortunately, when the main memory grows linearly with the number of processors, the total size of the directory memory grows as the square of the number of processors, which is prohibitive for large machines. To remedy this problem several schemes that use a limited number of pointers per directory entry have been suggested. These schemes often cause excessive invalidation traffic.

In this paper, we propose two simple techniques that significantly reduce invalidation traffic and directory memory requirements. First, we present the *coarse vector* as a novel way of keeping directory state information. This scheme uses as little memory as other limited pointer schemes, but causes significantly less invalidation traffic. Second, we propose *sparse directories*, where one directory entry is associated with several memory blocks, as a technique for greatly reducing directory memory requirements. The paper presents an evaluation of the proposed techniques in the context of the Stanford DASH multiprocessor architecture. Results indicate that sparse directories coupled with coarse

---

[*]This paper also appeared in the Proceedings of the International Conference on Parallel Processing, August 1990

vectors can save one to two orders of magnitude in storage, with only a slight degradation in performance.

INTRODUCTION

A critical design issue for shared-memory multiprocessors is the cache coherence scheme. In contrast to snoopy schemes [2], directory-based schemes provide an attractive alternative for scalable high-performance multiprocessors. In these schemes a directory keeps track of which processors have cached a given memory block. When a processor wishes to write into that block, the directory sends point-to-point messages to processors with a copy, thus invalidating all cached copies. As the number of processors is increased, the amount of state kept in the directory increases accordingly. With a large number of processors, the memory requirements for keeping a full record of all processors caching each memory block become prohibitive. Earlier studies [15] suggest that most memory blocks are shared by only a few processors at any given time, and that the number of blocks shared by a large number of processors is very small. These observations point towards directory organizations that are optimized to keep a small number of pointers per directory entry, but are also able to accommodate a few blocks with very many pointers.

We propose two methods for lowering invalidation traffic and directory memory requirements. The first is the *coarse vector* directory scheme. In the most common case of a block being shared between a small number of processors, the directory is kept in the form of several pointers. Each points to a processor which has a cached copy. When the number of processors sharing a block exceeds the number of pointers available, the directory switches to a different representation. The same memory that was used to store the pointers is now treated as a coarse bit vector, where each bit of the state indicates a group of processors. We term this new directory scheme $Dir_i CV_r$, where i is the number of pointers and r is the size of the region that each bit in the coarse vector represents. With all bits set, the equivalent of a broadcast is achieved. While using the same amount of memory, the proposed scheme is at least as good as the limited pointer scheme with broadcast—presented as $Dir_i B$ in [1].

The second method we propose reduces directory memory requirements by organizing the directory as a cache, instead of having one directory entry per memory block. Since the total size of main memory in machines is much larger than that of all cache memory, at any given time most memory blocks are not cached by any processor and the corresponding directory entries are empty. The idea of a *sparse directory* that only contains the active entries is thus appealing. Furthermore, there is no need to have a backing store for the directory cache. The state of a block can safely be discarded after invalidation messages have been sent to all processor caches with a copy of that block. Our scheme of sparse directories brings down the storage requirements of main-memory-based directories close to that of cache-based linked list directory schemes such as the SCI scheme [8]. However, we avoid the longer latencies and more complicated protocol associated with cache-based directories.

Note that our two proposals are orthogonal. Sparse directories apply equally well to other directory entry formats as to the coarse vector scheme.

In this paper we compare the full bit vector scheme and existing limited pointer schemes with our coarse vector scheme. We also evaluate the performance of sparse directories. The performance results were obtained using multiprocessor simulations of four parallel applications. The multiprocessor simulator is based on the Stanford DASH architecture [11]. Our results show that the coarse vector scheme always does at least as well as all other limited-pointer schemes and is much more robust in response to different applications. While some applications cause one or the other directory scheme to degrade badly, coarse vector performance is always close to that of the full bit vector scheme. Using sparse directories adds less than 17% to the traffic while reducing directory memory overhead by one to two orders of magnitude.

The next section briefly introduces the DASH multiprocessor architecture currently being developed at Stanford. It will be used as a base architecture for our studies throughout the paper. The DASH architecture section is followed by background information on directory-based cache coherence schemes, with emphasis on the memory requirements of each scheme. Section introduces the directory schemes proposed in this paper. Section describes the experimental environment and the parallel applications used for our performance evaluation studies. Section presents the results of these studies. Sections and contain a discussion of the results, future work, and conclusions.

THE DASH ARCHITECTURE

The performance analysis of the different directory schemes depends on the implementation details of a given multiprocessor architecture. In this paper we have made our schemes concrete by evaluating them in the context of the DASH multiprocessor currently being built at Stanford. This section gives a brief overview of DASH [11].

The DASH architecture consists of several processing nodes (referred to as *clusters*), interconnected by a mesh network (see Figure 1). Each processing node contains several processors with their caches, a portion of the global memory and the corresponding directory memory and controller. Caches within the clusters are kept consistent using a bus-based snoopy scheme [13]. Inter-cluster consistency is assured with a directory-based cache coherence scheme [10]. The DASH prototype currently being built will have a total of 64 processors, arranged in 16 clusters of 4. The prototype implementation uses a full bit vector for each directory entry. With one state bit per cluster and a single dirty bit, the corresponding directory memory overhead is 17 bits per 16 byte main memory block, i.e., 13.3%.

What follows is a brief description of the protocol messages sent for typical read and write operations. This information is useful for understanding the message traffic results presented in Section . For a read, the cluster from which the read is initiated

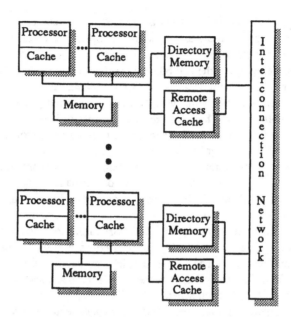

Figure 1: DASH Architecture.

(local cluster) sends a message to the cluster which contains the portion of main memory that holds the block (home cluster). If the directory determines the block to be clean or shared, it sends the response to the local cluster. If the block is dirty, the request is sent to the owning cluster, which replies directly to the original requestor. For a write, the local cluster again sends a message to the home cluster. A directory look-up occurs and the appropriate invalidations are sent to clusters having cached copies (remote clusters). At the same time, an ownership reply is returned to the local cluster. This reply also contains the count of invalidations sent out, which equals the number of acknowledgement messages to expect. As each of the invalidations reaches its destination, invalidation acknowledgement messages are sent to the local cluster. When all acknowledgements are received by the local cluster, the write is complete.

DIRECTORY SCHEMES FOR CACHE COHERENCE

Existing cache coherent multiprocessors are built using bus-based snoopy coherence protocols [12, 7]. Snoopy cache coherence schemes rely on the bus as a broadcast medium and the caches snoop on the bus to keep themselves coherent. Unfortunately, the bus can only accommodate a small number of processors and such machines are not scalable. For scalable multiprocessors we require a general interconnection network with scalable bandwidth, which makes snooping impossible. *Directory-*

based cache coherence schemes [4, 14] offer an attractive alternative. In these schemes, a directory keeps track of the processors caching each memory block in the system. This information is then used to selectively send invalidations/updates when a memory block is written.

For directory schemes to be successful for scalable multiprocessors, they must satisfy two requirements. The first is that the bandwidth to access directory information must scale linearly with the number of processors. This can be achieved by distributing the physical memory and the corresponding directory memory among the processing nodes and by using a scalable interconnection network [11]. The second requirement is that the hardware overhead of using a directory scheme must scale linearly with the number of processors. The critical component of the hardware overhead is the amount of memory needed to store the directory information. It is this second aspect of directory schemes that we focus on in this paper.

Various directory schemes that have been proposed fall into the following three broad classes: (i) the full bit vector scheme; (ii) limited pointer schemes; and (iii) cache-based linked-list schemes. We now examine directory schemes in each of these three classes and qualitatively discuss their scalability and performance advantages and disadvantages. Quantitative comparison results are presented in Section .

Full Bit Vector Scheme (Dir$_P$)

This scheme associates a complete bit vector, one bit per processor, with each block of main memory. The directory also contains a dirty-bit for each memory block to indicate if some processor has been given exclusive access to modify that block in its cache. Each bit indicates whether that memory block is being cached by the corresponding processor, and thus the directory has full knowledge of the processors caching a given block. When a block has to be invalidated, messages are sent to all processors whose caches have a copy. In terms of message traffic needed to keep the caches coherent, this is the best that an invalidation-based directory scheme can do.

Unfortunately, for a multiprocessor with P processors, M bytes of main memory per processor and a block size of B bytes, the directory memory requirements are $P^2 \cdot M/B$ bits, which grows as the square of the number of processors. This fact makes full bit vector schemes unacceptable for machines with a very large number of processors.

Although the asymptotic memory requirements look formidable, full bit vector directories can be quite attractive for machines with a moderate number of processors. For example, the prototype of the Stanford DASH multiprocessor [11] will consist of 64 processors organized as 16 clusters of 4 processors each. While a snoopy scheme is used for intra-cluster cache coherence, a full bit vector directory scheme is used for inter-cluster cache coherence. The block size is 16 bytes and we need a 16-bit vector per block to keep track of all the clusters. Thus the overhead of directory memory as a fraction of the total main memory is 13.3%, which is quite tolerable for the DASH multiprocessor.

We observe that one way of reducing the overhead of directory memory is to increase the cache block size. Beyond a certain point, this is not a very practical approach because increasing the cache block size can have other undesirable side effects. For example, increasing the block size increases the chances of false-sharing [6] and may significantly increase the coherence traffic and degrade the performance of the machine.

Limited Pointer Schemes

Our study of parallel applications has shown that for most kinds of data objects the corresponding memory locations are cached by only a *small* number of processors at any given time [15]. One can exploit this knowledge to reduce directory memory overhead by restricting each directory entry to a small fixed number of pointers, each pointing to a processor caching that memory block. An important implication of limited pointer schemes is that there must exist some mechanism to handle blocks that are cached by more processors than the number of pointers in the directory entry. Several alternatives exist to deal with this *pointer overflow*, and we will discuss three of them below. Depending on the alternative chosen, the coherence and data traffic generated may vary greatly.

In the limited pointer schemes we need $\log_2 P$ bits per pointer, while only one bit sufficed to point to a processor in the full bit vector scheme. Thus the full bit vector scheme makes more effective use of each of the bits. If we ignore the single dirty bit, the directory memory required for a limited pointer scheme with i pointers is $(i \cdot \log_2 P) \cdot (P \cdot M/B)$, which grows as $(P \log_2 P)$ with the number of processors.

Limited Pointers with Broadcast Scheme (Dir$_i$B)

The Dir$_i$B scheme [1] solves the pointer overflow problem by adding a broadcast bit to the state information for each block. When pointer overflow occurs, the broadcast bit is set. A subsequent write to this block will cause invalidations to be broadcast to *all* caches. Some of these invalidation messages will go to processors that do not have a copy of the block and thus reduce overall performance by delaying the completion of writes and by wasting communication bandwidth.

The Dir$_i$B scheme is expected to do poorly if the typical number of processors sharing a block is just larger than the number of pointers i. In that case numerous invalidation broadcasts will result, with most invalidations going to caches that do not have a copy of the block.

Limited Pointers without Broadcast Scheme (Dir$_i$NB)

One way to avoid broadcasts is to disallow pointer overflows altogether. In the Dir$_i$NB scheme [1], we make room for an additional requestor by invalidating one of the caches already sharing the block. In this manner a block can never be present in more than i caches at any one time, and thus a write can never cause more than i invalidations.

The most serious degradation in performance with this scheme occurs when the application has read-only or mostly-read data objects that are actively shared by a large number of processors. Even if the data is read-only, a continuous stream of invalidations will result as the objects are shuttled from one cache to another in an attempt to share them between more than i caches. Without special provisions to handle such widely shared data, performance can be severely degraded (Section presents an example).

Superset Scheme (Dir$_i$X)

Yet another way of dealing with pointer overflow is the *superset* or Dir$_i$X scheme (our terminology) suggested in [1]. In this scheme, two pointers are kept per entry. Once the pointers are exhausted, the same memory is used to keep a single composite pointer. Each bit of this composite pointer can assume three states: 0, 1, and X— where X denotes *both*. When an entry is to be added, its bit pattern is compared with that of the existing pointer. For each bit that the patterns disagree, the pointer bit is flipped to the X state.

When a write occurs and invalidations have to be sent out, each X in the composite pointer is expanded to both the 0 and 1 states. A set of pointers to processor caches result, which is a superset of the caches which actually have copies of the block. Unfortunately the composite pointer representation produces a lot of extraneous invalidations. In Section we will show that the superset scheme is only marginally better than the broadcast scheme at accurately capturing the identities of processors caching copies of the block.

Cache-Based Linked List Schemes

A different way of addressing the scalability problem of full vector directory schemes is to keep the list of pointers in the processors caches instead of a directory next to memory [9, 16]. One such scheme is currently being formalized as the Scalable Coherent Interface [8]. Each directory entry is made up of a doubly-linked list. The head and tail pointer to the list are kept in memory. Each cache with a copy of the block is one item of the list with a forward and back pointer to the remainder of the list. When a cache wants to read a shared item, it simply adds itself to the head of the linked list. Should a write to a shared block occur, the list is unraveled one by one as all the copies in the caches are invalidated one after another.

The advantage of this scheme is that it scales naturally with the number of processors. As more processors are added, the total cache space increases and so does the space in which to keep the directory information. Unfortunately, there are several disadvantages. For one thing, the protocol required to maintain a linked list for each directory entry is more complicated than the protocol for a memory-based directory scheme, because directory updates cannot be performed atomically. Secondly, each write produces a serial string of invalidations in the linked list scheme, caused by having to walk through the list, cache-by-cache. In contrast, the memory-based directory scheme can send invalidation messages as fast as the network can accept them. Thirdly, while a memory-based directory can operate at main memory speeds and can thus be made of cheap and dense DRAM, the linked list needs to be maintained in expensive high-speed cache memory. The exploration of tradeoffs between memory-based and cache-based directories is currently an active area of research. In this paper, however, we only focus on memory-based directories as used in DASH-like architectures.

NEW PROPOSALS

We propose two techniques to reduce memory requirements of directory schemes without significantly compromising performance and communication requirements. The first is the *coarse vector* scheme, which combines the best features of the limited pointer and full bit vector schemes. The second technique is the *sparse directory*, which uses a cache without a backing store.

Coarse Vector Scheme (Dir$_i$CV$_r$)

To overcome the disadvantages of the limited pointer scheme, without losing the advantage of reduced memory requirements, we propose the coarse vector scheme (Dir$_i$CV$_r$). In this notation, i is the number of pointers and r is the size of the region that each bit in the coarse vector represents. Dir$_i$CV$_r$ is identical to the other limited pointer schemes when there are no more than i processors sharing a block. Each of the i pointers stores the identity of a processor that is caching a copy of the block. However, when pointer overflow occurs, the semantics are switched, so that the memory used for storing the pointers is now used to store a coarse bit vector. Each bit of this bit vector stands for a group of r processors. The region size r is determined by the number of directory memory bits available. While some accuracy is lost over the full bit vector representation, we are neither forced to throw out entries (as in Dir$_i$NB) nor to go to broadcast immediately (as in Dir$_i$B).

Figures 2 and 3 make the different behaviour of the broadcast and coarse vector schemes apparent. In the graph, we assume that the limited pointer schemes each have three pointers. The graph shows the average number of invalidations sent out on a write to a shared block as the number of processors sharing that block is varied. For each invalidation event, the sharers were randomly chosen and the number of invalidations required was recorded. After a very large number of events, these invalidation figures were averaged and plotted.

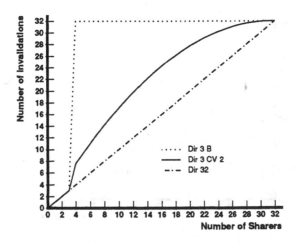

Figure 2: Average invalidation messages sent as a function of the number of sharers (32 Processors).

In the ideal case of the full bit vector (stipple line) the number of invalidations is identical to the number of sharers. For the other schemes, we do not have full knowledge of who the sharers are, and *extraneous* invalidations need to be sent. The areas between the stipple line of the full bit vector scheme and the lines of the other schemes represent the number of extraneous invalidations for that scheme. For the Dir_3B scheme, we go to broadcast as soon as the three pointers are exhausted. This results in many extraneous invalidations. The Dir_3X scheme uses a composite pointer once pointer overflow occurs, and the graph shows that its behaviour is almost as bad as that of the broadcast scheme. The composite vector soon contains mostly Xs and is thus close to a broadcast bit. The coarse vector scheme, on the other hand, retains a rough idea of which processors have cached copies. It is thus able to send invalidations to the *regions* of processors containing cached copies, without having to resort to broadcast. Hence the number of extraneous invalidations is much smaller.

The coarse vector scheme also has advantages in multiprogramming environments, where a large machine might be divided between several users. Each user will have a set of processor regions assigned to his application. Writes in one user's processor space will never cause invalidation messages to be sent to caches of other users. Even in single application environments we can take advantage of data locality by placing processors that share a given data set into the same processor region.

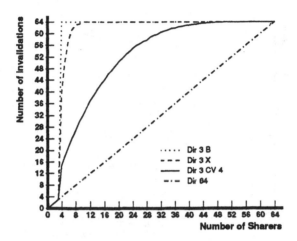

Figure 3: Average invalidation messages sent as a function of the number of sharers (64 Processors).

Sparse Directories

Typically the total amount of cache memory in a multiprocessor is much less than the total amount of main memory. If the directory state is kept in its entirety, we have one entry for each memory block. Most blocks will not be cached anywhere and the corresponding directory entries will thus be empty. To reduce such a waste of memory, we propose the *sparse directory*. This is a directory *cache*, but it needs no back-up store because we can safely replace an entry of the sparse directory after invalidating all processor caches which that entry points to.

As an example, if a given machine has 16 MBytes of main memory per processor and 256 KBytes of cache memory per processor, no more than 1/64 or about 1.5% of all directory entries will be used at any one time. By using a directory cache of suitable size, we are able to drastically reduce the directory memory. Thus either the machine cost is lowered, or the designer can choose to spend the saved memory by making each entry wider. For example, if the $Dir_i CV_r$ scheme were used with a sparse directory, more pointers i and smaller regions r would result. The directory cache size should be chosen to be at least as large as the total number of cache blocks. An additional factor of 2 or 4 will reduce the probability of contention over sparse directory entries if memory access patterns are skewed to load one directory more heavily than the others. This contention occurs when several memory blocks mapping to the same directory entry exist in processor caches and thus keep knocking each other out of the sparse directory. Similar reasoning also provides a motivation for making the sparse directory set-associative. Since sparse directories contain a large fraction of main memory blocks, tags need only be a few bits wide. Sparse

Table 1: Sample machine configurations.

no. of clusters	no. of procs	tot. main memory (MByte)	total cache (MByte)	block size (Byte)	directory scheme	dir. ovrhd.
16	64	1024	16	16	Dir_{16}	13.3%
64	256	4096	64	16	Dir_{64} (sparsity 4)	13.1%
256	1024	16384	256	16	Dir_8CV_4 (sparsity 4)	13.3%

directories are expected to do particularly well with a DASH-style architecture. In DASH, no directory entries are used if data from a given memory module is cached only by processors in that cluster. Since we expect processes to allocate their non-shared data from memory on the same cluster, no directory entries will be used for such data. Furthermore with increasing locality in programs, fewer data items will be remotely allocated and thus fewer directory entries will be needed.

The ratio of main memory blocks to directory entries is called the *sparsity* of the directory. Thus if the directory only contains 1/16 as many entries as there are main memory blocks, it has sparsity 16. Table 1 shows some possible directory configurations for machines of different sizes. For these machines, 16 MBytes of main memory and 256 KBytes of cache were allocated per processor. A directory memory overhead of around 13% has been allowed throughout. Processors have been clustered into processing nodes of 4—similar to DASH. The first line of the table is close to the DASH prototype configuration. There are 64 processors arranged as 16 clusters of 4 processors. For this machine, the full bit vector scheme Dir_{16} is easily feasible. As the machine is scaled to 256 processors, we keep the directory memory overhead at the same level by switching to sparse directories. The sparse directories contain entries for 1/4 of the main memory blocks (sparsity 4). As we shall see in Section , even much sparser directories still perform very well. For the 1024 processor machine, the directory memory overhead is kept constant and the entry size is kept manageable by using a coarse vector scheme (Dir_8CV_4) in addition to using a directory with sparsity 4. Note that this is achieved without having to resort to a larger cache block size.

EVALUATION METHODOLOGY

We evaluated the directory schemes discussed in the previous sections using an event-driven simulator of the Stanford DASH architecture. Besides studying overall execution time of various applications, we also looked at the amount and type of message traffic produced by the different directory schemes.

Our simulations utilized Tango [5] to generate multiprocessor references. Tango allows a parallel application to be executed on a uniprocessor while keeping the correct global event interleaving intact. Global events are references to shared data and synchronization events such as lock and unlock requests. Tango can be used to generate multiprocessor reference traces, or it can be coupled with a memory system simulator to yield accurate multiprocessor simulations. In the latter case the memory system simulator returns timing information to the reference generator, thus preserving a valid interleaving of references. We used this second method for our simulations.

Our study uses four benchmark applications derived from four different application domains. LU comes from the numerical domain and computes the L-U factorization of a matrix. DWF is from the medical domain and is a string matching program used to search gene databases. MP3D comes from aeronautics. It is a 3-dimensional particle simulator used to study airflow in the upper atmosphere. Finally, LocusRoute is a commercial quality standard cell routing tool from the VLSI-CAD domain.

Table 2: General application characteristics.

Application	shared refs (mill)	shared reads (mill)	shared writes (mill)	sync ops (thou)	shared space (MBytes)
LU	8.9	6.0	2.9	13	0.65
DWF	17.5	16.2	1.0	277	3.89
MP3D	13.5	8.8	4.7	1	3.46
LocusRoute	21.3	20.2	1.1	24	0.72

Table 2 presents some general data about the applications. It shows the total number of shared references in the application run and the breakdown into reads and writes. Shared references are defined as references to the globally shared data sections in the applications. The number of shared references varied slightly from run to run for the non-deterministic applications (LocusRoute and MP3D). We show the values for the full cache, non-sparse, full bit vector runs. The table also gives the amount of shared data touched during execution, which is an estimate of the data set size of the program.

All runs were done with 32 processors and a cache block size of 16 bytes. We did not use more processors because currently few of our applications achieve good speedup beyond 32 processors. For our evaluation studies, we assumed that a directory memory overhead around 13% was tolerable, which allowed us about 17 bits of directory memory per entry. This restricts the limited pointer schemes to three pointers and the coarse vector scheme to regions of size two. The schemes examined in this study are thus Dir_3CV_2, Dir_3B and Dir_3NB. We also used Dir_{32}, the full bit vector scheme, for comparison purposes. Once sparse directories are introduced, the overhead naturally drops dramatically—by one to two orders of magnitude, depending on sparsity. For example, a full bit vector directory with sparsity 64 requires 32 bits to keep track of the processor caches, 1 dirty bit, and 6 bits of tag. Instead of 33 bits per 16-byte block we now have 39 bits for every 64 blocks, a savings factor of 54.

The DASH simulator is configured with parameters that correspond to those of the DASH prototype hardware. The processors have 64 KByte primary and 256 KByte secondary caches. Local bus requests take on the order of 23 processor cycles. Remote requests involving two clusters take about 60 cycles and remote requests with three clusters have a latency of about 80 processor cycles. In the simulator, main memory is evenly distributed across all clusters and allocated to the clusters using a round-robin scheme.

The following messages classes are used by the simulator:

- Request messages are sent by the caches to request data or ownership.

- Reply messages are sent by the directories to grant ownership and/or send data.

- Invalidation messages are sent by the directories to invalidate a block.

- Acknowledgement messages are sent by caches in response to invalidations.

The simulator also collects statistics on the distribution of the number of invalidations that have to be sent for each write request. The invalidation distribution helps explain the behaviour of the different directory schemes.

SIMULATION RESULTS

The results presented in this section are subdivided as follows. The first subsection gives invalidation distributions for the different directory schemes. These impart an intuitive feel for how the different schemes behave and discusses their advantages and disadvantages. The next two subsections present the results of our main study. The first one contrasts the performance of our coarse vector scheme with that of other limited-pointer schemes. The second subsection presents results regarding the effectiveness of sparse directories.

Invalidation Distributions

Figures 4-7 give the invalidation distributions of shared data for the LocusRoute application. We do not present results for other applications for space reasons. Also, the LocusRoute distributions illustrate the trends of the different schemes well. In

Figure 4 we see the distribution for the full bit vector scheme (Dir_{32}) which is the *intrinsic* invalidation distribution and is the best that can be achieved. In the case of the Dir_{32} scheme, only writes that miss or hit a clean block are invalidation events. We note that most writes cause very few invalidations, but that there are also some writes that cause a large number of invalidations. The number of invalidation events is 0.26 million and each event on average causes 0.98 invalidations for a total of 0.25 million invalidations.

Figure 5 shows the invalidation distribution for Dir $_3$NB. Since no broadcasts are allowed, no more than three caches can share a given block at any one time. This also means that we never see more than three invalidations per write. Unfortunately, there are also many new single invalidations, caused by replacements when a block wants to be shared by more than three caches. For Dir$_3$NB it is possible for reads to cause invalidations, and this is why the number of invalidation events is so much larger. Although the average number of invalidations per event has decreased to 0.88, the total number of invalidations has increased to 0.37 million.

The distribution for Dir $_3$B is shown in Figure 6. We see that the number of smaller invalidations goes back to the level seen for the full vector scheme. However, any writes that caused more than three invalidations in the full vector scheme now have to broadcast invalidations. For most broadcasts, 30 clusters have to be invalidated, since the home cluster and the new owning cluster do not require an invalidation. This serves to drive the average invalidations per event up to 3.9 and the total to 1.01 million invalidations.

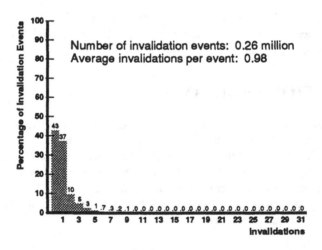

Figure 4: Invalidation distribution, LocusRoute, Dir$_{32}$.

In the Dir$_3$CV$_2$ scheme, shown in Figure 7, we are able to respond to the larger invalidations without resorting to broadcast. The peaks at odd numbers of

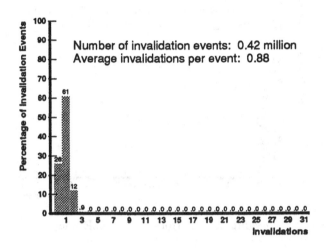

Figure 5: Invalidation distribution, LocusRoute, Dir$_3$NB.

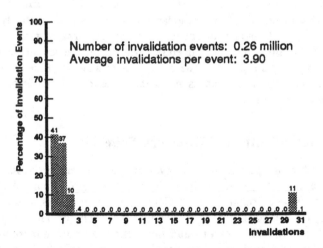

Figure 6: Invalidation distribution, LocusRoute, Dir$_3$B.

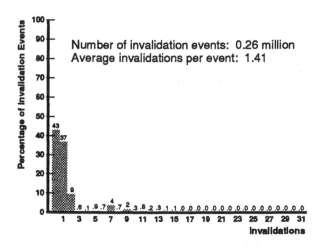

Figure 7: Invalidation distribution, LocusRoute, Dir_3CV_2.

invalidations are caused by the granularity of the bit vector. Also note the absence of the large peak of invalidations at the right edge that was present for the broadcast scheme. There are an average of 1.41 invalidations per event and 0.36 million total invalidations.

In conclusion, we see that the both the broadcast and non-broadcast schemes can cause invalidation traffic to increase. In the case of the broadcast scheme this increase is due to the broadcast invalidations, which can be relatively frequent if there are only a small number of pointers. For the non-broadcast scheme, the extra invalidations are caused by replacing entries when more caches are sharing a block than there are pointers available. The coarse vector scheme strikes a good balance by avoiding both of these drawbacks and is thus able to achieve performance closer to the full bit vector scheme.

Performance of Different Directory Schemes

Figures 8-11 show the performance achieved and data/coherence messages produced by the different directory schemes for each of the four applications. All runs use 32 processors, 64 KByte primary and 256 KByte secondary caches, and a cache block size of 16 bytes. The total number of messages is broken down into requests (which include writebacks), replies, and invalidation+acknowledgement messages.

Observe that the number of request and reply messages is about the same for the first three schemes (Dir_P, Dir_iCV_r and Dir_iB) for a given application. This is expected since all three schemes have similar request and reply behaviour. Dir_iCV_r and Dir_iB occasionally send out extraneous invalidations, but that is the only difference compared to the full bit vector scheme. For Dir$_i$NB, on the other hand, invalidations sometimes have to be sent even for *read* requests, when pointer overflow occurs. These invalidations can later cause additional read misses with the associated increase in request and reply messages.

Let us now look at each of the applications individually and discuss the results. LU exhibits the problem discussed in the previous paragraph. In Figure 8, we see a greatly increased number of request and reply messages as well as a very large number of invalidation and acknowledgement messages for the Dir$_i$NB scheme. In LU each matrix column is read by all processors just after the pivot step. This data is actively shared between many processors and Dir$_i$NB does very poorly.

Read-shared data is also the cause of the poorer performance of Dir$_i$NB for DWF. The pattern and library arrays are constantly read by all the processes during the run. The other schemes are virtually indistinguishable.

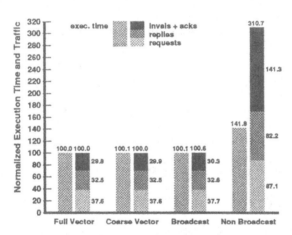

Figure 8: Performance for LU.

In MP3D (Figure 10) most of the data is shared between just one or two processors at any given time. This sharing pattern causes an invalidation distribution that all schemes can handle well. The coarse vector and broadcast schemes show almost no increase in execution time or message traffic, and even the non-broadcast scheme takes only 0.4% longer to run.

LocusRoute (Figure 11) is interesting in that it is the only application in which the Dir$_i$NB scheme outperforms Dir$_i$B. The central data structure of LocusRoute is shared amongst several processors working on the same geographical region. Whenever the number of sharers exceeds the number of pointers in Dir$_i$B, a broadcast results on a write. The Dir$_i$NB scheme does better with this kind of object, because the invalidations due to pointer overflow often do not cause re-reads.

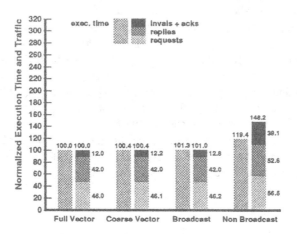

Figure 9: Performance for DWF.

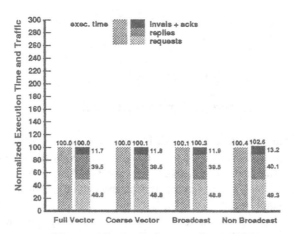

Figure 10: Performance for MP3D.

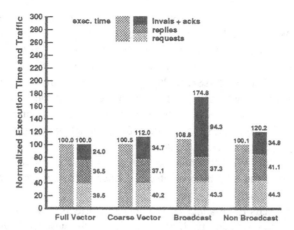

Figure 11: Performance for LocusRoute.

Throughout this section the message traffic numbers diverge more than the execution times for the various schemes. Since we simulate a 32 cluster multiprocessor with 32 processors, there is only one processor per cluster. The local cluster bus is thus underutilized. In a real DASH system, with four processors to a cluster, the cluster bus will be much busier. We consequently expect the performance degradation due to an increased number of messages to be larger than shown here.

Comparing the performance of the different schemes for the various applications, we see that the $Dir_i NB$ does much worse than the other schemes for most applications. Only in LocusRoute does it perform better than one of the other schemes. Secondly, while we expect the $Dir_i CV_r$ scheme to always perform as well as the broadcast scheme, we see that it can do significantly better for some applications. Finally, we note that the coarse bit vector scheme sends very few extraneous messages. For the worst case application (LocusRoute) $Dir_i CV_r$ only sends about 12% more messages than the ideal full bit vector scheme.

Performance of Sparse Directories

The method used for evaluating sparse directories was very similar to that used to evaluate the different directory schemes. There were two key differences. Firstly, the simulator was configured to use a sparse directory instead of keeping a complete directory. Secondly, we used *scaled* processor caches to achieve a more realistic size relationship of the sparse directories and processor caches. The slow speed of the simulator limited us to relatively small application data sets. As a result, if we had used the regular 256 KBytes of cache per processor, the whole data set would have fit into the caches. In such a case we would have been unable to experiment with sparse directories larger than the processor caches but smaller than the total memory blocks in the system. Instead, the caches were scaled to keep the ratio of data set size to cache size of our runs similar to that of data set size to cache size for a full blown application problem on a real DASH multiprocessor. For example, for DWF a full blown problem on a 64-processor DASH would occupy all of the 1 Gbyte of main memory (see Table 1). This is 64 times the total cache space. In our simulation, the data set size was 3.9 MBytes. So to preserve the data set to cache ratio, the total cache space for our 32-processor simulation was reduced to 64 KBytes, which is 2 KBytes per processor. We experimented with sparse directories that have entries from one to four times the total number of cache lines in the system (shown as size factor 1 to 4 in the graphs).

When an entry needs to be allocated in the sparse directory, we first look to see whether the slot it maps to is empty. If so, it is filled. Otherwise we have to replace an existing entry. Invalidations are sent out and the now empty slot is filled. Empty slots are also created when a processor cache replaces and writes back a dirty line.

Effect of Sparsity

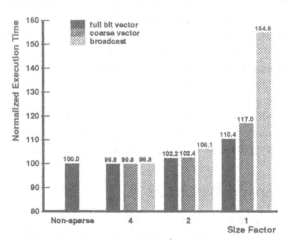

Figure 12: Sparse directory performance for LU.

Figures 12-13 show the effect of directory sparsity on performance. We chose to present results for LU and DWF only. The results for MP3D were very similar to those of DWF, so for lack of space we omit them here. For LocusRoute, even for full-scale runs the data set is expected to be small enough that sparse directories will perform as well as non-sparse directories. So again we omit the results in this

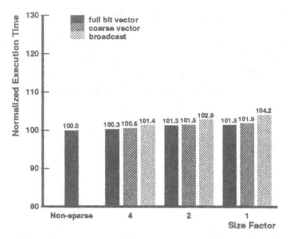

Figure 13: Sparse directory performance for DWF.

subsection.

In Figures 12 and 13 we show execution times for LU and DWF as the directory sparsity is varied. We consider the cases where the number of directory entries in the system is a factor of 1, 2, or 4 times the total number of cache blocks in the system. For these runs we used sparse directories of associativity 4 and use a random replacement policy (see below). The results suggest that even directories with the same size as the processor caches perform well. The worst case application (LU) shows only a 10.4% increase in execution time when going from a non-sparse, full bit vector directory to a sparse directory equal in size to the processor caches. When the directory size is increased to 2 or 4 times the cache size, the performance degradation of sparse directories is very small.

For the size factor 1 directory in LU we see a large performance difference between the coarse vector and the broadcast schemes. In LU, the pivot column is shared between all processors. When directory replacements are more frequent, as is the case for very sparse directories, only some of the processes may get a chance to access this data between replacements. When the replacement does occur, enough sharers exist to cause a broadcast for the $Dir_i B$ scheme while the $Dir_i CV_r$ only needs to send a few invalidations.

For DWF the performance is fairly flat across schemes and size factors. The performance does not vary much from scheme to scheme because the invalidation behaviour of DWF is handled equally well by all schemes. The performance is flat across size factors because DWF is a wave-front algorithm that has a relatively small working set at any moment in time. This ensures that even very sparse directories do not suffer from excessive replacements.

188

Effect of Associativity and Replacement Policy

Since a sparse directory has fewer entries than main memory has blocks, it is possible for several active blocks to map to the same directory entry. While a set-associative sparse directory can handle this situation, entries in a direct mapped sparse directory would keep bumping each other out, leading to poor directory performance.

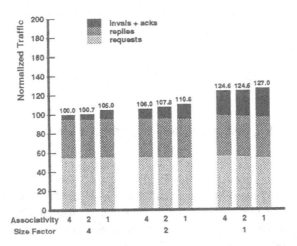

Figure 14: Effect of associativity in sparse directory (LU).

We used LU as a sample application to study the effect of sparse directory associativity and replacement policy. The full bit vector scheme was used in these studies. Figure 14 shows message traffic numbers for associativities of 1, 2 and 4 with directory size factors 1, 2 and 4. We show traffic numbers because they show the trends better than the execution time results. For each of the size factors, associativity 4 is equal to or slightly better than associativity 2, which in turn is better than direct-mapped by a larger margin. The benefits from set-associativity seem to be small, but we do expect associativity to make sparse directories more robust to different application behaviours.

For set-associative directories, there is a choice of replacement policies. We explored random, least-recently-used (LRU) and least-recently-allocated (LRA) schemes. LRU keeps the different sets in each entry ordered by time of access and replaces the least recently used one. LRA only keeps track of the allocation time of each set in the entry and replaces the one that was allocated first. The results for an LU run using a sparse directory with set-associativity 4 and a full bit vector scheme are shown in Figure 15. LRU is the most difficult to implement, and also performs the best. Even though random is the easiest to implement in hardware, it actually does better than LRA. With LRA the possibility of replacing entries that were allocated early, yet are used frequently exists. This soon leads to more

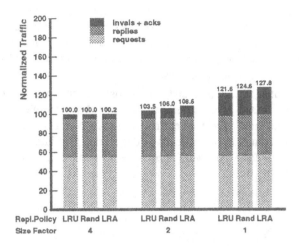

Figure 15: Effect of replacement policies in sparse directory (LU).

replacements when the frequently used entries are accessed again.

DISCUSSION

The question arises whether our proposals introduce additional complexities into the architecture. The answer is very few. The coarse vector scheme does not require any modification to the protocol used for the full bit vector scheme. It merely ends up sending some extraneous invalidations. For sparse directories, on the other hand, some protocol modification is required. When an entry is being replaced in the sparse directory, and is thus effectively removed from the system, we have to invalidate all copies of the corresponding memory block cached in processor caches. Some entity has to keep track of when all the acknowledgements for these invalidations have been received. Such an entity must already exist in systems that implement weak consistency, in order to keep track of outstanding invalidations. In DASH, we have the Remote Access Cache (RAC). When a block is to be replaced in the sparse directory, the RAC allocates an entry for that block and invalidations are sent out to all cached copies. The RAC receives the acknowledgement messages sent in response to these invalidations. The operation is complete when all acknowledgements have been received.

Another hardware issue concerns synchronization. In DASH, the directory bit vectors are also used to keep track of processors queued for a lock. In the case of the full bit vector we have enough space to keep track of all nodes. Consequently, when a lock is released, it is granted to exactly one of the waiting nodes. Once we switch to a coarse vector scheme, that is no longer the case. We are only able to keep track of which processor *regions* are queued for a lock. When the lock is released, and we wish to grant it to another node, we have to release all processors in that region and let them try to regain the lock. While this mechanism is slightly less efficient, it still avoids having to release *all* waiting processors and causing a hot spot when they all try to obtain the lock.

There are many other techniques that can be used to reduce the memory requirements of directory-based cache coherence schemes. For example, as suggested in [3], we can associate small directory entries with each memory block and allow these to overflow into a small cache of much wider entries. Similarly, we can make multiple memory blocks share one wide entry. We plan to evaluate some of these alternative schemes in the future.

CONCLUSIONS

We have presented two techniques for reducing the memory overhead and data/coherence traffic of directory cache coherence schemes—the coarse vector scheme and sparse directory scheme. The performance of the new schemes was analysed and compared to existing directory schemes. Our results show that the savings achieved in memory overhead and the traffic reduction are significant. Depending on the application, the coarse vector scheme produces up to 8% less memory message traffic than the next best limited pointer scheme and several factors less than the worst limited pointer scheme. The coarse vector scheme is also more robust than the other limited pointer schemes—its performance is always closest to the full bit vector scheme. While sparse directories add up to 17% to the memory coherence traffic, they can significantly reduce the directory memory overhead—by one to two orders of magnitude, depending on sparsity. We believe that a combination of the two techniques presented will allow machines to be scaled to hundreds of processors while keeping the directory memory overhead reasonable.

ACKNOWLEDGEMENTS

We would like to thank Helen Davis and Steven Goldschmidt for creating and supporting Tango. Dan Lenoski, Jim Laudon and Kourosh Gharachorloo provided insightful discussions. Dan Lenoski also provided Figure 1. Thanks to all the people who patiently stood by while we brought their machines to their knees with our runs. Lastly we would like to thank Henk Goosen, Jim Laudon, Dan Lenoski, Margaret Martonosi, Ed Rothberg and Mike Smith for reviewing an early version of this paper. Anoop Gupta and Todd Mowry are supported by DARPA contract N00014-87-K-0828. Wolf-Dietrich Weber is supported by an IBM Graduate Fellowship.

References

[1] Anant Agarwal, Richard Simoni, John Hennessy, and Mark Horowitz. An Evaluation of Directory Schemes for Cache Coherence. In *15th International Symposium on Computer Architecture*, 1988.

[2] James Archibald and Jean-Loup Baer. Cache Coherence Protocols: Evaluation Using a Multiprocessor Simulation Model. *ACM Transactions on Computer Systems*, 4(4):273–298, 1986.

[3] James K. Archibald. *The Cache Coherence Problem in Shared-Memory Multiprocessors*. PhD thesis, Department of Computer Science, University of Washington, February 1987.

[4] M. Censier and P. Feautier. A New Solution to Coherence Problems in Multicache Systems. *IEEE Transactions on Computers*, C-27(12):1112–1118, December 1978.

[5] H. Davis, S. Goldschmidt, and J. Hennessy. Tango: A Multiprocessor Simulation and Tracing System. Stanford Technical Report – in preparation, 1989.

[6] S. Eggers and R. Katz. The Effect of Sharing on the Cache and Bus Performance of Parallel Programs. In *Proceedings of the Third International Conference on Architectural Support for Programming Languages and Operating Systems*, pages 257–270, May 1989.

[7] Encore Computer Corporation. *Multimax Technical Summary*, 1986.

[8] P1596 Working Group. P1596/Part IIIA - SCI Cache Coherence Overview. Technical Report Revision 0.33, IEEE Computer Society, November 1989.

[9] Tom Knight, March 1987. Talk at Stanford Computer Systems Laboratory.

[10] D. Lenoski, J. Laudon, K. Gharachorloo, A. Gupta, and J. Hennessy. The Directory-Based Cache Coherence Protocol for the DASH Multiprocessor. In *Proceedings of 17th International Symposium on Computer Architecture*, 1990.

[11] Dan Lenoski, James Laudon, Kourosh Gharachorloo, Anoop Gupta, John Hennessy, Mark Horowitz, and Monica Lam. Design of Scalable Shared-Memory Multiprocessors: The DASH Approach. In *Proceedings of COMPCON'90*, pages 62–67, 1990.

[12] Tom Lovett and Shreekant Thakkar. The Symmetry Multiprocessor System. In *Proc. of the International Conference on Parallel Processing*, volume I, pages 303–310, August 1988.

[13] M. Papamarcos and J. Patel. A low Overhead Coherence Solution for Multiprocessors with private Cache Memories. In *Proceedings of 11th International Symposium on Computer Architecture*, pages 348–354, 1984.

[14] C. K. Tang. Cache Design in the Tightly Coupled Multiprocessor System. In *AFIPS Conference Proceedings, National Computer Conference, NY, NY*, pages 749–753, June 1976.

[15] Wolf-Dietrich Weber and Anoop Gupta. Analysis of Cache Invalidation Patterns in Multiprocessors. In *Proceedings of the Third International Conference on Architectural Support for Programming Languages and Operating Systems*, pages 243–256, April 1989.

[16] John Willis. Cache Coherence in Systems with Parallel Communication Channels & Many Processors. Technical Report TR-88-013, Philips Laboratories – Briarcliff, March 1988.

Multiprocessor Consistency and Synchronization Through Transient Cache States

Erik Hagersten, Anders Landin and Seif Haridi

Swedish Institute of Computer Science

Box 1263

S-164 28 Kista, Sweden

Abstract

A transient state can be used to mark a cache lines for which an access have started, but not yet completed. It can be used to implement cache-coherence protocols for split transaction buses.

Transient states can also be used to implement nonblocking writes, i.e. the processor never stalls on a write, while providing processor consistency for a certain class of networks. This has earlier only been achieved for looser forms of consistency at an extra hardware cost.

The same technique can be used to resolve data dependencies at run-time, implementing a functionality similar to that of Dataflow's I-structure memory, at no extra hardware cost.

Keywords: Multiprocessor, hierarchical architecture, hierarchical buses, multilevel cache, split-transaction bus, cache coherence, transient cache state, synchronization, processor consistency.

1 INTRODUCTION

Shared-memory multiprocessors with caches local to the processors often rely on a cache-coherence protocol to enable the programmer to observe a shared-memory view of the system. The protocol also provides some consistency level, specifying the order in which processors observe accesses from each other.

We have earlier shown how transient states can be used to implement a cache-coherence protocol for hierarchical buses [Hagersten et al., 1990]. The protocol makes use of transient states to implement a split-transaction protocol, allowing a bus to be released between a request and its reply. The consistency level provided by that protocol is the strongest level most often assumed by the programmer: sequential consistency [Lamport, 1979].

The weaker orders of consistency [Dubois et al., 1986, Gharachorloo et al., 1990] that have been proposed rely on special synchronization operations recognized by hardware. They allow for accesses to bypass each other, resulting in improved performance. However, the solutions ask for extra hardware support and introduce a new model to the programmer.

Processor consistency is an intermediate level of consistency introduced by Goodman [Goodman, 1989]. It provides a programming model closer to that of sequential consistency, while providing nearly the same performance as the weaker orders of consistency [Gharachorloo et al., 1991].

This paper discusses the use of transient states in processor caches. We have summarized the assumptions about the rest of the architecture in Section 2. The next section, Section 3, describes the general use of transient states in a cache-coherent protocol. Section 4 describes the sequentially consistent protocol reported earlier [Hagersten et al., 1990]. It features an efficient handling of write-invalidate, where a write acknowledge might be received before all other copies are erased. The protocol introduced in Section 5 implements processor consistency, allowing multiple outstanding writes, and where reads are allowed to bypass writes, by the use of transient states at (almost) no extra hardware cost.

The paper ends with a section about synchronization showing how transient states can be used to implement a synchronization similar to that of the I-structure memory in Dataflow [Arvind and Nikhil, 1989].

2   ASSUMPTIONS ABOUT THE ARCHITECTURE

The work presented here is targeted for the Data Diffusion Machine (DDM), currently being prototyped at the Swedish Institute of Computer Science. The presented solutions, however, can be generalized to apply to other architectures as well. The DDM is a cache-only memory architecture (COMA) characterized by a memory system consisting of caches only, and lacking the shared memory. A COMA architecture needs a cache replacement strategy different from most other architectures [Hagersten *et al.*, 1990]. Such a replacement is not included in this paper. The data entity handled by the protocol is referred to as an *item*, normally equal to a cache line.

We assume the following architectural properties in the rest of the paper:

- The network is a race-free network [Landin *et al.*, 1991], which is an acyclic network where transactions can not overtake each other. A tree with the processor/cache at its tips is an example of a race-free network.

- A *read* request will propagate in the network to a cache with a copy of the requested item.

- A *data* transaction being sent as a reply to a *read* request will propagate in the network to the requesting cache (or caches in combining-read situations)

- An *erase* request will propagate in the network to all caches with copies of the item and to all caches having sent a *read* request.

3   TRANSIENT STATES IN CACHE COHERENCE PROTOCOLS

The protocol we are about to describe has several similarities with the protocols of coherent caches reported over the last couple of years [Goodman, 1983, Archibald and Baer, 1986]. Most cache-coherent protocols reported are intended for single-bus systems. In such systems all caches snoop the transaction on the common bus at the same time, therefore making the consistency problem easy to solve. The protocol described here is intended to work for a network different from (and larger than) a single bus. When issuing a request (for example a read request) to the network, not all processors can monitor the transaction at once. It is not known how long time will elapse before an answer appears. In order to allow for the network to be used while waiting for the answer, we use a protocol of the split-transaction type; i.e., the request and its reply are not performed during the same bus tenure. For example in a system with a bus-based network, after sending a *read* request, the bus is released. Eventually there will be a *data* transaction on the bus, as a reply to the request. Items with outstanding requests are marked with transient states; e.g., example the transient state **reading**.

4 SEQUENTIAL CONSISTENCY

The strongest consistency level and the one most often used by programmers is called sequential consistency. The term was first defined by Lamport [Lamport, 1979]:

> [A system is sequentially consistent if] the result of any execution is the same as if the operations of all the processors were executed in some sequential order, and the operation of each individual processor appear in this sequence in the order specified by the program.

Uniprocessor systems with a single memory fulfill this requirement in a natural way. Multiprocessors, especially those with arbitrary network, often have to forfeit performance in order to maintain the high consistency level. Introducing multiple copies of data in caches makes the situation even worse. Normally sequential consistency is maintained in a system allowing for caching of shared data can be obtained if all processors issue their accesses in program order, and no access is performed by a processor until its previous access has been globally performed [Scheurich and Dubois, 1987]. This is an often used but not necessary condition.

4.1 A Sequentially Consistent Protocol

The protocol described in Figure 1 has been proven to ensure sequential consistency even though an acknowledge might be received, allowing the processor to continue, before all other copies in the system are erased [Landin *et al.*, 1991]. The branching point in the network whose subsystem contain all copies of the item, can send the acknowledge.

Figure 1 shows the implementation of the protocol, called *slow write*, using the behavior provided by our network. The protocol uses three stable states: **invalid (I)**, **exclusive (E)** and **shared (S)**. The protocol does

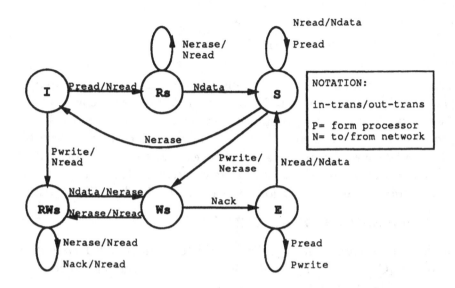

Figure 1: The slow write protocol. While providing sequential consistency, it requires the processor to stall both for read- and write-misses (states ending with an "s").

not need the "exclusive modified" state commonly used in other protocols, since there is no main memory that holds any old value. Transient states are **reading** (Rs), **waiting to become exclusive** (Ws) and **reading waiting to become exclusive,** (RWs). The "s" after the state letters indicates that the processor is stalled.

SUMMARY OF THE STATES:
I - Invalid. The cache does not contain this item.
E - Exclusive. This is the only copy of the item in the system.
S - Shared. There might be other copies of the item in the system.
Rs - Reading (stalled). A *read* request has been sent for this item.
Ws - Waiting (stalled). Waiting for an acknowledge before writing.
RWs - Reading waiting (stalled). A *read* request has been sent for this item, for which a write is intended.
TRANSACTIONS:
Pread - a *read* transaction from the processor
Pwrite - a write transaction from the processor
Nread - a *read* request to/from the network
Ndata - a *data* reply to/from the network

Nerase - an *erase* request to/from the network

Nack - acknowledge to an *erase* request to/from the network

The processor is allowed to read items in states **shared** or **exclusive**. Trying to read an item in state I results in a *read* request being sent to the network. The processor is stalled until *data* transaction is received. A processor is allowed to write to an item in **exclusive**. Trying to write to an item in **shared** results in an *erase* being sent to the network. The processor is stalled until the acknowledge is received. Trying to write to an item in **invalid** results in actions similar to a read followed by a write.

5 PROCESSOR CONSISTENCY

Goodman introduced an intermediate consistency level called *processor consistency* [Goodman, 1989]. He also noted that existing processors (e.g., VAX 8800) rely on this consistency model.

> A multiprocessor is said to be *processor consistent* if the result of any execution is the same as if the operations of each individual processor appear in the sequential order specified by its program.

> Thus the order in which writes from two processors occur, as observed by themselves or a third processor need not be identical, but writes issuing from any processor may not be observed in any order other than that in which they are issued.

This allows for reads to bypass writes in systems with general networks [Gharachorloo *et al.*, 1991], but in systems with a race-free network, writes may also be pipelined [Landin *et al.*, 1991].

We will here show how transient cache states can be used to implement processor consistency in a multiprocessor based on a race-free network without any extra cost in hardware. We call this the *fast write* scheme.

5.1 Processor Consistency by Transient States

For processor consistency the processor never needs to stall on a write. Instead, the newly changed, –or created, –item is marked as not yet public, while a write request is sent to the network. The item turns public upon the reception of an acknowledge. The replies to any read request for nonpublic items will have to be repeated after the acknowledge is received.

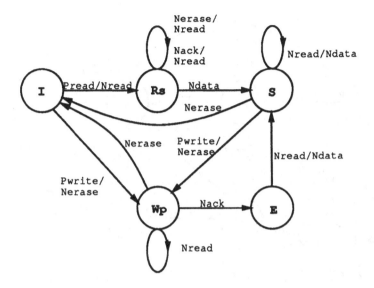

Figure 2: The fast write protocol for item-sized writes. Note that writes use the state write-pending without stalling the processor.

Processor consistency require all processors to observe the two consecutive writes: first A then B from a processor P in the exact order. A processor Q can violate processor consistency by reading first the new value of B and then the old value of A. The race-free network, however, guarantees that in order for Q to observe the new value of B, the write request for A must also have reached Q. This ensures that Q can not contain any old value of A. The properties of the race-free network also ensure that no other old copy of A can reach Q.

5.2   A Protocol for Item-Sized Writes

A fast write protocol for items equal in size to the smallest writable entity is shown in Figure 2. The protocol assumes a network similar to that for the slow-write protocol, where acknowledge is sent by the network handling the write races. The new transient state **write pending** (Wp) is used to mark an item not yet public. Upon reception of the acknowledge, the item is made public by its transition to **exclusive**. A *read* request for an item in state Wp will not be answered until an acknowledge has been received from the network. *Read* requests to items in **write pending** are forced to be repeated rather than answered. The probability of delaying

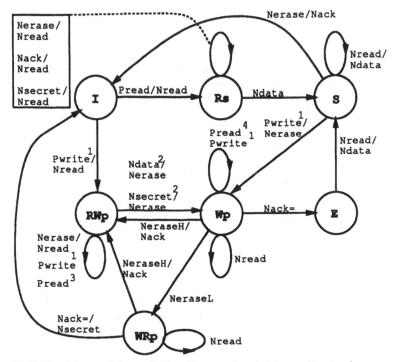

1) Write the portion of the item and set the write-mask.
2) Do not overwrite the masked portion of the item.
3) Stall processor.
4) Stall processor.

Figure 3: The fast write protocol for items larger than the smallest writable entity.

remote *reads* in that way is of course much lower than of stalling the processor for each write miss as in the slow-write protocol.

Note that the processor will not stall for writing items in state I. This is of great importance when an item is first used (e.g. cold start).

5.3   Increasing the Item-Size

The protocol for item-sized writes has one one winner and the rest losers in a write race. The item will hold the value of the winner when it goes public. Having an item size larger than the smallest writable entity requires a more complicated solution. When only one portion of an item in **invalid** is modified, the value of the remaining portion of the item has to be retrieved before the item goes public. In a write race, the value of the item can not be made public until all portions of the item with pending writes are updated.

This can be achieved by an extension to the fast write protocol as shown in Figure 3. The processor still never stalls on a write. A write attempt to an item in **invalid** will first retrieve the remaining part of the item while waiting in the new transient state **reading write pending** (RWp) before entering the write race by sending the *erase* transaction and moving to **write pending**. The write attempt will also set a write mask local to the cache, specifying what portion of the item has been modified.

The contenders in a write race add their modification to the item one by one in a strictly defined order. The order can for example be defined by the processor numbers, carried by the *erase* and *acknowledge* transactions. In Figure 3 the letter "L" marks a transaction with a lower priority than the pending write of the current cache, while the letter "H" marks a higher priority and "=" the same priority.

In the schema presented here, the acknowledge is produced by the processors rather than by the network. This allows for a simple way of describing how write races are detected, defined as receiving an *erase* while waiting for an *acknowledge*. The acknowledges will be combined by the network, so that the source node will receive its acknowledge first when all the processors with copies of the item have performed the erase.

The losers of a write race will receive an *erase* of a higher priority while in **write pending**, forcing them back into **reading write pending**. The winner of a write race will receive at least one *erase* transaction of a lower priority, forcing it into **write race pending**. When it finally receives the *acknowledge*, it changes state to **invalid** and transmits the new transaction *secret* containing the new value of the item. Note that only participants of the write race can make use of the *secret* transaction, and that the item is only made public after a write attempt that is not part of a write race.

5.4 Further Optimizations

The described protocol allows for starvation; i.e., a processor with a high priority that frequently writes an item might prevent any other processor from writing or reading that item. This can be resolved by introducing fairness in a write race by not letting any more processors enter the write race until it is completely resolved. The losers of a write race will transit to a new transient state **write looser pending**. Only contenders in **write loser pending** will be allowed to make use of the *secret* transaction. Footnotes 3 and 4 in Figure 3 are not required for implementing processor consistency, but will provide global ordering among write transactions from different processors for two different items to all other processors. Processor consistency will also be achieved for the following looser requirements of the footnotes: 3) Stall processor if the portion read is not included in the write mask. 4) Continue.

The write race detection can be migrated to the network, allowing for acknowledges to be sent from the network instead of from the leaves, similar to the slow-write protocol in section 4, reducing the number of transactions in the system [Hagersten *et al.*, 1991].

6 SYNCHRONIZATION

In dynamic Dataflow, the execution of each operation is dynamically scheduled. An operation is not enabled until all its needed inputs become available; i.e., the dependency graph controls the execution at runtime. A memory model called I-structure memory is introduced in order to support synchronization not only directly between operations $OP1 \to OP2$ but also to synchronize operations that communicate through memory, $OP1 \to MEM \to OP2$. This enables the introduction of more commonly used structures, like arrays, into Dataflow.

The memory is accessed by a select operation sending a *read* request of an item to the memory. If the value of that identifier is not yet available, the response is delayed until the location is written to. The memory has a state associated with each data element. The item might be in one of the states: **present(P)**, **absent (A)**, and **waiting (W)**. Initially all elements of the memory are in **absent**. Upon writes, they change state to **present**. *Read* requests to elements still in **absent** will cause a state change to **waiting** and will store a pointer (address) to the operator requesting the item. More than one request for the same element will be recorded as a linked list of pointers. Writing to an element in **waiting** results in a state transition to **present** and a reply message being sent to the operation(s) waiting for the value.

6.1 Per-Item Synchronization Protocol

In a COMA, I-structure memory can be implemented by transient states at almost no extra cost, by simply adding the states **locked** (for absent) and **answering** (for waiting). The old states **shared** and **exclusive** will be used to implement **present**. **Invalid** differs from **locked** in that the first is the implicit state for "the item is not here," while the latter has the meaning "this is the only copy of the item, but it can not yet be read."

Any processor can lock an item by issuing a *lock* operation: retrieving an exclusive copy of the item and changing its state to *locked*. Reading an item in **locked** results in a transition to **answering**, but no reply.

An item in **locked** or **answering** can be written to, but any read attempts will be delayed. It will be replaced like any other item, but it keeps its **locked** or **answering** state in its "new home." Any processor can release the item by issuing an unlock changing the state either from **locked** to **exclusive** or from **answering** to **shared**, in the latter case it should also transmit a *data* transaction. In case of the item being replaced, the unlock will be sent remotely to the "new home," resulting in similar actions remotely.

We still have the same assumptions about architecture in that the *data* transaction will by guided to the requesting node(s).

6.2   The Use of Per-Item Synchronization

The Dataflow processor makes a process switch for every instruction, and can benefit from such a synchronization in an efficient way. The memory model has been introduced without any restrictions to the parallelism explored by Dataflow. A process producing a big array of values does not need any explicit synchronization to its consumer(s) of the data. All producers and consumers start at the same time, and each operation will be enabled to execute as soon as its input becomes available. A parallelism explored by a Dataflow graph has been shown to benefit significantly by the use of I-structure memory in comparison with the use of barrier synchronization [Arvind and Nikhil, 1989].

A more conventional processor could also benefit from resolving data dependencies at runtime. The producer/consumer synchronization example above could be implemented. The implementation could benefit from a node delaying a *read* immediately sending the reply *item is locked* to the requesting node, allowing it to make a (lightweight) process switch.

7 ACKNOWLEDGMENTS

SICS is a nonprofit research foundation sponsored by the Swedish National Board for Technical Development (STU), Swedish Telecom, LM Ericsson, ASEA Brown Boveri, IBM Sweden, Bofors Electronics, and, the Swedish Defence Material Administration (FMV). Work on the DDM is being carried out as part of the Esprit project 2741 "PEPMA". We thank our many colleagues involved in or associated with the project.

References

[Adve and Hill, 1990] S. Adve and M. Hill. Implementing sequential consistency in cache-based systems. In *Proceedings of the 1990 International Conference on Parallel Processing*, pages 47–50, 1990.

[Archibald and Baer, 1986] James K. Archibald and Jean-Loup Baer. An evaluation of cache coherence solutions in shared-bus multiprocessors. *ACM Transactions on Computer Systems*, 4(4):273–298, November 1986.

[Arvind and Iannucci, 1983] Arvind and Robert A. Iannucci. Two fundamental issues in multiprocessing: the dataflow solution. MIT/LCS/TM 241, MIT, 1983.

[Arvind and Nikhil, 1989] Arvind and R. S. Nikhil. A dataflow approach to general-pupose parallel computing. Laboratory for Computer Science, MIT, SCG Memo 302, July 1989.

[Dubois *et al.*, 1986] M. Dubois, C. Scheurich, and F.A. Briggs. Memory access buffering in multiprocessors. In *Proceedings of the 13th Annual International Symposium on Computer Architecture*, pages 434–442, 1986.

[Gharachorloo *et al.*, 1990] K. Gharachorloo, D. Lanoski, J. Laudon, P. Gibbons, A. Gupta, and J. Hennessy. Memory consistency and event ordering in scalable shared-memory multiprocessors. In *Proceedings of the 17th Annual International Symposium on Computer Architecture*, pages 15–26, 1990.

[Gharachorloo *et al.*, 1991] K. Gharachorloo, A. Gupta, and J. Hennessy. Performance evaluation of memory consistency models. In *Proceedings of the 4th Annual ASPLOS*, 1991.

[Goodman, 1983] J. R. Goodman. Using cache memory to reduce processor-memory traffic. In *Proceedings of the 10th Annual International Symposium on Computer Architecture*, pages 124–131, 1983.

[Goodman, 1989] J. R. Goodman. Cache consistency and sequential consistency. Technical Report 61, SCI Commitee, 1989.

[Hagersten *et al.*, 1990] E. Hagersten, S. Haridi, and D.H.D. Warren. The cache-coherence protocol of the data diffusion machine. In *Proc. Cache and Interconnect Workshop*. Kluwer Academic Publisher, Norwell, Mass, 1990.

[Hagersten *et al.*, 1991] E. Hagersten, A. Landin, and S. Haridi. A processor-consistent protocol for a hierarchical architecture. Swedish Institute of Computer Science, DDM-memo, 1991.

[Lamport, 1979] L. Lamport. How to make a multiprocessor computer that correctly executes multiprocess programs. *IEEE Transactions on Computers*, 28(9):690–691, September 1979.

[Landin *et al.*, 1991] A. Landin, E. Hagersten, and S. Haridi. Race-free interconnection networks and multiprocessor consistency. In *To appear in Proceedings of the 18th Annual International Symposium on Computer Architecture*, 1991.

[Pfister and others, 1985] G.F. Pfister et al. The IBM Research Parallel Processor Prototype (RP3). In *Proceedings of the 1985 International Conference on Parallel Processing, Chigago*, 1985.

[Scheurich and Dubois, 1987] C. Scheurich and M. Dubois. Correct memory operation of cache-based multiprocessors. In *Proceedings of the 14th Annual International Symposium on Computer Architecture*, pages 234–243, 1987.

[Warren and Haridi, 1988] David H. D. Warren and Seif Haridi. Data Diffusion Machine–a scalable shared virtual memory multiprocessor. In *International Conference on Fifth Generation Computer Systems 1988*. ICOT, 1988.

DELAYED CONSISTENCY*

Michel Dubois

Department of Electrical Engineering Systems
University of Southern California
Los Angeles, CA90089-2562
(213) 740-4475
dubois@priam.usc.edu

Abstract

In weakly-ordered systems, coherence need only be enforced
at synchronization points, and therefore coherence enforcement
can be delayed. A delayed consistency protocol can be designed
from any on-the-fly (non-delayed) protocol. In this paper, we
present a write-invalidate delayed protocol.

The first gain is in the reduced number of invalidations due
to block sharing and a corresponding hit ratio increase. The
second gain is in the overlap of coherence actions such as invalidations with processor accesses to the cache.

INTRODUCTION

The design of shared memory systems that can scale up for large number of processors is a current topic of active research. There are two
approaches. In one approach, private caches are associated with each
processor and coherence is maintained among caches in hardware with
possible compiler assistance [Stenstrom, 1990]. The second approach
consists in emulating shared memory on a distributed system [Stumm
and Zhou, 1990]. The techniques presented in this paper are applicable
to both cases, but here we concentrate on cache coherence.

---

*This research is supported by NSF Research Grant No. CCR-8709997.

It has been argued that cache coherence and synchronization are related [Dubois and Scheurich, 1990]. When sequential consistency is not enforced, memory accesses are weakly ordered. In all existing multiprocessors coherence is enforced as soon as possible, on the fly. The major reason is that on-the-fly write-invalidate protocols rely on the acquisition of unique or exclusive block copies for Stores; they cannot cope with the multiple, exclusive copies, which may result from delays in sending invalidations.

In delayed protocols, some coherence actions are deliberately delayed, and multiple, inconsistent block copies may exist in different processors at any one time. Therefore the hardware complexity is increased, but the pay off is a greater concurrency in accessing shared cache blocks. In-coming invalidations are buffered in the processor; similarly, when a cache must send invalidations to acquire a unique (exclusive) copy of a block on a Store, the propagation of these invalidations can occur asynchronously with processor accesses to the cache: neither the processor nor the cache are blocked and the time to propagate invalidations may be selected optimally by the hardware. More importantly, delayed consistency increases concurrency by reducing the coherence activity on shared blocks due to false sharing.

FALSE SHARING

False sharing is the sharing of cache blocks without actual sharing of data. In parallel applications, shared data structures are partitioned statically or dynamically and different processes work on different partitions of the structures. In general, partition boundaries do not coincide with cache block boundaries. As a result, a cache block can be shared while no data in the block are actually shared. A more rigorous definition of false sharing can be found in [Torrellas et al., 1990].

To demonstrate occurrences of false sharing we will show two simple examples. The first example is an algorithm with static partitioning of the data, the Successive Over Relaxation (S.O.R.) iterative algorithm to solve Laplace's equation. In this algorithm, an array (grid) of iterate components is updated iteratively by a linear combination of the iterate and its four neighbors in the 2-dimensional grid. In the example of Figure 1.a, the grid has been partitioned among four processors. There are private iterate components, and shared iterate components, as indicated

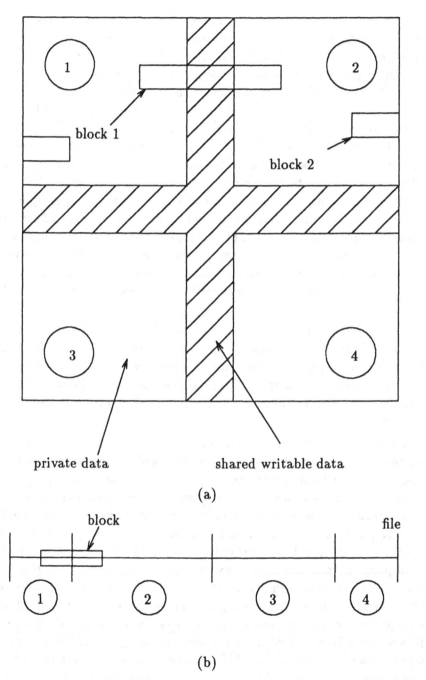

Figure 1: Illustration of false sharing in the S.O.R. (a) and Quicksort (b) algorithms

in the Figure. In a shared memory, organized as a linear address space, the array is stored row-wise or column-wise. Assume that it is stored row-wise (i.e., first row 1, then row 2, and so on), and assume that the row size is not a multiple of the block size. Then false sharing occurs for blocks of type 2. False sharing (and true sharing) occurs also for blocks of type 1. Clearly, in this static case, the compiler could easily deal with the problem by allocating an integer number of blocks per row. However, for blocks of type 1, it will be difficult to achieve this in general, without wasting a lot of cache space or complicating drastically the addressing to contiguous array components. In real-life PDE algorithms, grid partitions are more complex than in the simple case of Figure 1.a, and the compiler will not always be able to reduce false sharing significantly. Some simple compiling techniques, which in some cases can reduce the effect of false sharing, are introduced in [Torrellas et al., 1990]. For a given problem size the amount of false sharing increases as the granularity of parallelism decreases, ie for larger number of processors.

The second example, in Figure 1.b, is an algorithm with dynamic partitioning of the shared data structure, the dynamic quicksort algorithm. In this algorithm, a processor acquires exclusive access to a subfile and splits it in two. False sharing occurs at the boundaries between consecutive subfiles. The boundary between two subfiles cannot be predicted at compile time.

False sharing results in non-optimum protocols. In the case of a write-invalidate protocol, such as the Illinois protocol [Papamarcos and Patel, 1984], more invalidations are sent than strictly needed by the parallel application and its data-sharing requirements. Invalidations create traffic, and delays in the processor issuing them; moreover they increase the miss rate, because an invalidated block must be reloaded if it is accessed again. If the protocol enforces coherence on the fly, then a block may "ping-pong" several times between two processors, even if they reference different data elements in the block. For a given number of processors, the effect of the block size is very similar to the effect of the block size in uniprocessor systems, but for different reasons. As the block size increases, the miss rate first decreases because of spatial locality, then for larger block sizes, it increases. This behavior is observed even in caches of infinite sizes. It is caused by the increase in false sharing, which quickly offsets the gains due to spatial locality. Because of these effects, some researchers have advocated a block size of one and extensive prefetching for shared data [Lee *et al.*, 1987].

These effects are clear from the curves of Figures 2 and 3, which show the effect of false sharing on the total number of misses for executions of the S.O.R. algorithm (Figure 2) and the quicksort (Figure 3). The results in these Figures were obtained through execution-driven simulations, following a technique introduced in [Dubois *et al.*, 1986]. In these simulations, all caches have infinite sizes and each simulated processor executes in turn until it accesses a shared data; at that point, the simulator simulates a different processor. This is done in a round-robin fashion. In Figure 2 we have plotted the total number of shared-data misses for the S.O.R. algorithm with four processors, a grid size of 128x128 and 100 iterations. Two curves are shown: in one curve it is assumed that all processors are working at the same speed and start each iteration at the same time (best case); in this case the effect of false sharing as the block size increases is very small. In the second curve (worst case), processor 2 is slightly slower so that it reaches a given block of type 2 at the same time as processor 1 (and similarly for processors 3 and 4); this could happen because of the order in which the processors reach and execute the barrier synchronization; the effect of false sharing is maximum here.

The plots for the quicksort are shown in Figure 3; the number of processors is 32, the file to sort is made of 32K random integers drawn from a uniform distribution; each point is the average of the number of misses for 10 files. For 32 processors, the miss rate curve bottoms out for block sizes of 8x4=32 bytes.

WEAK ORDERING

The class of concurrent programs for which delayed consistency is applicable has been defined in [Adve and Hill, 1990]. It is based on a weakly-ordered concurrency model called DRF (Data-Race Free). Programs assuming sequential consistency will not run correctly in general on machines with delayed consistency. In the DRE model, processes must synchronize in such a way that no set of processes can ever access a shared variable at the same time unless all these accesses are Loads. Clearly, critical sections and semi-critical sections are required to access shared writable data in such programs.

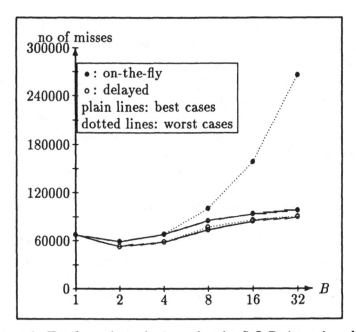

Figure 2: Total number of misses for the S.O.R. iterative algorithm

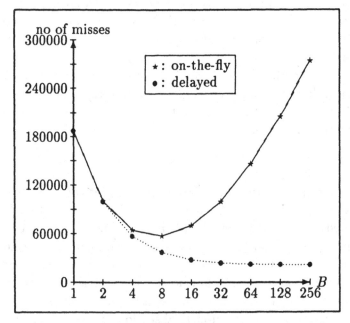

Figure 3: Total number of misses for the dynamic quicksort ($P=32$)

In the following, we call a *datom* the smallest unit of addressing in the machine. This is usually a byte (8 bits), but could also be a 32-bit word. Under DRF, a datom goes through different phases. These are Read/Write phases by a single process, and/or Read phases by multiple processes. To enforce DRF in asynchronous multiprocessors, these phases must be "framed" by explicit, hardware-recognized synchronizations.

When a process needs to enter a Read/Write phase (critical section) for a datom, it must first acquire a lock; then, at the end of the phase, it must release the lock. Critical sections are present in both algorithms introduced above. In the S.O.R. algorithm, each process executes a barrier synchronization between consecutive sweeps of the grid, and in each sweep, different iterates are updated exclusively by different processes. In the quicksort example, when a process fetches a new subfile descriptor, some form of hardware synchronization is assumed, so that updates to a given subfile are done exclusively by one process; similarly, when a process has completed the split of a subfile, it must execute some form of hardware-recognized synchronization.

PROTOCOL

We describe in this Section a write-invalidate delayed protocol. In an on-the-fly protocol, updates on non-owned blocks require the sending of invalidations; later, these invalidations are received and executed by individual processors. Each of these two phases can be delayed, ie the sending of invalidations, and the execution of these invalidations. To maximize the delay, we also assume that at the hardware level, distinction can be made between acquiring a lock (*lock* operation) and releasing a lock (*unlock* operation).

When a processor modifies a clean block, it does not need to acquire a unique copy, and furthermore, the modification does not have to be *visible* to other processors before the execution of the next *unlock* (at the latest). The modifications are temporarily stored in an Invalidation Send Buffer (ISB). Similarly, when a cache receives an invalidation for a block, the local copy can remain valid and accessible by the local processor until the execution of the next *lock* instruction; we say that the copy is *stale*. Note that a stale copy is only valid for the local processor, which can read and modify the block copy; the rest of the system considers it as invalid.

In particular, in a directory based system such as the one described in [Censier and Feautrier, 1978], the presence bit in the directory for a stale copy is reset. Therefore, when we talk about the state of a block copy we have to distinguish between the *system* point of view (state stored in memory directories) and the *processor* point of view (state stored in the cache directory).

System Point of View

From the system point of view, a block copy can be in three states in any one cache: I (stale, invalid, or not in cache), O (Owner), or K (Keeper). The *Owner* of a copy has a dirty copy, which must be unique, and must respond to a miss by another processor; otherwise, if the cache has a valid copy but is not the owner, then the cache is a *Keeper* of the block.

At the system level, the protocol is a conventional write-invalidate protocol. It will be effective for private data, and by by-passing all buffers, it will also work for accesses to synchronization variables.

The following commands can be issued by one processor node to the memory system:

- **ReqO** (Request Ownership): If there are copies in other caches, they must be invalidated. If there is an owned copy, a *Inv* (Invalidate Command) is sent to the owner.

- **ReqKC** (Request Keeper Copy): If there is an owned copy, a *RelO* (Release Ownership) command is sent to the owner. The memory copy is then sent to the requesting processor.

- **WB**: Write back the block to memory.

- **ReqU**: Write the block modifications in ISB to memory and notify all keepers or the owner by sending *Inv's* (Invalidate Commands).

Processor Point of View

When a copy of a block is *stale*, part of the block is valid and part is invalid; however, the processor can still access the copy (Read and Write) for as long as it accesses the valid part (in practice until the next *lock* instruction). The stale state can be implemented with a stale bit in the cache.

From the previous discussion, it appears that a cache may receive two commands from the memory system. They are:

- **Inv** (Invalidate): The block copy becomes stale and if it was owned it must update memory.

- **RelO** (Release Ownership): This command can be received only if the block is owned by the cache. The cache must become a keeper and the copy must update memory.

Let's now examine the state transitions due to accesses made by the local processor.

- **Read hit:** No action.

- **Read Miss:** The processor sends a $ReqKC$ command to the memory system. The cache becomes a keeper.

- **Write hit:** If the copy is owned, no action is taken. If the cache is a keeper or if the copy is stale, an entry is allocated for the block in the ISB (unless an entry is already present). The new values are stored in the ISB (with a dirty bit set for the modified datum).

- **Write Miss:** The cache issues a $ReqO$ command. It also receives a copy and becomes owner.

- **Replacement:** If the cache is the owner, then a WB command is sent to memory. A $ReqU$ command is sent to memory if the copy is a stale or a keeper copy which have been modified; in this case the modifications are in the ISB.

- **Removing an Entry from ISB:** The keepers or the owner (if any) must be notified; if the block was invalid or stale in the cache then a $ReqU$ request is sent to memory and the block stays invalid or stale in the cache. If the cache was a keeper then a $ReqO$ command is sent to the memory controller (in this case, there cannot be an owner).

- **Acquiring a lock** *(lock)*: All stale blocks become invalid right after the successful acquisition of the lock.

- **Releasing a lock** (*unlock*): All entries in the ISB must be removed before releasing the lock.

EFFECTS ON FALSE SHARING

The miss rate improvement due to the delayed protocol (with an ISB of 2 entries) is shown in Figures 2 and 3 for the SOR and the quicksort algorithm. The on-the-fly protocol used for Figure 2 and 3 is the protocol described above for the system point of view with no delays in the processors. For a given problem size, the delayed protocol reduces the number of false sharing misses as the number of processor increases. For these examples, it appears that delayed protocols are more scalable than on-the-fly consistency protocols.

CONCLUSIONS

In this paper, we have introduced a delayed consistency protocol in which the coherence overhead due to false sharing is reduced with respect to on-the-fly consistency protocols. Another advantage of delayed consistency is that the sending of invalidations and the receiving of invalidations can be done asynchronously with the local processor execution; the time to propagate these invalidations can be selected by the hardware to reduce conflicts and multiple invalidations pending in the SIB may be sent at the same time. This feature reduces the coherence penalty seen by the processor and is critical to good processor efficiency. From our preliminary evaluations (which only include the effect on false sharing), it appears that delayed protocols are more scalable than traditional protocols; this increased scalability is obtained with no assistance from the programmer and the compiler, and therefore it is particularly useful for general-purpose multiprocessors.

Synchronization variables must be stored in different regions of shared memory than other shared data. Accesses to the region of memory reserved for synchronization variables must by-pass all buffers, so that the on-the-fly protocol is enforced on these variables.

Much more work remains to be done. First of all, the protocol may not be optimum and it may be possible to refine it once simulation results are available. Second, we need to investigate the effect of delays on write-broadcast protocols. Third, we need to study physical implementations of the protocol in bus-based systems, in directory-based systems (implemented by linked lists or by tables), and in systems with multi-level caches.

ACKNOWLEDGEMENTS

I wish to acknowledge the work of Jin-Chin Wang, with whom I was able to discuss some of the problems associated with delayed consistency protocols. Andy Glew gave me the idea of the stale state to implement partial invalidation of blocks. Finally, several discussions with Philip Bitar were very useful. Philip coined the word "datom."

References

[Adve and Hill, 1990] S. V. Adve and M. D. Hill. Weak Ordering-A New Definition. *Proc. of the 17th Int. Symp. on Computer Architecture*, pages 2–14, 1990.

[Censier and Feautrier, 1978] L. M. Censier and P. Feautrier. A New Solution to Coherence Problems in Multicache Systems. *IEEE Trans. on Computers, Vol. C-27, No. 12*, pages 1112–1118, Dec. 1978.

[Dubois and Scheurich, 1990] M. Dubois and C. Scheurich. Memory Access Dependencies in Shared Memory Multiprocessors. *IEEE Trans. on Software Engineering, Vol. 16, No. 6*, June 1990.

[Dubois et al., 1986] M. Dubois, F. A. Briggs, I. Patil, and M. Balakrishnan. Trace-driven Simulations of Parallel and Distributed Algorithms in Multiprocessors. *Proc. Int. Conf. on Parallel Processing*, pages 909–916, Aug. 1986.

[Lee et al., 1987] R. L. Lee, P. C. Yew, and D. H. Lawrie. Multiprocessor Cache Design Considerations. *Proc. of the 14th Int. Symp. on Computer Architecture*, pages 253–262, 1987.

[Papamarcos and Patel, 1984] M. Papamarcos and J. Patel. A Low Overhead Coherence Solution for Multiprocessors with Private Cache Memories. *Proc. of the 11th Int. Symp. on Computer Architecture*, pages 348–354, 1984.

[Stenstrom, 1990] Per Stenstrom. A Survey of Cache Coherence Schemes for Multiprocessors. *IEEE Computer, Vol. 23, No. 6*, June 1990.

[Stumm and Zhou, 1990] M. Stumm and S. Zhou. Algorithms Implementing Distributed Shared Memory. *IEEE Computer, Vol. 23, No. 5*, May 1990.

[Torrellas *et al.*, 1990] J. Torrellas, M. S. Lam, and J. L Hennessy. Measurement, Analysis, and Improvement of the Cache Behavior of Shared Data in Cache Coherent Multiprocessors. Technical Report CSL-TR-90-412, Stanford University, February 1990.

The SCI Cache Coherence Protocol

Stein Gjessing
University of Oslo
P.O.B. 1080 Blindern
N-0316 Oslo 3
NORWAY

David B. Gustavson
SLAC Computation Research Group
Stanford University,
P.O. Box 4349, M/S 88
Stanford, CA 94309

James R. Goodman
Computer Sciences Dept.
4211 Computer Sci. & Stat. Bldg.
1210 West Dayton Street
Madison, Wisconsin 53706

David V. James
Advanced Technology Group
Apple Computer, MS 76-2H
20525 Mariani Avenue
Cupertino, CA 95014

Ernst H. Kristiansen
Dolphin Server Technology A.S.
P.O. Box 52, Bogerud
N-0621 Oslo 6
NORWAY

Abstract

This article discusses the current status of the Scalable Coherent Interface (SCI), IEEE standards project P1596. The SCI cache coherence protocol is scalable (up to 64K processors can be supported), efficient (memory is not involved in the common pairwise-sharing updates), and robust (data can be reliably recovered by software after transmission errors). Scalability is achieved by having the memory directory identify only the first processor sharing a cache line; other processors sharing the same line are identified by entries in a distributed doubly linked list.

1 Introduction

To simplify programming, multiprocessors have often assumed a shared-memory data-access model. When caches are used to improve the performance of these processors, cache-coherence protocols are needed to maintain the simple shared-memory model assumed by software. Such coherence is achieved by exchanges of read or write transactions between processors or between processors and memory. In a traditional bus-based multiprocessor, coherence is enforced by broadcasting all or a subset of these transactions to other processors (Goodman 83). Such a protocol is usually called snooping or eavesdropping.

This paper focuses on the directory-based cache coherence protocol being defined for the Scalable Coherent Interface (SCI). SCI is an IEEE standards project (P1596), which began as a spin-off from the Futurebus standardization work (Sweazey 86). Brief presentations of preliminary results of the SCI cache coherence protocol design effort are given in (Sweazey 89) and (James 90).

It became clear early in the SCI work that no bus-based connection scheme could handle the demands of the next generation of processor chips in multiprocessor configurations. The speed of buses is inadequate because of multidrop transmission line physics problems and because buses are inherently a bottleneck, i.e. they can be used by only one processor at a time.

SCI solved these problems by using a large collection of point-to-point links instead of a bus. Because links have better physical properties than buses, their signalling rates can be much higher (1000 MegaBytes/sec in the first version). Also, the bus bottleneck is avoided: distinct packets can be sent concurrently over different links within the system.

However, new protocols were needed to provide the desired bus-like services without re-introducing the bus-related bottlenecks. For example, snooping cache coherence mechanisms depend on having all transactions serialized so that all participants can snoop, thus the coherence protocols developed for Futurebus cannot be used by SCI.

A major effort was required to develop protocols to achieve these goals. Our design goals included scalability (up to 64K nodes), high performance (faster than eavesdrop or memory-directory based protocols), and robustness (recovery from an arbitrary number of transmission errors).

For a long time SCI's success was in doubt because the feasibility of meeting such ambitious goals was not obvious. However, we have been pleasantly surprized; although SCI's distributed-list structure was mandated by the scalability goal, this distributed-list structure has been found to be efficient and robust as well. We know of no other cache-coherence protocol that addresses all these goals as comprehensively as SCI does.

The rest of this paper is organized as follows: we first give a brief overview of directory-based cache coherence protocols and discuss the basic design of the SCI cache coherence protocol. We then describe its special properties, which include scalability, high performance, and robustness.

2 Previous Directory-Based Protocols

Directory-based protocols use tags to identify the processors that are actively sharing the same cache line. For each coherently cached memory line, a directory identifies the set of caches that contain this line (called the sharing set), the state of the memory line, and the state of the cache lines. In central-directory schemes the directory is contained in one system memory; in distributed-directory schemes there may be multiple memory controllers, each of which has a directory for the addresses that it supports. We are primarily concerned with distributed-directory schemes, since the bottleneck of central-directory schemes limits their usefulness to a small number of processors.

We use the terms central list and distributed list to differentiate between the coherence protocols that maintain the lists of sharing caches in memory and the coherence protocols that distribute the list among the sharing caches.

One of the first directory-based cache coherence protocols was suggested by Tang (Tang 76). Tang uses a central list to keep track of caches that cache lines. He also uses a "write-back" model, i.e. the data of a cache line is written back into memory only when needed. Store back is needed only when the cache line is dirty, the cache space is needed by another line, or the line is about to be shared by another cache. The amount of directory space used in this solution can become large (it is proportional to the number of used cache lines) and the central directory can become a performance bottleneck.

In (Agarwal 88b) it is observed that there are two difficulties in making scalable central lists: broadcasts are sometimes required, and the memory can become a performance bottleneck. For example, Archibald and Baer (Archibald 84), proposed a central list which keeps the state of the memory lines but not the location of the sharing caches, thus requiring broadcasts in order to access the caches. The Aquarius project (Carlton 90) uses directories to selectively route transactions from one bus to a grid of buses. With their interconnect topology (a bus mesh) and selective routing, the Aquarius-project computer provides scalability by increasing the bandwidth when the number of processors increases. Other computers also use hierarchical cache organizations (Wilson 87).

The cache protocol described by Censier and Feautrier (Censier 78) also uses the "write-back" model, but they call it "nonstore-through". They maintain a MODIFIED bit for each memory line, and a PRIVATE flag for each cache line. In addition there are as many PRESENT bits in each memory line as there are caches in the system. Such coherence protocols where the complete sharing set is stored with the memory line is called a "full-mapped directory" in (Chaiken 90).

(Chaiken 90) also introduces the notion of a "limited directory." A limited directory can hold only a portion of the largest potential sharing set. The sharing-set size can be reduced by invalidating old cache copies when the set size would be exceeded (Agarwal 88b). In the DASH computer (Lenoski 89) the limited directory is used to hold multicast lists when the set size has been exceeded.

In the Alewife computer (Agarwal 90) a limited directory is implemented in hardware, but a software based overflow mechanism is provided. This lets the directory overflow into RAM when the sharing set becomes large.

The last class of directories defined in (Chaiken 90) is called "chained directories." John Willis reports that variations of the chained directory protocol have been used in several research computers including Lawrence Livermore's S-1 Mark III, Symbolic's Aurora and Philips Laboratory's Strand (Willis 88). In a linked list protocol the directory information for each memory line is distributed over all cache lines that cache this memory line. Hence such a directory is also called a "distributed directory". The Stanford Distributed-Directory protocol (Thapar 90) and the SCI protocol are of this class.

The Stanford Distributed Directory uses a singly linked list to define the sharing set. The main memory line contains a (head) pointer to the last cache to access this line. The cache line in that cache contains a pointer to the previous cache that accessed the line, etc. Insertions are done at the head of the list. When one cache line wants to be deleted from the list it invalidates itself and the rest of the list.

The SCI directory uses a doubly linked list to identify the sharing set, and the list entries are distributed among the sharing caches. The memory or directory bottleneck that is reported in (Agarwal 88b) is minimized by distributing many of the directory-update operations out to the caches themselves, and by simplifying the few memory directory operations that are left. For example, memory operations can always be performed immediately, independent of the processor-cache state.

Sharing lists scale better when distributed, since the directory at the memory needs only be large enough to identify the cache at the head of the sharing list.

3 The SCI Standard

The SCI standard defines the physical and logical interface and interaction protocol for up to 64K nodes. A node is a processor (or a multiprocessor), a memory module, an I/O adapter or a combination of these, as shown in Figure 1.

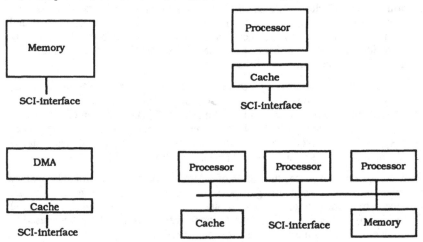

Figure 1: Four possible SCI configurations.

Note that a DMA adapter needs a cache with at least one line in order to participate in the coherence protocols.

Physical SCI memory addresses are 64 bits long; the most significant 16 bits are the node identification, while the remaining 48 bits are the physical address within the memory of the node. The coherent transactions are split into a request message and a response message. The request and response messages are called subactions.

A subaction also contains command, data, and status fields. A 16-bit CRC is included to detect transmission errors reliably. Any damaged subactions are discarded when the damage is detected; timeouts are used to detect the loss of a request or response subaction.

To simplify the coherence protocols, a standard coherence line-size of 64 bytes has been assumed. For this transfer size, the size of the subaction headers (16 bytes) is significantly less than the size of the data transfers (64 bytes). We expect to keep the same coherence line size as technological improvements increase the bandwidth of our links, since the ratio of the header size to the data size is independent of the link bandwidth for SCI.

The SCI interface consists of an input link and an output link, operating at 1 GByte/sec in initial implementations. For small systems neighboring input and output links may be directly connected, forming a ring. For larger systems these links could be dynamically connected by a switch, or a large number of small rings could be interconnected by bridging nodes. The SCI protocols were designed to support all these models transparently.

4 SCI Sharing Lists

4.1 Sharing List Structure

There are three basic operations on the SCI list: The insertion of a new cache element, the deletion of an element, and the reduction to a single-entry list. The insertion operation is used when a new cache wants to get a readable copy of the line. The deletion operation is used when a cache needs a cache line for other uses (also called roll-out). The reduction operation is used when data is written, to remove all but one of the duplicate copies in the sharing set. The remaining copy is then private and can be modified.

To facilitate these operations the SCI sharing set is identified as a doubly linked list. There is a pointer in memory to the first node in the sharing list and the other nodes in the list contain pointers to their predecessor and successor in the list (Figure 2). In memory each line that may be coherently cached contains (in addition to its data) some status information and a 16-bit node identifier which points to the first cache line (node) in the sharing list. In the caches each cache line contains (in addition to its status and data) two 16-bit node identifiers that are the backward and forward pointers to other nodes in the sharing list.

The cache coherence protocol is built on the transaction mechanism described in the previous section. The directory is modified by requests sent from one cache line to another or from a cache line to memory. These requests contain the destination address (the node identification of another cache) as well as the 64-bit physical memory address. Given a memory line address, a sharing set is a set of nodes actively sharing that memory line address, as illustrated in Figure 2.

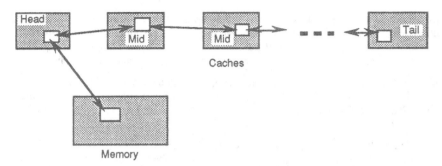

Figure 2: An SCI sharing list.

The status field of a cache line defines the meaning of the forward and backward pointers; if the line is not in a sharing list, the pointers are undefined; at the head of a list, only the forward pointer is defined; at the middle of a list, both pointers are defined; at the tail of a list only the backward pointer is defined. The status field of a memory line defines whether a list exists, and whether the memory data is valid.

The linked list data structure also makes SCI scalable in the sense that the size of the SCI directory is proportional to the total cache and memory sizes; all (maximum 64K) nodes can theoretically be members of one sharing set. In Section 9 we will discuss optimizations that improve the efficiency of updating such large sharing sets.

4.2 Sharing-List States

As stated above, the status fields in cache lines and memory lines define not only the meaning of the pointers, but also the privileges and status of the data in cache or memory. In this section we describe these status values in more detail. The coherence protocols support the stable states shown in Table 1 (to simplify the descriptions, some optional states are not described).

mem	first	(other)	last	Description
home	----	----	----	Uncached data
fresh	only_fresh	----	----	One fresh copy
"	head_fresh	----	tail_valid	Two fresh copies
"	head_fresh	mid_valid	tail_valid	More fresh copies
gone	only_dirty	----	----	One dirty copy
"	head_dirty	----	tail_valid	Two dirty copies
"	head_dirty	mid_valid	tail_valid	More dirty copies
gone	head_excl	----	tail_stale	Two copies, stale tail
"	head_stale	----	tail_excl	Two copies, stale head

Table 1: Stable Sharing-List States.

When the sharing set is empty the memory line is in the state *home*. Otherwise memory is in one of the two states *fresh* or *gone*. In the state *fresh*, memory is known to contain valid data, while in the state *gone*, memory data may be stale. When the memory state is *gone*, valid data is found in one or more cache lines of the sharing set. Since memory updates are always completed indivisibly, memory has no transient intermediate states.

A cache line that is not in use is in the state *invalid* (shown as ---- in the table). The data in a cache line is always valid for at least one entry in the sharing list. The head node knows when memory contains *fresh* data, and reflects this by being in the state *only_fresh or head_fresh*. The contents of head entries in other states must be written back to memory when the sharing list collapses.

Additional cache line state information gives the position of the cache line in the sharing list: *head, mid* and *tail*. A cache line that is both the head and the tail is in the state *only*. Special two-entry list states (*head_excl&tail_stale* or *head_stale&tail_excl*) are provided to efficiently support pairwise sharing. A cache line in the *only_dirty, head_excl*, or *tail_excl* states can be modified.

The basic sharing-list updates are described in the following sections. The optional pairwise-sharing updates are described in a later chapter.

5 Sharing-List Updates

5.1 Insertion

On a load miss, a node joins an existing sharing list by sending a *prepend request* (R1 in Figure 3) to the addressed memory line. The target of this subaction is defined by the 16-bit node identification of the memory controller, plus the 48-bit physical line address within the node. The memory controller swaps its old head pointer with a pointer to the new node, and returns the old head pointer in an immediate *response* (S1 in Figure 3) back to the requester.

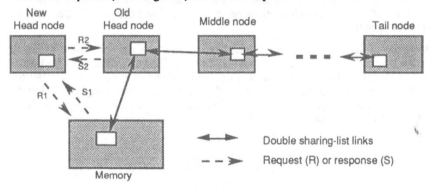

Figure 3: Sharing list insertion initiated.

After receiving this response, the new head (if the sharing list was not empty) informs the old head of its predecessor in the list by sending a *new-head* request, R2, to the old head. The old head updates its pointers and (if asked) returns a copy of its data in the response, S2. After these two transactions have completed, the sharing list has one more entry and a new head, as illustrated in Figure 4.

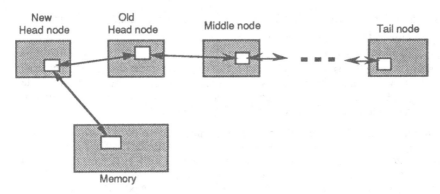

Figure 4: Sharing list insertion completed.

Several new nodes might (nearly) simultaneously prepend themselves to an existing list. Memory immediately responds to the prepend requests in the order that they are received. The new head, however, delays other would-be new heads until it has prepended itself to the sharing list. This scheme is fast and ensures forward progress. Insertion bandwidth is however limited by the constant time it takes to execute the prepend request in memory. A truly scalable architecture would insert elements into the sharing set even faster; we will briefly elaborate on this in Section 9.

5.2 Deletions

When a node no longer wants to share a memory line, it deletes its entry from the sharing list. The entry in a single-entry list is deleted by writing the data back to memory. Otherwise, the delete operation involves transfers between adjacent entries in the sharing list.

A middle-of-list cache line (called ML) has a forward pointer with value Vf and a backward pointer with value Vb, as illustrated in Figure 5. Note that backward pointers point to the left while forward pointers point to the right. If the deleting node is in the middle of the list, it first sends an *update backward* request (R1) to its successor. This request contains the node identification Vb, which normally updates the backward pointer in the successor.

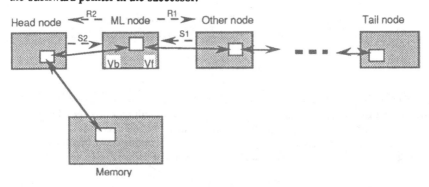

Figure 5: Sharing set deletion.

The deleting node then sends an *update forward* request (R2) to the predecessor, containing the identification, Vf, of the successor. This leaves the sharing list with one less entry, as illustrated in Figure 6.

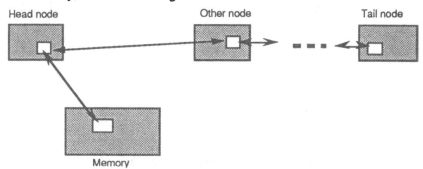

Figure 6: Sharing set deletion.

Note that these are the normal protocols for deleting an entry from a doubly-linked list. However, special care is required to resolve conflicts when deletions are concurrently performed by adjacent nodes.

The above described deletion algorithm is scalable to a large set of nodes, since many deletions can occur in parallel. In the extreme case, however, deletions in one sharing list will be serialized when all nodes delete themselves at the same time. In this case, the deletions occur only at the (dynamically changing) tail entry.

5.3 Reduction to Single-Entry Sharing List

The SCI cache coherence protocol is invalidation based: in order to write, a node must invalidate copies in the other sharing list entries. A head node has the privilege to delete all the other nodes from the list, and hence may reduce the sharing set to a single-entry list with itself as the only member. The head deletes or purges the rest of the list by first sending a purge request to the second node in the list. This node responds by returning the identification of its successor (the third node in the list). The head then sends a purge request to this next node (as seen in Figure 7). This node gives a purge reply, containing the identification of the next node in the list, etc.

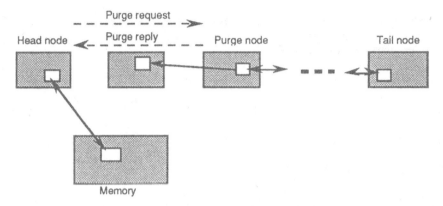

Figure 7: Reduction to single-entry list.

The time used to reduce the sharing list to a single-entry list when the data structure is a linear list is proportional to the size of the list. Previous studies have shown that sharing sets are usually not large (Eggers 88, Agarwal 88b). Hence the linear time that this operation uses will normally not be of any concern.

In the future, however, new highly parallel algorithms will perhaps not have such characteristics. An optimization of this purge operation is defined in optional extensions to the SCI base protocol: a node can, under certain circumstances, forward the purge request to both the adjacent and further distant nodes. In this way, the purge process can be concurrently active at multiple sites within the sharing list. In Section 9 we will briefly describe the data structures which support these more-efficient sharing list reductions.

SCI supports both weak and strong ordering. Strong ordering is enforced by waiting for the purge to complete before allowing the processor to proceed; for weak ordering, the processor may proceed before the purge is complete, only checking completion as needed for program correctness.

6. Scalability

A computer architecture is scalable if it is possible to add new components (e.g. processors or memory modules) and get an increased performance appropriate to the added cost.

SCI supports up to 65,000+ nodes, hence it has the potential to be scalable up to this limit. The SCI coherence protocol is scalable in the sense that that there is no central control and no globally-shared resource. Any number of memory or sharing-list operations can take place at the same time provided they do not use conflicting resources (the same part of the interconnect, the same memory module, or the same cache).

The SCI directory is scalable in the sense that any number of nodes can share the same memory line, and the size of the directory is proportional to the number of memory lines and cache lines. Deletion of elements from the sharing set is fully scalable. This operation is executed in a decentralized way and does not (usually) involve the central directory (in memory) at all.

Ideally a shared-memory system should be able to handle a large (proportional to the total number of nodes in the system) number of accesses to the same memory location "at the same time." We define a system to be logarithmically scalable if the maximum delay for any operation is proportional to $\log(N)$, where N is the number of nodes in the system. We are considering extensions to the base protocol that make SCI scalable even according to this definition. The implementation of the sharing set as a list makes two operations linear: 1) set insertion (including distribution of data to all new members), and 2) the reduction of the set. In order to make these two operations scalable, the sharing set can optionally be structured as a tree. See Section 9 for details.

7. Performance

Previous sections have described the basic SCI sharing-list operations required for coherently-shared data. SCI also provides a rich set of interoperable performance-enhancement options, which (at some cost in complexity) can be implemented as required to enhance system performance. Several of these options (DMA, pairwise-sharing, and QOLB) are discussed in the following sections.

7.1 DMA

In some of the existing RISC-based systems, DMA I/O transfers are performed non-coherently into what are otherwise coherently managed pages of memory address space. For data transfers, this dramatically complicates the I/O driver software, which has to explicitly manage the flushing of relevant cache lines. For instruction-page replacements, the problems are significant but less severe (since the data is read-only). However, special treatment of instruction-cache pages is less practical for languages which support or encourage the use of self-modifying code.

To simplify software, SCI provides coherence check options for DMA transfers; these options improve the performance of DMA-related coherence checking, while reducing the complexity of their implementation. These simple protocol optimizations are possible because of the nature of DMA participation – a DMA controller doesn't need to be added to the sharing list. However, the DMA controller is required to have a minimal (one line) cache in order to participate in the coherence protocols.

For example, consider the coherent DMA read protocols. If the memory state is home or fresh, the memory read returns the data and leaves the sharing-list state unchanged. The DMA reader is prepended to the existing sharing list (from which the read data is copied) only when the memory state is gone. We rejected the idea of reading from the sharing-list without prepending to it, since the structure of the sharing list (and hence its validity) may change between the time that memory is read and the old sharing-list head is accessed.

7.2 Pairwise sharing

The pairwise sharing option is invoked when the sharing set consists of two nodes and is constant over a period of time. At most one of the nodes may modify the data at a time, but this capability can be negotiated between the nodes without involving memory. If processor A needs to modify the line (that was last read by processor B), it sends a request (R1) to processor B. When the request is processed at processor B, its state is changed to *stale* and a (modifiable) *excl* copy is returned (S1) to processor A, as illustrated in Figure 8 (showing processors A and B as the head and tail respectively).

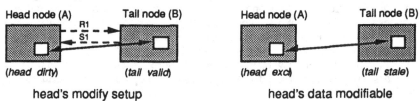

Figure 8: Pairwise sharing (head's data modified).

Similarly, when node B needs to read the line (that was last written by processor A), it sends a request (R2) to processor A. When the request is processed at processor A, its state is changed to *dirty* and a (readable) *valid* copy is returned (S2) to processor B. These steps are illustrated in Figure 9.

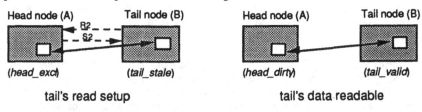

Figure 9: Pairwise sharing (tail's data read).

In this way data can be transferred directly between the caches of the two processors sharing the data. This is a fundamental advantage of distributed-list protocols over their central-list counterparts, since the memory bottleneck is avoided and the transfers are much more efficient. The performance advantages (when compared to central-list protocols) can be calculated when the pairwise-write components and node delays (as illustrated in Figure 10) are considered.

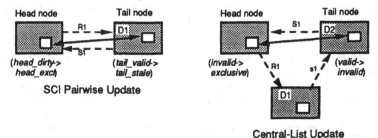

Figure 10: Pairwise-Sharing Write Sequences (SCI and Central Lists).

To simplify the comparison, assume that the node-access delays are twice the subaction transmission delays (a reasonable assumption for SCI). The pairwise performance of SCI and central-list protocols (which require an additional transaction and node-access delay) is summarized in Table 2.

Parameter	SCI	Central List
Total transaction latency	4	7
Number of subactions	2	3
Nodes accesses performed	1	2

Table 2: Pairwise-write Performance Comparison (smaller is better).

This performance distinction indirectly affects system performance, since pairwise-sharing is only one form of data sharing. However, we expect to see large amounts of pairwise-sharing, so this distinction should significantly affect overall system performance. Note that this performance comparison does not consider the performance loss associated with implementing specialized 3-phase transaction sequences (R1,s1,S2), which are assumed by the central-list coherence protocols (DASH and SDD).

7.3 QOLB

In a multiprocessor computer, implementation of primitives for data sharing and synchronization is of vital importance. Sharing and synchronization operations can be done by software, with simple coherence hardware support. Special software algorithms, based on the use of the indivisible swap and compare&swap primitives, are sufficient to implement a variety of efficient non-blocking enqueue and dequeue operations. These algorithms can be designed to minimize the number of unnecessary coherence transactions sent through the interconnect (Mellor-Crummey 90b).

However, better performance is possible when the synchronization mechanisms are integrated with the cache coherence protocol. These generally involve direct cache-to-cache transactions that are delayed until the data is in a useful (unlocked) state. It should then be possible (and easy) to write efficient programs that utilize the shared memory and the caches in an optimal way.

In SCI, a special QOLB (Queue On Lock Bit, Goodman 89) mechanism creates a queue of processors, where only the first processor has access to the line in question. When this first processor has finished using the data, the ownership is automatically transferred to the next processor in the queue. Where possible, enrollment in the queue also effects a prefetch of the desired data.

The SCI version of QOLB uses a sharing list where all but one processing node (at the tail) is in the *head_idle* or *mid_idle* states, and the owner of the cache line is in the *tail_need* state. The processing nodes prepend themselves into the sharing list and passively wait in the idle state until the tail's copy is passed to them. When a QOLB lock is released, the tail passes its copy to the previous entry in the sharing list, which becomes the new tail.

The QOLB protocols use the sharing-list tags provided by the basic SCI protocols, but additional cache-line states (like *head_idle* and *mid_idle*) are required to support this optional extension. The QOLB mechanism also works efficiently for two-element sharing lists, using the pairwise-sharing protocols described previously.

Such an SCI QOLB mechanism only assures exclusive access to a line as long as it resides in cache. Therefore, the QOLB locks are only used for scheduling synchronization instruction sequences; indivisible instruction sequences (such as swap) are relied on to maintain the integrity of shared data structures.

8 Fault tolerance and error recovery

The SCI transaction protocol ensures that requests and responses are correctly transferred between the nodes. The SCI cache coherence protocol is based on split transactions (request and response subactions) that time out when a response is not returned within a software-specified timeout interval. When the timeout is exceeded, software is expected to invoke a fault recovery routine.

The SCI cache coherence protocol can recover from any number of transmission errors. To support this recovery, the deletion of a previously dirty cache line is always delayed until after the dirty data has been reliably copied to another location. Otherwise, dirty data could be lost if the transaction containing the dirty data were dropped.

When data is being modified, for example, a new head prepends to an *only_dirty* entry and leaves this entry in the *tail_stale* state. If the prepend transaction (which contains the dirty data) is damaged, the dirty data can be recovered from the *tail_stale* copy. Note that the robust prepend algorithm also leaves the sharing-list entries in efficient pairwise-sharing states (*head_excl* and *tail_stale*).

Special care is also required when an *only_dirty* copy is returned to memory; a two transaction sequence is required. The dirty data is first written back to memory (transaction 1) and the cache-line ownership of the clean line is then returned to memory (transaction 2). The increased use of interconnect bandwidth is small, since the data (which is the largest part of the packet) is only transmitted once.

Recovery from errors is handled by fault-recovery software that is activated by the transaction-timeout error. The recovery strategy is to 1) disable coherent memory accesses to the affected cache-line address(es), 2) return dirty cache-line copies to memory, 3) discard the residual sharing-list structures, and 4) re-enable coherent access to the affected cache-line addresses.

To simplify the recovery, the fault-recovery software is expected to use a non-coherent memory-access mode. Special transactions are provided to selectively disable coherent memory accesses while the recovery is being performed. The recovery software extracts the affected cache lines from remote processors and leaves their cumulative state in a pre-reserved range of memory address space. Software searches through these residual sharing-list states and identifies the cache line with the most-recently modified data. After the modified data is copied to its proper memory location, the memory is re-enabled for accesses to the affected cache line.

No attempt is made to reconstruct the sharing-list structure, since similar structures can be dynamically re-created after the fault-recovery process has completed. Identifying the cache-line with the most-recently modified data can be a complex task, but with our low transmission error rates the performance of the recovery process should not be a concern.

9 Ongoing Research

The linear list structures appear to be adequate for moderate-sized systems, but in very large systems (thousands of processors) more efficient structures may become important. We are working on extensions to the SCI protocols that have logarithmic rather than linear performance, supporting combining of requests in the interconnect when congestion occurs, rapid parallel distribution of responses to combined requests, and fast purging of lists.

The strategy we are pursuing uses a third pointer for each line in each cache controller, that points to a distant (or at least non-adjacent) part of the list. Each sharing-list would have its forward and backward pointers (to its adjacent neighbors) as well as an approximate pointer to a more distant (but closer to the tail) sharing-list entry, as illustrated in Figure 12. Note that this is an illustration of an approximate pointer structure; the analysis and selection of approximate pointer structures is being addressed as an extension to the base SCI standard.

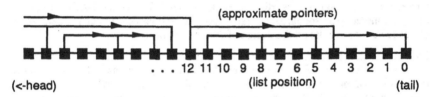

Figure 11: Approximate pointer structures.

These pointers allow tree structures to be created in order to achieve logarithmic performance. However, the tree is not maintained (which would be prohibitively expensive) so the pointer is checked for validity as it is used (in case the target node has subsequently rolled out the line, for example). Thus we call them approximate pointers: they approximately formed an optimal tree when created, and they may still point to a useful place when they are used.

Memory requests can be combined in the interconnect (Gottlieb 83, Edler 85) or at the memory controller. As requests combine, the originating nodes are informed of their position in the list (measured as distance from the tail). Each node uses its position value to determine how to create its approximate pointer, following the linear list pointers initially, in a series of hops we call recursive doubling. Choosing optimal pointer strategies is a subject of our current SCI extensions work. One needs good performance in both directions (the initial data fetch as well as the final data purge), with gradual degradation of performance when a few of the nodes leave the list.

The linear lists are always correct, and are relied on for correct performance wherever the approximate pointers fail. The approximate pointer scheme is thus merely an optimization that gives logarithmic performance in many situations, and can be added to the SCI standard at some later date when it is well understood.

10 Conclusion

The cache coherence protocol of SCI is invalidation based and uses distributed sharing lists and directories. The basic cache coherence operations are efficient and simple. The high performance is particularly due to the fact that a new cache line can join the set of sharers by one simple and extremely fast memory operation. Other operations such as deletion and breaking down of the sharing set are executed decentralized and possibly in parallel while new caches concurrently join the sharing list at full speed.

The SCI cache directory is scalable. The directory overhead is a maximum of 3.5% of the memory and 7.4% of the cache size. In this data structure up to a theoretical maximum of 65,000+ caches can share the same line.

The SCI cache coherence protocol is based on point-to-point subactions arranged as transactions, where the request subaction is sent and a response subaction is returned. By avoiding specialized 3-party transactions (as are used in the SDD and DASH protocols), the simpler SCI transactions should be faster and more reliable (errors can be trapped at the earliest possible moment). Unlike the DASH protocols, the SCI coherence protocols allow transactions to be completed in any order, which places fewer constraints on the design of the interconnect.

The distributed-list protocols have other advantages over their memory-list counterparts. The size of the memory-resident directory remains largely constant as the number of processors is increased; special directory overflow protocols (as implemented in the DASH and Alewife protocols) are not required. The memory-update protocols can always be completed immediately, which eliminates the livelock/deadlock conditions that arise if memory rejects new requests while processing others.

We are not aware of any other coherence protocol that has addressed the issue of data recovery after transmission errors. SCI not only addresses this issue, but supports recovery from an arbitrary number of transmission errors. Although other protocols might be extendable to provide such capabilities, we suspect that the specialized transaction-set requirements of some distributed protocols (3-party transactions and constrained ordering, for example) would make them difficult to extend.

Because it is based on three simple directory operations, the SCI cache coherence protocol is relatively easy to understand. However, SCI supports a high degree of parallelism, and several of these directory operations could be performed simultaneously on the same sharing list. Thus, it is not immediately obvious that the operations will give correct results in all cases of interaction. Simulations are being performed in order to find errors in the draft specifications of the cache coherence algorithms. Since the SCI coherence protocols are specified as C-code routines, exact simulations of the specification can be performed.

Given the large numbers of combinations of transient states, these simulations might not find all errors in the draft specifications. A mathematical proof is therefore being performed on the cache coherence protocol (Gjessing 90a-c).

The SCI cache coherence protocol has been designed based on currently known technology and research results. Since no real execution traces exist for directory-based shared-memory multiprocessors, some design choices have probably been made without sufficiently sound arguments. When the first SCI based computers are operational we will be able to evaluate the design and eventually correct and improve it. It will be very interesting to see what kinds of new algorithms evolve when new large-scale cache-coherent multiprocessors are in regular use.

11 Acknowledgements

The SCI cache protocol was designed by a number of people. The first initiative was taken by Paul Sweazey, former leader of the cache coherence task group for the IEEE P896 Futurebus, when he started the SuperBus study group in the IEEE Computer Society. Others initially or currently involved with cache-coherence issues include Knut Alnes, Bjørn Bakka, Håkkon Bugge, Craig Hansen, Marit Jensen, Sverre Johansen, Ross Johnson, Michael Koster, Stein Krogdahl, John Moussouris, Ellen Munthe-Kaas, Randy Rettberg, Alan Smith, Guri Sohi, and Phil Woest. Thanks are due to these and all others that have contributed to SCI in one way or another.

12 References

Agarwal, A., Hennessy, J., Horowitz, M.: Cache Performance of Operating System and Multiprogramming Workloads. ACM Trans. on Computer Systems, Vol. 6, No. 4, Nov. 1988a.

Agarwal, A., Simoni, R., Hennessy, J., Horowitz, M.: An Evaluation of Directory Schemes for Cache Coherence. 15th Annual International Symposium on Computer Architecture, 1988b.

Agarwal, A., Chaiken, D., Fields, C., Johnson, K., Kranz, D., Kubiatowicz, J., Kurihara, K., Lim, B.H., Maa, G., Nussbaum, D.: The MIT Alewife Machine: Promoting a Fuzzy Hardware-Software Boundary. Workshop on Scalable Shared-Memory Architectures, Seattle, May 1990.

Archibald, J., Baer, J-L.: An Economical Solution to the Cache Coherence Problem. 11th International Symposium on Computer Architecture, 1984.

Borg, A., Kessler, R.E., Wall, D.W.: Generation and Analysis of Very Long Address Traces. 17th Annual International Symposium on Computer Architecture, Seattle, Washington, 1990.

Bugge, H.O., Kristiansen, E.H., Bakka, B.O.: Trace-driven Simulations for a Two-level Cache Design in Open Bus Systems. 17th Annual International Symposium on Computer Architecture, Seattle, Washington, 1990.

Carlton, M., Despain, A.: Aquarius Project. IEEE Computer, June 1990.

Censier, L.M., Feautrier, P.: A New Solution to Coherence Problems in Multicache Systems. IEEE Trans. on Computers, Vol. 27, No. 12, Dec. 1978.

Chaiken, D., Fields, C., Kurihara, K., Agarwal, A.: Directory-Based Cache Coherence in Large-Scale Multiprocessors. IEEE Computer, June 1990.

Edler, J., Gottlieb, A., Kruskal, C.P., McAuliffe, K.P., Rudolph, L., Snir, M., Teller, P.J., Wilson, J.: Issues Related to MIMD Shared-Memory Computers: the NYU Ultracomputer Approach. 12th International Symposium on Computer Architecture, 1985.

Eggers, S., Katz, R.: A Characterization of Sharing in Parallel Programs and its Application to Coherency Protocol Evaluation. 15th Annual International Symposium on Computer Architecture, 1988.

Eggers, S., Katz, R.: The Effect of Sharing on the Cache and Bus Performance of Parallel Programs. 3rd Symposium on Architectural Support for Programming Languages and Operating Systems, 1989.

Gjessing, S., Krogdahl, S., Munthe-Kaas, E.: Formal Specification and Verification of SCI Cache Coherence, Univ. of Oslo Dept. of Informatics Research Report No. 142, ISBN 82-7368-048-7, August 1990a.

Gjessing, S., Krogdahl, S., Munthe-Kaas, E.: Approaching Verification of the SCI Cache Coherence Protocol, Univ. of Oslo Dept. of Informatics Research Report No. 145, ISBN 82-7368-051-7, August 1990b.

Gjessing, S., Krogdahl, S., Munthe-Kaas, E.: A Top Down Approach to the Formal Specification of SCI Cache Coherence, Univ. of Oslo Dept. of Informatics Research Report No. 146, ISBN 82-7368-052-5, August 1990c.

Goodman, J.R.: Using Cache Memory to Reduce Processor-Memory Traffic. 10th International Symposium on Computer Architecture, 1983.

Goodman, J., Vernon, M., Woest, P.: Efficient Synchronization Primitives for Large-Scale Cache-Coherent Multiprocessors. 3rd Symposium on Architectural Support for Programming Languages and Operating Systems, 1989.

Gottlieb, A. et al.: The NYU Ultracomputer — Designing an MIMD Shared Memory Parallel Computer. IEEE Trans. on Computers, C-32, 2 pp 175-189 Feb. 1983.

James, D.V., Laundrie, A.T., Gjessing, S., Sohi, G.S.: Scalable Coherent Interface. IEEE Computer, June 1990.

Lamport, L.: How to Make a Multiprocessor Computer that Correctly Executes Multiprocess Programs. IEEE Trans. on Computers, Vol. 28, No. 9, pp 690–691, Sept. 1979.

Lenoski, D., Laudon, J., Gharachorloo, K., Gupta, A., Hennessy, J.: The Directory-Based Cache Coherence Protocol for the DASH Multiprocessor. Technical Report No. CSL-TR-89-404, Computer Systems Laboratory, Stanford University, December 1989.

Mellor-Crummey, J.M.: Concurrent Queues: Practical Fetch-and-Φ Algorithms. Technical Report 229, University of Rochester, Computer Science Department, November 1987.

Mellor-Crummey, J.M.: private communication, May 1990a.

Mellor-Crummey, J.M., Scott, M.L.: Algorithms for Scalable Synchronization on Shared-Memory Multiprocessors. Rice Technical Report COMP TR90-114, Rice University, Department of Computer Science, May 1990b.

Przybylski, S., Horowitz, M., Hennessy, J.: Characteristics of Performance-Optimal Multi-Level Cache Hierarchies. 16th International Symposium on Computer Architecture, 1989.

Sweazey, P., Smith, A.J.: A Class of Compatible Cache Consistency Protocols and their Support by the IEEE Futurebus. 13th International Symposium on Computer Architecture, 1986.

Sweazey, P.: Cache Coherence on SCI. IEEE/ACM Computer Architecture Workshop, Eilat, Israel, May 1989.

Tang, C.K.: Cache System Design in Tightly Coupled Multiprocessor Systems. AFIPS Conference Proceedings, Vol 45, National Computer Conference, 1976.

Thapar, M., Delagi, B.: Stanford Distributed-Directory Protocol. IEEE Computer, June 1990.

Willis, J.: Cache Coherence in Systems with Parallel Communication Channels and Many Processors. Document no. TR-88-013, Philips Laboratories – Briarcliff, March 1988.

Wilson Jr., A.W.: Hierarchical Cache/Bus Architecture for Shared Memory Multiprocessors. 14th International Symposium on Computer Architecture, 1987.

The MIT Alewife Machine: A Large-Scale Distributed-Memory Multiprocessor

Anant Agarwal, David Chaiken, Kirk Johnson, David Kranz,
John Kubiatowicz, Kiyoshi Kurihara, Beng-Hong Lim,
Gino Maa, and Dan Nussbaum
Laboratory for Computer Science
Massachusetts Institute of Technology
Cambridge, MA 02139

Abstract

The Alewife multiprocessor project focuses on the architecture and design of a large-scale parallel machine. The machine uses a low dimension direct interconnection network to provide scalable communication bandwidth, while allowing the exploitation of locality. Despite its distributed memory architecture, Alewife allows efficient shared memory programming through a multilayered approach to locality management. A new scalable cache coherence scheme called LimitLESS directories allows the use of caches for reducing communication latency and network bandwidth requirements. Alewife also employs run-time and compile-time methods for partitioning and placement of data and processes to enhance communication locality. While the above methods attempt to minimize communication latency, remote communication with distant processors cannot be completely avoided. Alewife's processor, Sparcle, is designed to tolerate these latencies by rapidly switching between threads of computation. This paper describes the Alewife architecture and concentrates on the novel hardware features of the machine including LimitLESS directories and the rapid context switching processor.

1 Introduction

High-performance computer design is driven by the need to solve important problems efficiently and at a reasonable cost. While single-processor performance is limited by physical constraints, advances in technology make machines with thousands of processors feasible. Highly parallel machines offer significant cost-performance benefits over single processor machines.

Parallel machines are commonly organized as a set of nodes that communicate over an interconnection network, each node containing a processor and some memory. From the perspective of a node in a real machine built in three dimensional space, some nodes will be physically closer than others. Informally, a program running on a parallel machine displays *communication locality* (or memory reference locality) if the probability of communication (or access) to various nodes decreases with physical distance. Communication locality in parallel programs depends on the application as well as on partitioning and placement of data and processes.

Parallel machines are *scalable* if they can exploit communication locality in parallel programs. That is, for programs that display communication locality, scalable machines can offer proportionally better performance with more processing nodes [29]. Scalable machines are *easily programmable* if they provide automatic enhancement of communication locality in parallel programs.

The Alewife experiment explores methods for automatic enhancement of locality in a scalable parallel machine. The Alewife multiprocessor uses a distributed shared-memory architecture with a low-dimension direct network. Such networks are cost-effective, modular, and encourage the exploitation of locality [34, 19, 2]. Unfortunately, non-uniform communication latencies usually make such machines hard to program because the onus of managing locality invariably falls on the programmer. The goal of the Alewife project is to discover and to evaluate techniques for automatic locality management in scalable multiprocessors.

Alewife uses a multilayered approach to achieve this goal, consisting of techniques for *latency minimization* and *latency tolerance*. The compiler, runtime system, and hardware cooperate to enhance communication locality, thereby reducing average communication latency and required network bandwidth. Because remote communication with distant processors cannot always be avoided, Alewife's processor tolerates the resulting latencies by rapidly switching between threads of computation.

This paper focuses on the organization of the Alewife machine and describes its hardware features for automatic locality management. These features include shared-data caching, made possible by a new cache coherence scheme called LimitLESS directories, and rapid context switching. We present an overview of our approach to locality management in Section 2, and describe the machine organization and the programming environment in Section 3. Section 4 discusses the LimitLESS directory scheme, and Section 5 outlines our approach to latency tolerance. We also discuss the performance of the machine on a few applications. Other details of the machine are presented elsewhere [4, 8, 28]. Section 6 discusses related work, and Section 7 offers some perspective and summarizes the paper.

2   System Overview

The Alewife compiler, runtime system, and hardware try to reduce the communication latency where possible, and attempt to tolerate the latency otherwise. We are developing compiler technology to enhance the static communication locality of applications. Programs are first transformed into an intermediate task graph representation called WAIF [27], where the communication between threads is exposed through program analysis. Succeeding stages of the compiler map the task graph on to the machine and attempt to minimize overall execution time. When the compiler lacks enough information to make good placement decisions, it relegates the responsibility to the runtime layer.

Run-time software participates in enhancing locality through lazy task creation, a novel dynamic partitioning method [28], and intelligent scheduling. In a dynamic partitioning system the programmer or compiler can expose all of the parallelism in an application, but new tasks will be created at runtime only when there are idle processors. To enhance the likelihood of placing related tasks close to each other, a locality-based tree scheduler determines the order in which idle processors search for new tasks. To reduce the network bandwidth consumed by the searching processors, only single representatives from neighborhoods search for work. Simulations of several parallel applications with 64 processors showed that a mesh network yielded roughly the same speedup as a more expensive multistage network, when both used lazy task partitioning, a tree scheduler, and coherent caches.

Caching shared data is Alewife's hardware method for reducing memory access latency. With caches, the software does not need to worry as much about careful initial data placement; the caches dynamically move data objects close to the processor, so accesses are satisfied completely within a node. A new scalable scheme called *LimitLESS directories* solves the cache coherence problem. The LimitLESS directory is a small set of pointers (say 4) distributed along with each block of main memory that tracks copies of cached data and maintains memory consistency by transmitting invalidation messages over the network. The LimitLESS scheme allows a memory module to interrupt its local processor for software emulation of a full-map directory when the small set of pointers overflows. Section 4 describes and evaluates this scheme.

If the system cannot avoid a remote memory request, Alewife's processor can rapidly schedule another task in place of the stalled process. Alewife also tolerates synchronization latencies and provides fast traps through the *same* context switching mechanism. Because context switches are forced only on memory requests that require the use of the interconnection network and on synchronization faults, the processor achieves high single-thread performance.

We believe such a layered approach is necessary to build truly general-purpose parallel machines. Real applications are composed of phases, which will benefit in different proportions from the various layers. For example, matrix computations can benefit from static compiler analysis, while combinatorial search problems will profit from the runtime and cache layers. Finally, efficient execution of phases without inherent locality, such as matrix transpose, is possible when the processors can mask the latency of remote requests.

3   Hardware Organization of Alewife

Figure 1 depicts the Alewife machine as a set of processing nodes connected in a mesh topology. Each Alewife node consists of a processor, a cache, a portion of globally-shared distributed memory, a cache-memory-network controller, a floating-point coprocessor, and a network switch.

A single-chip controller on each node holds the cache tags and implements the cache coherence protocol by synthesizing messages to other nodes. While the Alewife architecture is scalable, the number of directory pointer bits in the current implementation of our controller will limit the maximum size of the machine to 512 nodes. The controller uses a simple message-based interface with the network. Various forms of shared memory coherence models are maintained by the controller via messages to other nodes. Alewife has a simple memory mapping scheme. The top few bits of the address determine the node number, and the rest of the address is the index within the specific module.

As shown in Figure 1, each node contains a network switch chip, specifically the Frontier series Mesh Routing Chip (FMRC) from Caltech. The mesh network uses wormhole routing [11] – a variant of cut-through routing [21]. The network has eight-bit channels, with a throughput of roughly 100M bytes per second in each direction. Free ports on peripheral nodes of the network are used for I/O, monitor, and host connections. The prototype Alewife system will attach to a host SUN backplane by interfacing a network switch to the VME bus.

The processor uses a *memory-reference-based interface* with the controller, although the controller uses a *message-based interface* for internode communications. Using a control word associated with each memory reference, various types of synchronization or communication types are synthesized by the processor. This interface allows a simple implementation of the processor.

Sparcle, a first-round prototype based on modifications to LSI Logic's SPARC processor [36] implementation, will clock at 33 MHz and context switch in 11 cycles. Each node has 64K bytes of direct-mapped cache and 4M bytes of globally-shared main memory. Each node has and an additional 4M bytes of

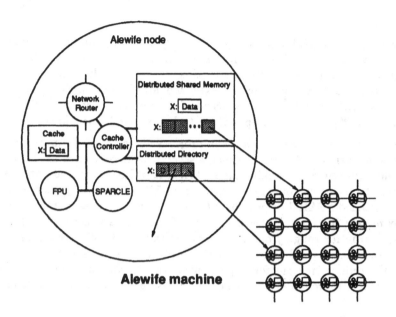

Figure 1: The Alewife machine, showing the LimitLESS directory extension.

local memory, a portion of which is used for the coherence directory. Alewife's cache and floating-point units are SPARC compatible. Sparcle uses a block multithreaded architecture [4].

Initially, our software system will be based on Mul-T [23]. A parallel C-like language is also under development. Mul-T's basic mechanism for generating concurrent threads is the future construct. The expression (future X), where X is an arbitrary expression, creates a task to evaluate X and also creates an object known as a *placeholder* to hold eventually the value of X. When created, the future is in an *unresolved* or *undetermined* state. When the value of X becomes known, the future *resolves* to that value, effectively mutating into the value of X and losing its identity as a future. Concurrency arises because the expression (future X) returns the future as its value without waiting for the future to resolve. Thus, the computation containing (future X) can proceed concurrently with the evaluation of X. The act of suspending computation if an object is an unresolved future and then proceeding when the future resolves is known as *touching* the object.

Our processor will allow operators to check for resolved futures with no overhead, disposing of the 60-100% overhead incurred by the system on other processors. Support for lightweight full-empty bit synchronization [35] in the processor will allow use of efficient fine-grain parallelism. In addition, the modified SPARC implementation is competitive in raw performance to contemporary sequential machines.

We propose to use Mul-T as our intermediate compiler language, augmented with primitives for specifying explicit partitioning and placement of both data and processes. Our compiler will partition a program taking communication costs into account, and produce an extended Mul-T program consisting of a set of tasks with granularity and placement information. The Orbit optimizing compiler [13, 22] will then compile these tasks to Sparcle machine code.

The design of the Alewife machine is in progress and a detailed simulator called ASIM is operational. ASIM implements several cache coherence protocols and interconnection network architectures. When ASIM is configured with its full statistics-gathering capability, it runs at about 5000 processor cycles per second on an unloaded SPARCserver 330. At this rate, a 64 processor machine runs approximately 80 cycles per second. Most of the simulations that we chose for this paper run for roughly one million cycles (a fraction of a second on a real machine), which takes 3.5 hours to complete. This lack of simulation speed is one of the primary reasons for implementing the Alewife machine in hardware — to enable a thorough evaluation of our ideas on much larger applications.

4   LimitLESS Directories

Shared data caching is an important component of Alewife's multilayered system for automatic locality management. Caches reduce the volume of traffic imposed on the network by providing demand-driven data replication where needed. However, replicating blocks of data in multiple caches introduces the cache coherence problem [15, 38]. A number of cache coherence protocols have been proposed to solve the coherence problem in network-based multiprocessors [6, 37, 5, 20]. These message-based protocols allocate a section of the system's memory, called a directory, to store the locations and state of the cached copies of each data block. The protocols send messages with data requests or invalidation signals, and record the acknowledgment of each of these messages to ensure global consistency of memory.

Although directory protocols have been around since the late 1970's, the usefulness of the early protocols (e.g., [6]) was in doubt for several reasons: First, the directory itself was a *centralized* monolithic resource which serialized all requests. Second, directory accesses were expected to consume a disproportionately large fraction of the available network bandwidth. Third, the directory became prohibitively large as the number of processors increased. To store pointers to blocks potentially cached by all the processors in the system, the size of the directory memory in early *full-map* protocols grows as $\Theta(N^2)$, where N is the number of processors in the system.

As observed in [5], the first two concerns are easily dispelled: The directory can be *distributed* along with main memory among the processing nodes to match the aggregate bandwidth of distributed main memory. Furthermore, required directory bandwidth is not much more than the memory bandwidth, because accesses destined to the directory alone comprise a small fraction of all network requests. Thus, the challenge lies in alleviating the severe memory requirements of the distributed full-map directory schemes.

Scalable coherence protocols differ in the size and the structure of the directory memory. *Limited directory* protocols [5], for example, avoid the severe memory overhead of full-map directories by allowing only a limited number of simultaneously cached copies of any individual block of data. Unlike a full-map directory, the size of a limited directory grows as $\Theta(N \log N)$ with the number of processors. Once all of the pointers in a directory entry are filled, the protocol must evict previously cached copies to satisfy new requests to read the data associated with the entry. In such systems, widely shared data locations degrade system performance by causing constant eviction and reassignment, or *thrashing*, of directory pointers. However, previous studies have shown that a small set of pointers is sufficient to capture the *worker-set* of processors that concurrently read many types of data [7, 39, 30]. The worker-set of a memory block is defined as the set of processors that concurrently read a memory location, and corresponds to the number of active pointers it would have in a full-map directory entry.

4.1 Overview of the LimitLESS Protocol

Alewife implements the LimitLESS cache coherence protocol, which nearly realizes the performance of the full-map directory protocol, with the memory overhead of a limited directory, but without excessive sensitivity to widely shared data. The LimitLESS scheme implements a small set of pointers in the memory modules, as do limited directory protocols. But when necessary, the scheme allows a memory module to interrupt the processor for software emulation of a full-map directory. Its name reflects the above properties: *Limited* directory *Locally Extended through Software Support*.

Figure 1 depicts a set of directory pointers that correspond to the shared data block X, copies of which exist in several caches. In the figure, the software has extended the directory pointer array (which is shaded) into local memory.

The structure of the Alewife machine provides for an efficient implementation of this memory system extension. Since each processing node in Alewife contains both a memory controller and a processor, it is a straightforward modification of the architecture to couple the responsibilities of these two functional units, using the Sparcle processor's fast trap mechanism.

The LimitLESS scheme should not be confused with schemes previously termed

Component	Name	Meaning
Memory	Read-Only	Some caches have read-only copies of the data.
	Read-Write	Exactly one cache has a read-write copy.
	Read-Transaction	Holding read request, update is in progress.
	Write-Transaction	Holding write request, invalidation is in progress.
Cache	Invalid	Cache block may not be read or written.
	Read-Only	Cache block may be read, but not written.
	Read-Write	Cache block may be read or written.

Table 1: Directory states.

software-based, which require static identification of non-cacheable locations. Although the LimitLESS scheme is partially implemented in software, it dynamically detects when coherence actions are required; consequently, the software emulation should be considered a logical extension of the hardware functionality. To clarify the difference between protocols, schemes may be classified by function as *static* (compiler-dependent) or *dynamic* (using run-time information), and by implementation as *software-based* or *hardware-based*.

4.2   Protocol Specification

We now describe the LimitLESS directory protocol and the architectural interfaces needed to implement it.

The LimitLESS protocol has the same state transition diagram as the full-map protocol. The memory controller side of this protocol is illustrated in Figure 2, which contains the memory states listed in Table 1. These states are mirrored by the state of the block in the caches, also listed in Table 1. The state transition diagram specifies the states, the composition of the pointer set (P), and the transitions between the states. It is the responsibility of the protocol to keep the states of the memory and the cache blocks coherent. The protocol enforces coherence by transmitting messages between the cache/memory controllers. Every message contains the address of a memory block, to indicate which directory entry should be used when processing the message.

For example, Transition 2 from the Read-Only state to the Read-Write state is taken when cache i requests write permission (Write Request) and the pointer set is empty or contains just cache i ($P = \{\}$ or $P = \{i\}$). In this case, the pointer set is modified to contain i (if necessary) and the memory controller issues a message containing the data of the block to be written (Write Data).

Following the notation in [5], both full-map and LimitLESS are members of the $Dir_N NB$ class of cache coherence protocols. Therefore, from the point of view of the protocol specification, the LimitLESS scheme does not differ substantially from the full-map protocol. In fact, the LimitLESS protocol is also specified in

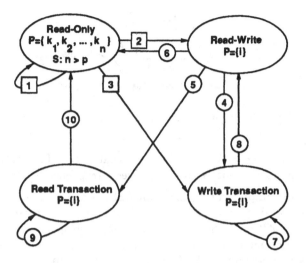

Figure 2: Directory state transition diagram.

Figure 2. The extra notation on the Read-Only ellipse ($S : n > p$) indicates that the state is handled in software when the size of the pointer set (n) is greater than the size of the limited directory (p). (See [8] for details). In this situation, the transitions with the square labels (1, 2, and 3) are executed by the interrupt handler on the processor that is local to the overflowing directory. When the protocol changes from a software-handled state to a hardware-handled state, the processor must modify the directory state so that the memory controller can resume responsibility for the protocol transitions.

4.3   Interfaces for LimitLESS

This section outlines the architectural features and hardware interfaces needed to support the LimitLESS directory scheme. To support the LimitLESS proto-col efficiently, a cache-based multiprocessor needs several properties. First, it must be capable of rapid trap handling. Sparcle permits execution of trap code within five to ten cycles from the time a trap is initiated.

Second, the processor needs complete access to coherence related controller state such as pointers and state bits in the hardware directories. Similarly the directory controller must be able to invoke processor trap handlers when necessary. The hardware interface between the Alewife processor and controller, depicted in Figure 3, is designed to meet these requirements. The address and data buses permit processor manipulation of controller state and initiation of actions via load and store instructions to memory-mapped I/O space. In Alewife, the directories are placed in this special region of memory distinguished

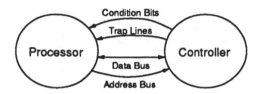

Figure 3: Signals between processor and controller.

from normal memory space by a distinct Alternate Space Indicator (ASI). The controller returns two condition bits and several trap lines to the processor.

Finally, a machine implementing the LimitLESS scheme needs an interface to the network that allows the processor to launch and to intercept coherence protocol packets. Although most shared-memory multiprocessors export little or no network functionality to the processor, Alewife provides the processor with direct network access through the Interprocessor-Interrupt (IPI) mechanism.

The Alewife machine supports a complete interface to the interconnection network. This interface provides the processor with a superset of the network functionality needed by the cache-coherence hardware. Not only can it be used to send and receive cache protocol packets, but it can also be used to send preemptive messages to remote processors (as in message-passing machines), hence the name Interprocessor-Interrupt.

We stress that the IPI interface is a single generic mechanism for network access – *not* a conglomeration of different mechanisms. The power of such a mechanism lies in its generality.

The current implementation of the LimitLESS trap handler is as follows: when an overflow trap occurs for the first time on a given memory line, the trap code allocates a full-map bit-vector in local memory. This vector is entered into a hash table. All hardware pointers are emptied and the corresponding bits are set in this vector. The directory state for that block is tagged Trap-On-Write. Emptying the hardware pointers allows the controller to continue handling read requests until the next pointer array overflow and maximizes the number of transactions serviced in hardware. However, the memory controller must interrupt the processor upon a write request. When additional overflow traps occur, the trap code locates the full-map vector in the hash table, empties the hardware pointers, and sets the appropriate bits in the vector.

Software handling of a memory line terminates when the processor traps on an incoming write request or local write fault. The trap handler finds the full-map bit vector and empties the hardware pointers as above. Next, it records the identity of the requester in the directory, sets the acknowledgment counter to the number of bits in the vector that are set, and places the directory in its normal Write Transaction state. Finally, it sends invalidations to all caches with bits set in the vector. The vector may now be freed. At this point, the memory line has returned to hardware control. When all invalidations are acknowledged, the hardware will send the data with write permission to the requester.

4.4 Performance Measurements

This section presents some preliminary results from the Alewife system simulator, comparing the performance of limited, LimitLESS, and full-map directories. The protocols are evaluated in terms of the total number of cycles needed to execute an application on a 64 processor Alewife machine. Using execution cycles as a metric emphasizes the bottom line of multiprocessor design: how fast a system can run a program.

The results presented below are derived from complete Alewife machine simulations and from dynamic post-mortem scheduler simulations. The complete-machine simulator runs programs written in the Mul-T language, optimized by the Mul-T compiler, and linked with a runtime system that implements both static work distribution and dynamic task partitioning and scheduling. Post-mortem scheduling, on the other hand, generates a parallel trace from a uniprocessor execution trace that has embedded synchronization information [9]. The post-mortem scheduler was implemented by Mathews Cherian with Kimming So at IBM. The post-mortem scheduler has been modified to incorporate feedback from the network in issuing trace requests [25].

To evaluate the benefits of the LimitLESS coherence scheme, we implemented an approximation of the new protocol in ASIM. During the simulations, ASIM simulates an ordinary full-map protocol, but when the simulator encounters a pointer array overflow, it stalls both the memory controller and the processor that would handle the LimitLESS interrupt for T_s cycles. The current implementation of the LimitLESS software trap handlers in Alewife suggests $T_s \approx 50$.

Table 2 shows the simulated performance of four applications, using a four-pointer limited protocol (Dir_4NB), a full-map protocol, and a LimitLESS (LimitLESS$_4$) scheme with $T_s = 50$. All of the runs simulate a 64-node Alewife machine with 64K byte caches and a two-dimensional mesh network.

Multigrid is a statically scheduled relaxation program, Weather forecasts the state of the atmosphere given an initial state, SIMPLE simulates the hydrodynamic and thermal behavior of fluids, and Matexpr performs several multiplications and additions of various sized matrices. The computations in Matexpr are partitioned and scheduled by a compiler. Weather and SIMPLE are measured using dynamic post-mortem scheduling of traces, while Multigrid and Matexpr are run on complete-machine simulations.

Since the LimitLESS scheme implements a full-fledged limited directory in hard-

Application	Dir_4NB	LimitLESS$_4$	Full-Map
Multigrid	0.729	0.704	0.665
SIMPLE	3.579	2.902	2.553
Matexpr	1.296	0.317	0.171
Weather	1.356	0.654	0.621

Table 2: Performance for three coherence schemes, in terms of millions of cycles.

ware, applications that perform well using a limited scheme also perform well using LimitLESS. Multigrid is such an application. All of the protocols require approximately the same time to complete the computation phase. This confirms the assumption that for applications with small worker-sets, such as multigrid, the limited (and therefore the LimitLESS) directory protocols perform almost as well as the full-map protocol. See [7] for more evidence of the general success of limited directory protocols.

To measure the performance of LimitLESS under extreme conditions, we simulated a version of SIMPLE with barrier synchronization implemented using a single lock (rather than a software combining tree). Although the worker-sets in SIMPLE are small for the most part, the globally shared barrier structure causes the performance of the limited directory protocol to suffer. In contrast, the LimitLESS scheme is less sensitive to wide-spread sharing.

The Matexpr application uses several variables that have worker-sets of up to 16 processors. Due to these large worker-sets time with the LimitLESS scheme is almost double that with the full-map protocol. The limited protocol, however, exhibits a much higher sensitivity to the large worker-sets.

Although software combining trees distribute barrier synchronization variables in Weather, one variable is initialized by one processor and then read by all of the other processors. Consequently the limited directory scheme suffers form hot-spot access to this location. As is evident from Table 2, the LimitLESS protocol avoids the sensitivity displayed by limited directories.

5   Using Multithreading to Tolerate Latency

While dynamic data relocation through caches reduces the average memory access latency, a fraction of memory transactions require service from remote memory modules. When transactions cause the cache coherence protocol to issue invalidation messages, the remote memory access latency is especially high. If the resulting remote memory access latency is much longer than the time between memory accesses, processors spend most of their time waiting for memory transactions to be serviced. Processor idle time also results from synchronization delays.

One solution allows the processor to have multiple outstanding remote memory accesses or synchronization requests. Alewife implements this solution by using a processor that can rapidly switch between multiple threads of computation, and a cache controller that supports multiple outstanding requests. The controller forces a context switch when a thread issues a remote transaction or suffers an unsuccessful synchronization attempt. Processors that rapidly switch between multiple threads of computation are called *multithreaded architectures*.

The prototypical multithreaded architecture is the HEP [35]. In the HEP, the processor switches every cycle between eight processor-resident threads. Cycle-by-cycle interleaving of threads is also used in other designs [31, 18]. Such architectures are termed *finely multithreaded*. Although fine multithreading offers the potential of high processor utilization, it results in relatively poor scalar performance observed by any single thread, when there is not enough parallelism to fill all of the hardware contexts.

In contrast, Alewife employs *block multithreading* or coarse multithreading – context switches occur only when a thread executes a memory request that must be serviced by a remote node in the multiprocessor. Context switches are also forced when a thread encounters a delay due to a synchronization variable access. Thus, as long as a thread's memory requests hit in the cache or can be serviced by a local memory module, the thread continues to execute. Block multithreading allows a single thread to benefit from the maximum performance of the processor.

A multithreaded architecture is not free in terms of either its hardware or software requirements. The implementation of such an architecture requires multiple register sets or some other mechanism to allow fast context switches, additional network bandwidth, support logic in the cache controller, and extra complexity in the thread scheduling mechanism. Other methods, such as weak ordering [12, 1, 26], incur similar implementation complexities in the cache controller to allow multiple outstanding requests. In Alewife, because the same context-switching mechanism is used for fast traps and for masking synchronization latencies as well, we feel the extra complexity is justified.

5.1   Implementing a Multithreaded Processor

This section describes the implementation of the Sparcle processor and evaluates its potential in masking communication latency. Alewife's processor is designed to meet several objectives: it must context switch rapidly; it must support fast trap dispatching; and it must provide fine-grain synchronization.

Alewife's block multithreaded processor uses multiple register sets to implement fast context switching. The same rapid switching mechanism coupled with widely-spaced trap vectors minimizes the delay between the trap signal and the execution of the trap code. The wide spacing between trap dispatch points allows inlining of common trap routines at the dispatch point. The processor supports word-level full-empty bit synchronization. On a synchronization fault, the trap handling routine can respond by:

1. *spinning* – immediately return from the trap and retry the trapping instruction.

2. *switch spinning* – context switch without unloading the trapped thread.

3. *blocking* – unload the thread.

Sparcle is based on the following modifications to the SPARC architecture.

- Register windows in the SPARC processor permit a simple implementation of block multithreading. A window is allocated to each thread. The current register window is altered via SPARC instructions (SAVE and RESTORE). To effect a context switch, the trap routine saves the Program Counter (PC) and Processor Status Register (PSR), flushes the pipeline, and sets the Frame Pointer (FP) to a new register window. [4] shows that even with a low-cost implementation, a context switch can be done in about 11 cycles. By maintaining a separate PC and PSR for each context, a custom processor could switch contexts even faster. We show that even with 11 cycles of overhead and four processor resident contexts, multithreading significantly improves the system performance. See [40] for additional evidence of the success of multithreaded processors.

- The effect of multiple hardware contexts in the SPARC floating-point unit is achieved by modifying floating-point instructions in a context dependent fashion as they are loaded into the FPU and by maintaining four different sets of condition bits. A modification of the SPARC processor will make the context window pointer available externally to allow insertion into the FPU instruction.

- Sparcle detects unresolved futures through *word-alignment* and *non-fixnum* traps.

- The SPARC definition includes the Alternate Space Indicator (ASI) feature that permits a simple implementation of the general interface with the controller. The ASI is available externally as an eight-bit field and is set by special SPARC load and store instructions (LDA and STA). By examining the processor's ASI bits during memory accesses, the controller can select between different load/store and synchronization behavior.

- Through use of the Memory Exception (MEXC) line on SPARC, it can invoke synchronous traps and rapid context switching. Sparcle adds multiple synchronous trap lines for rapid trap dispatch to common routines. The controller can suspend processor execution using the MHOLD line. Inter-processor interrupts are implemented via asynchronous traps.

5.2   Simulation Results and Analysis

We compare the behavior of a multithreaded architecture to a standard configuration, and analyze how synchronization, local memory access latency, and remote memory access latency contribute to the run time of each application. See [3] for additional analyses.

A thorough evaluation of multithreading will require a large parallel machine and a scheduler optimized for multithreaded multiprocessors. On the largest machines we can reasonably simulate (around 64 processors) and with our current scheduler, the scheduling cost of threads generally outweighs the benefits of latency tolerance. Furthermore, the locality enhancement afforded by our caches and the runtime system diminishes the effect of non-local communications. Indeed, multithreading is expected to be the last line of defense when locality enhancement has failed. However it is still possible to observe the benefits of multithreading for phases of applications with poor communication locality.

Our simulation results are derived from both post-mortem scheduled and full system simulation branches of ASIM. The post-mortem scheduled runs use traces of SIMPLE and Weather as described in Section 4.4 and the full system simulations represent a transpose phase for a 256 × 256 matrix. In addition to determining the execution time of an application, the multiprocessor simulator generates raw statistics that measure an application's memory access patterns and the utilization of various system resources. We will use these statistics to explain the performance of our multithreaded architecture. The simulations reported in the following sections use the parameters listed in Table 3.

5.3   Effect of Multithreading

Table 4 shows the run times for the various applications using one and two threads per processor. SIMPLE and Weather realize about a 20% performance increase from multithreading. Since neither of the application problem sets are large enough to sustain more than 128 contexts, no performance gain results from increasing the number of contexts from two to three per processor. For the matrix transpose phase, we realize a performance gain of about 20% with 2 threads and 25% with four threads.

Number of Processing Elements	64
Cache Coherence Protocol	LimitLESS$_4$
Cache Size	64KB (4096 lines)
Cache Block Size	16 bytes
Network Topology	2 Dimensional Mesh (8 × 8)
Network Channel Width	16
Network Speed	2 × processor speed
Memory Latency	5 processor cycles
Context Switch Time	11 processor cycles

Table 3: Default Simulation Parameters

Application	Contexts	Time
SIMPLE	1	2440123
	2	2034963
Weather	1	1405536
	2	1150325
Transpose	1	172242
	2	141571
	4	129450

Table 4: Effect of Multithreading

5.4 Cost Analysis

An analysis of the costs of memory transactions confirms the intuition that a multithreaded architecture yields better performance by reducing the effect of interprocessor communication latency. We refine the simulator statistics into the costs of four basic types of transactions.

1. *Application transactions* are the memory requests issued by the program running on the system. These transactions are the memory operations in the original unscheduled trace.

2. *Synchronization transactions* are memory requests that implement the barrier executed at the end of a parallel segment of the application.

3. *Local cache miss transactions* occur when an application or synchronization transaction misses in the cache, but can be serviced in the local memory module.

4. *Remote transactions* occur when an application or synchronization transaction misses in the cache or requires a coherence action, resulting in a network transmission to a remote memory module. Multithreading is designed to alleviate the latency caused by this type of transaction.

	SIMPLE		Weather	
Transaction Type	1 Thread	2 Threads	1 Thread	2 Threads
Application	1.00	1.00	1.00	1.00
Synchronization	1.17	1.08	0.76	0.45
Local Cache Miss	0.41	0.36	0.34	0.36
Remote	3.98	2.83	1.25	0.94
Total	6.56	5.27	3.35	2.75

Table 5: Memory access costs, normalized to application transactions.

The contribution of each type of transaction to the time needed to run an application is equal to the number of transactions multiplied by the average latency of the transaction. We assume that the latency of application and synchronization transactions is equal to 1 cycle, while the simulator collects statistics that determine the average latency of the cache miss transactions. Table 5 shows the cost of each transaction type, normalized to the number of application transactions for SIMPLE and Weather. For example, in the simulation of SIMPLE with one context per processor, the memory system spends an average of 3.98 cycles servicing remote transactions for every cycle it spends servicing an application data access.

The statistics in Table 5 are calculated directly from the raw statistics generated by the multiprocessor simulator, except for the cost of remote transactions in the multithreaded environment. A multithreaded architecture can overlap some of the cycles spent servicing remote transactions with useful work performed by switching to an active thread. We approximate the number of cycles that are overlapped from the average remote transaction latency, the context switch overhead, and the number of remote transactions. The number of overlapped cycles is subtracted from the latency of remote transactions in order to adjust the cost of remote transactions. For all of the simulations summarized in the table, the total cost multiplied by the number of application cycles is within 5% of the actual number of cycles needed to execute the application.

The analysis shows that remote transactions contribute a large percentage of the cost of running an application. This conclusion agrees with the premise that communication between processors significantly affects the speed of a multiprocessor. The multithreaded architecture realizes higher speed-up than the standard configuration, because it reduces the cost of remote transactions. Because communication latency grows with the number of processors in a system, the relative cost of remote transactions increases. This trend indicates that the effect of multithreading becomes more significant as system size increases.

6 Related Work

A hardware approach to the automatic reduction of non-local references that has achieved wide success in small-scale shared-memory systems is the use of high-speed caches to hold local copies of data needed by the processor. The memory consistency problem can be solved effectively on bus-based machines [15, 38] by exploiting their broadcast capabilities, but buses are bandwidth limited. Hence most shared-memory machines that deal with more than 8 or 16 processors do not support caching of shared data [17, 14, 32, 24].

Some recent efforts propose to circumvent the bandwidth limitation through various arrangements of buses and networks [41, 16, 26, 10]. However, buses cannot keep pace with improving processor technologies, because they suffer from clocking speed limitations in multidrop transmission environments. The DASH architecture does not really require the bus broadcast capability; rather, it uses a full-map directory scheme to maintain cache consistency. In contrast, Alewife is exploring the use of the LimitLESS directory for cache coherence, where the directory memory requirements grow as $\Theta(N \log N)$ with machine size

Chained directory protocols [20] are scalable in terms of their memory requirements, but they suffer from high invalidation latencies, because invalidations must be transmitted serially down the links. It is possible to use a block multithreaded processor such as Sparcle to mask the latency, or by implementing some form of combining. Accordingly, we have observed that chaining scheme enjoys a larger relative benefit from multithreading than the LimitLESS scheme. Chained protocols also require additional traffic to prevent fragmentation of the linked lists when cache locations are replaced. Furthermore, chained directory protocols lack the LimitLESS protocol's ability to couple closely with a multiprocessor's software.

Although caches are successful in automatic locality management in many environments, they are not a panacea. Caches rely on a very simple heuristic to improve communication locality. On a memory request, caches retain a local copy of the datum in the hope that the processor will reuse it before some other processor attempts to write to the same location. Thus repeat requests are satisfied entirely within the node, and communication locality is enhanced because remote requests are avoided. Caching and the associated coherence algorithms can be viewed as a mechanism for replicating and migrating data objects close to where they are used. Unfortunately, the same locality management heuristic is ill-suited to programs with poor data reuse; attempts by the programmer or compiler to maximize the potential reuse of data will not benefit all applications. In such environments, the ability to enhance the communication locality of references that miss in the cache and the ability to tolerate latencies of non-local accesses are prerequisites for achieving scalability.

The Alewife effort is unique in its multilayered approach to locality management: the compiler, runtime system and caches share the responsibility of intelligent partitioning and placement of data and processes to maximize communication locality. The block multithreaded processors mitigate the effects of unavoidable remote communication with their ability to tolerate latency.

7 Perspective and Summary

The class of MIMD machines is composed mainly of shared memory multiprocessors and message passing multicomputers. In the past, machine realizations of shared memory multiprocessors corresponded closely with the shared-memory programming model. Although the network took many forms, such as buses and multistage networks, shared memory was uniformly accessible by all the processors, closely reflecting the programmer's viewpoint. It was relatively easy to write parallel programs for such machines because the uniform implementation of shared memory did not require careful placement of data and processes. However, it has become abundantly clear that such architectures do not scale to more than few tens of processors, because an efficient implementation of uniform memory access is infeasible due to physical constraints.

Message passing machines, on the other hand, were built to closely match physical constraints, and message passing was the computational model of choice. In this model, no attempt was made to provide uniform access to all of memory, rather, access was limited to local memory. Communication with remote nodes required the explicit use of messages. Because they allowed the exploitation of locality, the performance of such architectures scaled with the size of the machine for applications that displayed communication locality. Unfortunately, the onus of managing locality was relegated to the user. The programmer not only had to worry about partitioning and placing data and processes to minimize expensive message transmissions, but also had to overcome the limitations of the small amount of memory within a node.

Recent designs reflect an increased awareness of the importance of simultaneously exploiting locality and reducing programming difficulty. Accordingly, we see a confluence in MIMD machine architectures with the emergence of distributed shared-memory architectures that allow the exploitation of communication locality, and message passing architectures with global addressability. A major challenge in such designs is the management of communication locality.

Alewife is a distributed shared-memory architecture that allows the exploitation of locality through the use of mesh networks. Alewife's network interface is message oriented, while the processor interface with the rest of the system is memory reference oriented. Alewife's approach to locality management is multilayered, encompassing the compiler, the runtime system, and the hardware.

While a more general compiler system is being developed, we have been experimenting with applications with special structure. Prasanna [33] has developed a compiler for expressions of matrix operations and FFTs. The system exploits the known structure of such computations to derive near-optimal process partitions and schedules. The Matexpr program used in Section 4 was produced by this system. The speedups measured on ASIM with this system outstrips the performance of parallel programs written using traditional heuristics.

A runtime system for Alewife is operational. The system implements dynamic process partitioning and near-neighbor tree scheduling. The tree scheduler currently uses the simple heuristic that threads closely related through their control flow are highly likely to communicate with each other. For many applications written in a functional style with the use of **futures** for synchronization the assumption is largely true, and the performance is superior to that of a randomized scheduler.

Caches are useful in enhancing locality for applications where there is a significant amount of reuse (assuming locality is related to the frequency and distance of remote communications). The LimitLESS directory scheme solves the cache coherence problem in Alewife. This scheme is scalable in terms of its directory memory use, and its performance is close to that of a full-map directory scheme.

The performance gap between LimitLESS and full-map is expected to become even smaller as the machine scales in size. Although in a 64-node machine, the software handling cost of LimitLESS traps is of the same order as the remote transaction latency of hardware-handled requests (about 50 cycles), the internode communication latency in much larger systems will be much more significant than the processors' interrupt handling latency. Furthermore, improving processor technology will make the software handling cost even less significant. If both processor speeds and multiprocessor sizes increase, handling cache coherence completely in software will become a viable option. Indeed, the LimitLESS protocol is the first step on the migration path towards interrupt-driven cache coherence.

Latency tolerance through the use of block multithreaded processors is Alewife's last line of defense when the other layers of the system are unable to minimize the latency of memory requests. The multithreaded scheme allows us to mask both memory and synchronization delays. The hardware support needed for block multithreaded also makes trap handling efficient.

The design of Alewife is in progress and a detailed simulator called ASIM is operational. The Sparcle processor has been designed; its implementation through modifications to an existing LSI Logic SPARC processor is in progress. A significant portion of the software system, including the dynamic partitioning scheme and the tree scheduler, is implemented and runs on ASIM. The Alewife compiler currently accepts hand partitioning and placement of data and threads; ongoing work focuses on automating the partitioning and placement. Several applications have been written, compiled, and executed on our simulation system.

8 Acknowledgments

The research reported in this paper is funded by DARPA contract # N00014-87-K-0825, and by grants from the Sloan foundation and IBM. Generous equipment grants from SUN Microsystems, Digital Equipment Corporation, and Encore are gratefully acknowledged.

References

[1] Sarita V. Adve and Mark D. Hill. Weak Ordering - A New Definition. In *Proceedings 17th Annual International Symposium on Computer Architecture*, June 1990.

[2] Anant Agarwal. Limits on Interconnection Network Performance. *IEEE Transactions on Parallel and Distributed Systems*, 1991. To appear.

[3] Anant Agarwal. Performance Tradeoffs in Multithreaded Processors. September 1989. MIT VLSI Memo 89-566, Laboratory for Computer Science. Submitted for publication.

[4] Anant Agarwal, Beng-Hong Lim, David A. Kranz, and John Kubiatowicz. APRIL: A Processor Architecture for Multiprocessing. In *Proceedings 17th Annual International Symposium on Computer Architecture*, pages 104–114, June 1990.

[5] Anant Agarwal, Richard Simoni, John Hennessy, and Mark Horowitz. An Evaluation of Directory Schemes for Cache Coherence. In *Proceedings of the 15th International Symposium on Computer Architecture*, IEEE, New York, June 1988.

[6] Lucien M. Censier and Paul Feautrier. A New Solution to Coherence Problems in Multicache Systems. *IEEE Transactions on Computers*, C-27(12):1112–1118, December 1978.

[7] David Chaiken, Craig Fields, Kiyoshi Kurihara, and Anant Agarwal. Directory-Based Cache-Coherence in Large-Scale Multiprocessors. *IEEE Computer*, June 1990.

[8] David Chaiken, John Kubiatowicz, and Anant Agarwal. LimitLESS Directories: A Scalable Cache Coherence Scheme. In *Fourth International Conference on Architectural Support for Programming Languages and Operating Systems (ASPLOS IV). To appear.*, ACM, April 1991.

[9] Mathews Cherian. *A Study of Backoff Barrier Synchronization in Shared-Memory Multiprocessors.* Technical Report, S.M. Thesis, Department of Electrical Engineering and Computer Science, Massachusetts Institute of Technology, May 1989.

[10] D. R. Cheriton, H. A. Goosen, , and P. D. Boyle. ParaDIGM: A Highly Scalable Shared-Memory Multi-computer Architecture. *IEEE Computer*. To appear.

[11] William J. Dally. *A VLSI Architecture for Concurrent Data Structures*. Kluwer Academic Publishers, 1987.

[12] Michel Dubois, Christoph Scheurich, and Faye A. Briggs. Synchronization, coherence, and event ordering in multiprocessors. *IEEE Computer*, 9–21, February 1988.

[13] David A. Kranz et al. ORBIT: An Optimizing Compiler for Scheme. In *Proceedings of SIGPLAN '86, Symposium on Compiler Construction*, June 1986.

[14] Daniel Gajski, David Kuck, Duncan Lawrie, and Ahmed Saleh. Cedar – A Large Scale Multiprocessor. In *International Conference on Parallel Processing*, pages 524–529, August 1983.

[15] James R. Goodman. Using Cache Memory to Reduce Processor-Memory Traffic. In *Proceedings of the 10th Annual Symposium on Computer Architecture*, pages 124–131, IEEE, New York, June 1983.

[16] James R. Goodman and Philip J. Woest. The Wisconsin Multicube: A New Large Scale Cache-Coherent Multiprocessor. In *Proceedings of the 15th Annual International Symposium on Computer Architecture*, pages 422–431, Hawaii, June 1988.

[17] A. Gottlieb, R. Grishman, C. P. Kruskal, K. P. McAuliffe, L. Rudolph, and M. Snir. The NYU Ultracomputer – Designing a MIMD Shared-Memory Parallel Machine. *IEEE Transactions on Computers*, C-32(2):175–189, February 1983.

[18] R.H. Halstead and T. Fujita. MASA: A Multithreaded Processor Architecture for Parallel Symbolic Computing. In *Proceedings of the 15th Annual International Symposium on Computer Architecture*, pages 443–451, IEEE, New York, June 1988.

[19] W. D. Hillis. *The Connection Machine*. The MIT Press, Cambridge, MA, 1985.

[20] David V. James, Anthony T. Laundrie, Stein Gjessing, and Gurindar S. Sohi. Distributed-Directory Scheme: Scalable Coherent Interface. *IEEE Computer*, 74–77, June 1990.

[21] Parviz Kermani and Leonard Kleinrock. Virtual Cut-Through: A New Computer Communication Switching Technique. *Computer Networks*, 3:267–286, October 1979.

[22] David A. Kranz. *ORBIT: An Optimizing Compiler for Scheme*. PhD thesis, Yale University, February 1988. Technical Report YALEU/DCS/RR-632.

[23] David A. Kranz, R. Halstead, and E. Mohr. Mul-T: A High-Performance Parallel Lisp. In *Proceedings of SIGPLAN '89, Symposium on Programming Languages Design and Implementation*, June 1989.

[24] James T. Kuehn and Burton J. Smith. The HORIZON Supercomputing System: Architecture and Software. In *Proceedings of Supercomputing '88*, November 1988.

[25] Kiyoshi Kurihara. *Performance Evaluation of Large-Scale Multiprocessors*. Technical Report, S.M. Thesis, Department of Electrical Engineering and Computer Science, Massachusetts Institute of Technology, September 1990.

[26] D. Lenoski, J. Laudon, K. Gharachorloo, A. Gupta, and J. Hennessy. The Directory-Based Cache Coherence Protocol for the DASH Multiprocessor. In *Proceedings 17th Annual International Symposium on Computer Architecture*, pages 49–58, June 1990.

[27] Gino Maa. The WAIF Intermediate Graphical Form. Oct. 1990. Alewife Memo.

[28] Eric Mohr, David A. Kranz, and Robert H. Halstead. Lazy task creation: a technique for increasing the granularity of parallel programs. In *Proceedings of Symposium on Lisp and Functional Programming*, June 1990.

[29] Dan Nussbaum and Anant Agarwal. Scalability of Parallel Machines. *Communications of the ACM*, March 1990. To appear.

[30] Brian W. O'Krafka and A. Richard Newton. An Empirical Evaluation of Two Memory-Efficient Directory Methods. In *Proceedings 17th Annual International Symposium on Computer Architecture*, June 1990.

[31] G. M. Papadopoulos and D.E. Culler. Monsoon: An Explicit Token-Store Architecture. In *Proceedings 17th Annual International Symposium on Computer Architecture*, June 1990.

[32] G. F. Pfister et al. The IBM Research Parallel Processor Prototype (RP3): Introduction and Architecture. In *Proceedings ICPP*, pages 764–771, August 1985.

[33] G. N. S. Prasanna. *Structure Driven Multiprocessor Compilation of Numeric Problems*. PhD thesis, Massachusetts Institute of Technology, Department of Electrical Engineering and Computer Science, 1990.

[34] Charles L. Seitz. Concurrent VLSI Architectures. *IEEE Transactions on Computers*, C-33(12):1247–1265, December 1984.

[35] B.J. Smith. Architecture and Applications of the HEP Multiprocessor Computer System. *SPIE*, 298:241–248, 1981.

[36] SPARC Architecture Manual. 1988. SUN Microsystems, Mountain View, California.

[37] C. K. Tang. Cache Design in the Tightly Coupled Multiprocessor System. In *AFIPS Conference Proceedings, National Computer Conference, NY, NY*, pages 749–753, June 1976.

[38] Charles P. Thacker and Lawrence C. Stewart. Firefly: a Multiprocessor Workstation. In *Proceedings of ASPLOS II*, pages 164–172, October 1987.

[39] Wolf-Dietrich Weber and Anoop Gupta. Analysis of Cache Invalidation Patterns in Multiprocessors. In *Third International Conference on Architectural Support for Programming Languages and Operating Systems (ASPLOS III)*, April 1989.

[40] Wolf-Dietrich Weber and Anoop Gupta. Exploring the Benefits of Multiple Hardware Contexts in a Multiprocessor Architecture: Preliminary Results. In *Proceedings 16th Annual International Symposium on Computer Architecture*, IEEE, New York, June 1989.

[41] Andrew Wilson. Hierarchical Cache/Bus Architecture for Shared Memory Multiprocessors. In *Proceedings of the 14th Annual International Symposium on Computer Architecture*, pages 244–252, June 1987.

Scalability Issues of Shared virtual Memory for Multicomputers

Kai Li

Department of Computer Science

35 Olden Street

Princeton University

Princeton, NJ 08544

li@princeton.edu

Abstract

A shared virtual memory (SVM) system provides a shared, coherent memory address space on a message-passing based architecture by maintaining memory coherence at the page level. Although previous research and early implementations of SVM systems are quite successful, new design issues arise when implementing SVM systems on large-scale multicomputers. One issue is that the sizes of certain data structures for maintaining memory coherence are linearly proportional to the number of processors. A system will not be scalable if such data structures are used for each SVM page. Another issue is how to take advantage of the fast data transmission among memories to implement large SVM address spaces. This paper addresses both issues and describes solutions.

INTRODUCTION

Much of the research on shared-memory multiprocessor architectures has concentrated on techniques of maintaining coherence of processor caches. Most early protocols are based on a shared-bus [Archibald and Baer, 1986]; they support relatively few processors. Recently, scalable cache coherence protocols such as hierarchical approaches [Cheriton, 1988, Goodman and Woest, 1988] and distributed directory-based schemes [Agarwal *et al.*, 1990, Bisiani and Ravishankar, 1990, Gharachorloo *et al.*, 1990, Thakkar *et al.*, 1990] have been proposed. Some of these schemes use weak coherence models [Dubois *et al.*, 1986] to further reduce memory coherence traffic. Maintaining memory coherence at the cache block level supports efficient, fine-grained updates to shared data. But such architectures not only require special hardware but also introduce complicated design issues when a memory hierarchy has multiple levels of caches.

An alternative is the shared virtual memory (SVM) approach [Li, 1986b, Li and Hudak, 1989] that maintains memory coherence at memory page level by software. The first SVM implementation on a network of workstations [Li, 1986b, Li, 1988] has shown that shared virtual memory is an effective approach to utilize both memory and processor power and that many parallel programs can obtain good speedups over a uniprocessor. The challenge is to implement shared virtual memory systems on large-scale multicomputers.

A large-scale multicomputer with hundreds or thousands of processors is different from a network of workstations in many aspects:

- The number of processors of a large-scale multicomputer is in the order of hundreds and thousands of processors, much larger than that of a network of workstations.

- The data transmission rate on a multicomputer is much faster than that on a network of workstations and the latency of a message transmission on a multicomputer is usually smaller than that on a network of workstations, due to fast hardware and simple protocols.

- The memory on each processor node is usually smaller than that on a stand-alone workstation, but the total amount of available physical memory of a large-scale multicomputer is usually larger than that of a network of workstations used for a shared virtual memory.

- Unlike a workstation, only a few nodes on a large-scale multicomputer have disks or other kinds of stable storage devices.

It is clear that these differences raise a number of design issues for implementing shared virtual memory systems for large-scale multicomputers. This paper addresses two issues we have encountered in designing and implementing a shared virtual memory system for the Intel iPSC/860 multicomputer.

The first issue is how to make system data structures scalable. A shared virtual memory system uses distributed data structures for maintaining its memory coherence. The data structure on each node is a table or directory with an entry for each shared virtual memory page. Without any compaction, such an entry requires $O(N)$ bits for its copyset field to keep track of read copy locations, where N is the the number of nodes in the system. A few copyset compaction methods were proposed in [Li, 1986b]. This paper refines two methods proposed in [Li, 1986b] and proposes a distributed copyset method.

Another issue is how to take advantage of fast interprocessor data transmission on large-scale multiprocessors in implementing large shared virtual memory address spaces. Usually, the data transfer rate on a commercially available multicomputer is an order-of-magnitude faster than that between a memory and a disk. It is clear that using other memory pages instead of disks as backing stores should significantly reduce the system overhead for implementing large virtual address spaces. This paper describes a strategy that uses no-access page frames and replicated read-only page frames to reduce page swapping overhead for implementing large shared virtual memory address spaces.

SHARED VIRTUAL MEMORY

Shared virtual memory implements coherent shared memory on a network of processors without physically shared memory. The concept of shared virtual memory was first proposed in [Li, 1986b] and the first prototype was implemented for a network of workstations [Li, 1988]. Figure 1 shows the coherent mapping of an SVM system on a message-passing based architecture, in which nodes in the system are connected by an communication network and each node consists of a processor and a memory.

An SVM system employs virtual addresses instead of physical addresses for memory references. Each virtual address space can be as large as a single node's Memory Management Unit (MMU) provides and is shared by all nodes in a system. As in traditional virtual memory [Denning, 1970], the address space is *virtual* since it is larger than the physical memory available on a node. The address space is kept coherent at all times. That is, the value returned by a read operation is always the same as the value written by the most recent write operation to that address.

An SVM address space is organized in pages which can be accessed by

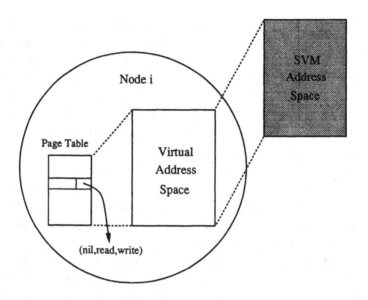

Figure 1: Shared virtual memory mapping.

any node in the system. A memory mapping manager on each node views its local memory as a large cache of pages for its associated processor. Pages that are marked read-only can have copies residing in the physical memories of many processors at the same time. A page currently being written can reside in the physical memory of only one processor. When a processor writes a page that is currently residing on other processors, it must get an up-to-date copy of the page and then invalidate all copies on other processors. A memory reference causes a page fault when the page containing the memory location is not in a processor's current physical memory. When the fault occurs, the memory mapping manager retrieves the page from the memory of another processor. If there is a page frame available on the receiving node, the page is simply moved between the nodes. Otherwise, the SVM system uses page replacement policies to find an available page frame, swapping its contents to the sending node.

A hardware MMU designed for supporting traditional virtual memory systems can be used to implement such a system. The protection mechanism of an MMU allows single instructions to trigger page faults and trap the faults in appropriate fault handlers. The system can set the access rights (nil, read-only or writable) so that a memory access which could violate memory coherence causes a page fault. Then, the memory coherence problem can be solved in a modular way with page fault handlers and their servers. To client programs, this mechanism is completely transparent: there is no distinction made between accessing data which is currently local or remote.

In general, the SVM presents clients with the same type of interface as a tightly-coupled shared-memory multiprocessor. The large virtual address space allows programs to be much larger in code and data space than the physical memory on a single node. Remote memory can serve as an added level of the memory hierarchy between the local memory and disks. In this way, the full potential of the large aggregate memory of a multicomputer can be utilized. Application programs are completely relieved from having to arrange data movement and availability across the network in an effort to effectively use the capabilities of a multicomputer.

DATA STRUCTURE COMPACTION

A large-scale multicomputer, by definition, has a large number of nodes. Each node has a processor and its memory. Because of cost and engineering constraints, the physical memory on each node is usually limited. In order to effectively use the physical memory on each node, it is important to compact SVM system data structures.

In addition to the MMU page table, the SVM page fault handlers and their servers use a table or directory on each node to maintain memory coherence. The table has an entry for each SVM page; the size of the table is proportional to that of its SVM address space. For example, if the size of an SVM address space is 2^{32} bytes and the page size is 2^{12} (4096) bytes, the table will have 2^{20} (or more than 1 million) entries. On a multicomputer such as the iPSC/860, each node is usually configured with 8 MBytes memory. Clearly, a large fraction of the physical memory will be consumed by such a table, even if each entry requires a few bytes.

Two methods can be used to compact the table: reducing the number of entries and compressing the size of each entry. The following presents a straightforward way to reduce the number of table entries and three basic methods to compact a table entry.

Hash Table

There is no way to reduce the number of table entries if every processor uses the whole shared virtual memory address space. Fortunately, this is not the common case. A parallel program based on a global memory model normally has a number of threads, at least one on each processor. Each thread usually accesses a portion of the shared data structures. This means that when a shared virtual memory system has a number of processors, each processor only accesses part of the address space. Obviously, if this is true, a hashing technique [Knuth, 1973] can be used to compact the table.

The hash table size can be adjusted according to the configuration of the system. For example, it can be the smallest prime number q such that $q > (cP)/N$ where P is the maximum number of pages in an SVM address space, N is the number of processors in the system, and c is a parameter to be adjusted. Each entry in the hash table is a linked page table entry list.

In order to keep the size of the hash table small, one can delete a table entry when the accessibility of the page is changed to nil. This can be done either when the memory coherence algorithm invalidates a page or when the total size of the table exceeds some threshold.

Table Entry

The size of the table also depends on the size of each entry. In the dynamic distributed manager algorithm, the page fault handlers and their servers maintain the following information for each page [Li and Hudak, 1989]:

- probOwner — a node number leading to the owner of the page. It requires $\lceil \log N \rceil$ bits.

- access — accessibility of the page (no-access, read-only, writable). It requires 2 bits.

- lock — to implement mutual exclusive accesses to per-page-based memory coherence data structures. It requires 1 bit for the test-and-set or equivalent instruction.

- queue — to keep track of blocked threads and remote requests.

- copyset — to remember which processor has a copy of the page. i is in the copyset if processor i has a copy. It requires N bits if bit-vector is used to represent a set [Aho et al., 1974].

On a multicomputer with a 32-bit address space, the size (in bits) of a table entry of a straightforward representation is: $N + \lceil \log N \rceil + 32$, assuming that the lock and queue fields can be implemented with 32 bits and that the access field is stored in the MMU page table. Since a large-scale multicomputer has a large number of nodes, the table entry size becomes a serious problem because the size of an entry is linearly proportional to N.

The probOwner field does not need to be compacted because $\lceil \log N \rceil$ bits is already quite small. A simple, yet effective method to compact the queue field is to use a hash table to store queues where the page number is used as the hashing key. The hash table size can be rather small because the number of queues is bounded by the maximum number of threads in the SVM address space. This method does not require any bits for each page table entry.

The copyset field is a set of processor numbers $S = \{0, \ldots, N-1\}$. It is used solely by the memory coherence algorithm with the following four operations:

- Insert(e, S) — inserts an element e into a set S.

- Next(S) — returns the next element in S in a round-robin fashion.

- Size(S) — returns the number of elements in set S.

- Empty(S) — removes all elements in S.

The speed of these operations is not very important, so the design can concentrate only on saving space.

The experience with shared virtual memory systems [Li, 1988, Li and Schaefer, 1989] shows that most pages either have copies on all processors or have fewer copies. Such a property suggests the following three methods to compact a copyset.

Linked Bit-vector

The linked bit-vector approach represents a copyset as a linked list. The main idea of this approach is to link the meaningful bit-vectors together to save space. Each element in the list has three fields: *link*, *base* and *bit-vector*. The link field points to the next element in the list. The bit-vector field is a zero-based bit vector of k bits. The base field tells the starting point of the bit vector. The definition of the bits in a bit-vector is that node $base + i$ is in the copyset if and only if the i-th bit of a bit-vector is 1. Figure 2 shows a compacted copyset $S = \{3, 995\}$ when $N = 1024$ and $k = 32$.

Insert(e, S) operation traverses down the linked list to find an element such that $base \le e < base + k$. If such an element is found, e will

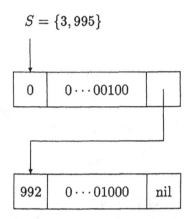

Figure 2: An example of linked bit-vector compaction.

be inserted into its bit vector. If such an element does not exist, a new element whose bit vector contains e will be created and linked to the list. Other operations are trivial. The link field in each element can usually be compacted with the compaction method proposed in [Li, 1986a].

The linked bit-vector compaction method does not require much storage when all nodes are in the copyset, but it may waste storage when there are few nodes in the copyset and they are evenly distributed.

Vaguely-defined Set

A *vaguely-defined set* is, as the name indicates, a set without precise definition. The idea of a vaguely-defined set was developed because the copyset field is only used by the invalidation operations in the memory coherence program. It is harmless to send a page invalidation request to a processor that does not have the page. This is why the memory coherence algorithms allow a processor to broadcast an invalidation request when the number of elements in a copyset exceeds a threshold.

The vaguely-defined set approach uses a tag together with a partial representation of a copyset. When the partial representation of a copyset is over its limit, the tag is set to indicate that the memory coherence algorithm can treat the copyset as if it contains all processors.

Figure 3 shows an example of using vaguely-defined set approach to compact an entry into a 32-bit representation for an 128-node multicomputer. As indicated in the figure, the lock field uses 1 bit and the tag uses 3 bits. The rest of the 28 bits are used to store 4 7-bit processor numbers. Since the page owner maintains its copyset, we know that the probOwner is the current processor itself when the copyset is not empty. The example uses this property to allow the partial representation of a copyset to contain up to 4 processor numbers instead of 3. When the value of the tag is 0, the copyset is empty and the right-most processor number (n_4) stores the probOwner processor number. When the value of the tag between 1 and 4, it indicates the number of processors in the copyset. When the value of the tag is 5, 6, or 7, it means that the copyset contains more than 4 processor numbers. In this case, the memory coherence algorithm treats the copyset as if it contains all processor numbers.

31	30	28	27	21	20	14	13	7	6	0
lock	tag		n_1		n_2		n_3		n_4	

$$0\ 0\ 0 \quad \text{probOwner} = n_4, \text{copyset} = \{\};$$
$$0\ 0\ 1 \quad \text{probOwner} = \text{self}, \text{copyset} = \{n_1\}$$
$$0\ 1\ 0 \quad \text{probOwner} = \text{self}, \text{copyset} = \{n_1, n_2\}$$
$$0\ 1\ 1 \quad \text{probOwner} = \text{self}, \text{copyset} = \{n_1, n_2, n_3\}$$
$$1\ 0\ 0 \quad \text{probOwner} = \text{self}, \text{copyset} = \{n_1, n_2, n_3, n_4\}$$
$$1\ 0\ 1 \quad \text{probOwner} = \text{self}, \text{copyset} = \{0, \cdots, N-1\}$$
$$1\ 1\ 0 \quad \text{probOwner} = \text{self}, \text{copyset} = \{0, \cdots, N-1\}$$
$$1\ 1\ 1 \quad \text{probOwner} = \text{self}, \text{copyset} = \{0, \cdots, N-1\}$$

Figure 3: An example of vaguely-defined set compaction.

The vaguely-defined set approach does not restrict the data structure of the partial copyset. It can be a list of processor numbers rather than the straightforward representation in the example. The list can be compacted by the method proposed in [Li, 1986a] so that normally only two bits are needed for each pointer field. The linked bit-vector can be also used to represent the partial copyset.

Distributed Copyset

The main idea of this approach is to distribute space requirements on different nodes in a tree fashion rooted at the owner of the page. The idea is based on the observation that for maintaining memory coherence, the copyset of a page is used only for the invalidation operation induced by a write fault. The location of the set is unimportant as long as the algorithm can invalidate all read copies of a page.

A copyset is represented by a number of subsets residing on different processors. Read page faults build distributed copysets as a tree for each page [Li and Hudak, 1989]. The tree of a distributed copyset is bidirectional, with the edges directed from the root formed by the copysets and the edges directed from the leaves formed by probOwner fields. On a read page fault, the faulting processor follows its probOwner field to look for a read copy. If any processor p along the path to the true owner has a read copy of the page, the faulting processor will receive a copy from processor p and the faulting processor number will be added into p's copyset. Figure 4 shows an example of how a read page fault builds up a tree. Figure 4 (a) shows a copyset = $\{2, 3, 6\}$ on processor 0, the owner of the page. When a read page fault occurs on processor 11 whose probOwner field points to processor 3, a read copy is made from processor 3, as shown in Figure 4 (b).

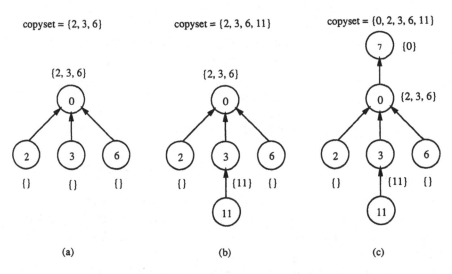

Figure 4: An example of distributing a copyset

When the copyset on the owner of the page exceeds its space limit, it can relinquish its ownership to the requesting processor and make the copyset of the new owner contain the old owner. If the maximum number of elements in a copyset on a processor is 3 in the example of Figure 4 (b), a read page fault on processor 7 will result in Figure 4 (c).

Such a distribution strategy requires no additional message to distribute copysets.

A write fault invalidates all copies in the tree by inducing a wave of invalidation operations starting at the owner and propagating to the processors in its copyset, which, in turn send invalidation requests to the processors in their copysets and so on. For the example shown in Figure 4 (b), processor 0 will send invalidation messages to processor 2, 3, and 6. Processor 3 will then send an invalidation message to processor 11.

The minimum space required for the copyset on each processor is that for a processor number ($\log N$ bits). In which case, the structure of a distributed copyset is a doubly-linked list starting at the owner. Obviously, it requires k serial messages to invalidate k copies. With more space for the copyset on each processor, the structure of a distributed copyset can be a tree. For example, with a space for 2 processor numbers on each processor, a distributed copyset can be a binary tree. With a space for 3 processor numbers, a distributed copyset can be a 2-3 tree.

Since a non-owner processor needs to have the probOwner field in its table entry, the space used for the probOwner field cannot be used to store a processor number in the copyset on an non-owner processor. The example in Figure 3 for a non-owner processor allows its copyset to contain up to 3 processor numbers instead of 4, leaving the last processor number for the probOwner field.

PAGE SWAPPING

Since the size of a physical memory on a processor is usually much less than the size of a shared virtual memory address space, the implementation of a shared virtual memory system must have page replacements between a physical memory and its backing store. Unlike traditional virtual memory implementations that use disks as backing stores, an SVM system on a multicomputer can use remote physical memories as backing stores to improve page swapping performance. This paper considers page replacement among physical memories in a multicomputer.

Page Types

Page swapping or replacement in an SVM system is quite different from that of traditional virtual memory systems for uniprocessor and shared-memory processors. In a traditional virtual memory system, there are two kinds of virtual pages: valid and invalid. A valid virtual page has a mapping to a physical page frame in its page table entry. An invalid virtual page either has a mapping to a disk page, or a mapping to a physical page frame. The latter means that the corresponding physical page is being reclaimed. The page replacement mechanism usually tries to reclaim the page frames of least-recently-used (LRU) pages when the number of free page frames is below a certain threshold. If a reclaimed physical page is dirty, its contents will be written to its disk backing store page.

Although in an SVM system there are also two kinds of virtual pages: valid and invalid, the accessibility and replication of a SVM page adds another dimension to page replacement. Any SVM page can be no-access, read-copy, read-owner, or writable. A no-access page is a page whose access bits in its page table entry have been set to nil by the SVM memory coherence algorithm. Both read-copy and read-owner pages are read-only. A read-owner page is owned by the current processor and a read-copy page is not. A writable page is owned by the processor and it allows both read or write accesses.

To minimize the system overhead for page replacement, The physical page frames of different kinds of SVM pages should be treated differently. It is intuitive that physical page frames whose virtual pages are no-access should have higher priority to be reclaimed because if the processor issues a memory reference to a no-access page, a page fault will occur anyway. Physical page frames whose SVM pages are read-copy should be reclaimed next because there is at least another copy of the page (namely, read-owner) in the system. Physical page frames whose SVM pages are read-owner should be chosen over those whose SVM pages are writable because it is less expensive to relinquish the ownership of a page than to transfer a page.

Reclaiming Page Frames

Two parameters are important for page frame reclamation: SVM page type and last-reference time. It is a bad strategy to reclaim all page frames of one type before starting the reclamation of another type, because recently referenced page frames may be reclaimed. Only using the last-reference time is not a good strategy either because page frames whose SVM pages are no-access may be referenced recently. Since parallel programs exhibit a high degree of special locality of reference [Eggers and Katz, 1988], a better strategy is to use both parameters to decide the reclamation priorities of page frames.

A practical approach is to use a list data structure to represent an ordered set for a particular type of page frames. Each set is ordered by its last reference time. Each set has thresholds to control when its page frames should be reclaimed. Figure shows a pipelined strategy controlled by thresholds of each page frame set.

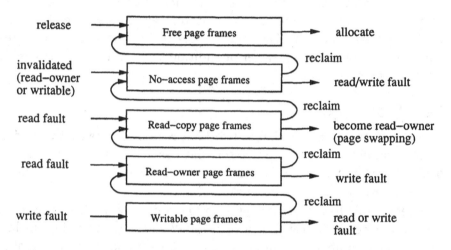

Figure 5: Reclaiming page frames

No access page frames will be reclaimed to the free set when the number of free page frames is below its threshold. When both the number of free page frames and the number of no-access page frames are below certain thresholds, certain read-copy page frames will be put into the no-access set. Such page frames are different from those due to the invalidations of the SVM memory coherence algorithm. When a read page fault occurs on a page whose physical page frame was moved from the read-copyset to the no-access set and the processor has not received an invalidation, the page accessibility can be changed to read-only without copying the page content from the page owner. Its physical page frame can be simply moved back to the read-copy set. Reclaiming a read-copy page does not require any message to its page owner because the page is already no-access when an invalidation message arrives.

The reclamation of a page frame whose SVM page is read-owner can be done by relinquishing its ownership to one of its copy holders. Since the page is still read-only, the local processor can still read memory locations without generating a fault. Such an operation usually requires a short message. It is possible that the copy holder has already changed its read-copy page to no-access without informing its owner. If no copy holder is found, the page frame will be moved to the writable page frame set and the accessibility of the page should be changed to writable.

The reclamation of writable page frames is similar to that of a read-owner page frame except that it asks another processor to make a read-copy page. It is possible to reclaim writable page frames directly to the read-copy page frame set. The disadvantage of doing so is that it requires a message for ownership transfer in addition to invalidation messages, if a write access occurs.

Page Replacement

When a writable page is changed to be a read-owner page, the paging mechanism needs to find a processor that has a relatively large number of free page frames. The goal is to minimize the overhead of related messages over the routing network.

A reasonable heuristic method is to maintain a table FreeFrames on each processor. FreeFrames is a vector of N elements indicating the latest information about the number of free page frames plus the number of page frames associated with no-access SVM pages. The information is initialized at the initialization stage and maintained by the page replacement mechanism. Each page swapping related message will carry such information of the sender to the receiver so that FreeFrames always has fairly recent information. This way it does not introduce additional packets in the replacement strategy.

A processor uses the hint information in its FreeFrames to find processor i such that FreeFrames[i] has the maximum value. Rather than starting with processor 0 each time, each processor can use a roving pointer indicating the last processor found. If i happens to be the current processor, no page replacement will occur. Otherwise, a loop may be generated.

An SVM address space reaches its limit when no page is replicated anywhere (no read-copy page). Clearly, the maximum size of an SVM address space without using disks as backing stores is bounded by the sum of the page frames used for the SVM address space on all processors. If the SVM address space requires more page frames than the multicomputer has, one will have to use disks as backing stores.

The performance of a page frame reclamation can be quite different. Table shows the number of messages required to reclaim different page frames.

Page types	# short msgs	# long msgs
no-access	0	0
read-copy	0	0
read-owner	≥ 1	0
writable	≥ 1	1

Table 1: Message overhead of reclaiming page frames.

The implementation of such page reclamations on a commercially available multicomputer such as the Intel iPSC/860 will significantly outperform the traditional virtual memory systems that use disks as page swapping backing stores. The latency of a short message on such a multicomputer is less than 400 microseconds. The latency of a long message is less than 3 milliseconds. The worst case page frame reclamation for page swapping is an order of magnitude faster than paging between memories and disks.

CONCLUSIONS

This paper addressed two issues critical to implementing shared virtual memory systems on large-scale multicomputers: data structure compaction and page swapping.

The paper has described three methods to compact the copyset data structure: linked-bit-vector, vaguely-defined-set, and distributed copyset. The linked bit-vector compaction method does not require much storage when all nodes are in the copyset, but it wastes storage when there are few nodes in the copyset and they are evenly distributed. The vaguely-defined set approach is simple and should be good for the case in which memory pages are either shared by all the processors, or very few processors. The distributed copyset approach is probably the best of the three. Since read page faults distribute copysets on demand, distributing a copyset requires minimum space and no additional network messages.

Another issue addressed in the paper is page swapping among physical memories. Since large-scale multicomputers usually have a large number of processors with a limited amount of physical memory on each node, page swapping is a technique to implement a large SVM address space without using disks as backing stores. This paper described a page swapping method that allows an SVM address space to span over the entire multicomputer. The overhead of a page swapping in the worst case on the commercially available multicomputer iPSC/2 is an order of magnitude faster than using disks as page backing stores.

References

[Agarwal et al., 1990] A. Agarwal, B. Lim, D. Kranz, and J. Kubiatowicz. APRIL: A Processor Architecture for Multiprocessing. In *Proceedings of the 17th Annual Symposium on Computer Architecture*, pages 104–114, May 1990.

[Aho et al., 1974] A.V. Aho, J.E. Hopcroft, and J.D. Ullman. *The Design and Analysis of Computer Algorithms*. Addison-Wesley Publishing Company, 1974.

[Archibald and Baer, 1986] J. Archibald and J. Baer. Cache Coherence Protocols: Evaluation Using a Multiprocessor Simulation Model. *ACM Transactions on Computer Systems*, 4(4):273–298, November 1986.

[Bisiani and Ravishankar, 1990] R. Bisiani and M. Ravishankar. PLUS: A Distributed Shared-Memory System. In *Proceedings of the 17th Annual Symposium on Computer Architecture*, pages 115–124, May 1990.

[Cheriton, 1988] David R. Cheriton. The VMP Multiprocessor: Initial Experience, Refinements and Performance Evaluation. In *Proceedings of the 14th Annual Symposium on Computer Architecture*, 1988.

[Denning, 1970] Peter J. Denning. Virtual Memory. *ACM Computing Surveys*, 2(3):153–189, September 1970.

[Dubois et al., 1986] M. Dubois, C. Scheurich, and F. Briggs. Memory Access Buffering in Multiprocessors. In *Proceedings of the 13th Annual Symposium on Computer Architecture*, pages 434–442, June 1986.

[Eggers and Katz, 1988] S.J. Eggers and R.H. Katz. A Characterization of Sharing in Parallel Programs and Its Applications to Coherence Protocol Evaluation. In *Proceedings of the 15th Annual International Symposium on Computer Architecture*, pages 373–383, June 1988.

[Gharachorloo *et al.*, 1990] K. Gharachorloo, D. Lenoski, J. Laudon, P. Gibbons, A. Gupta, and J. Hennessy. Memory Consistency and Event Ordering in Scalable Shared-Memory Multiprocessors. In *Proceedings of the 17th Annual Symposium on Computer Architecture*, pages 15–26, May 1990.

[Goodman and Woest, 1988] James R. Goodman and Philip J. Woest. The Wisconsin Multicube: A New Large-Scale Cache-Coherent Multiprocessor. In *Proceedings of the 15th Annual Symposium on Computer Architecture*, pages 422–431, June 1988.

[Knuth, 1973] Donald E. Knuth. *The Art of Computer Programming, Volume III*. Addison-Wesley Publishing Company, 1973.

[Li and Hudak, 1989] Kai Li and Paul Hudak. Memory Coherence in Shared Virtual Memory Systems. *ACM Transactions on Computer Systems*, 7(4):321–359, November 1989.

[Li and Schaefer, 1989] Kai Li and Richard Schaefer. A Hypercube Shared Virtual Memory. In *Proceedings of the 1989 International Parallel Processing Conference*, volume Vol:I Architecture, pages 125–132, August 1989.

[Li, 1986a] Kai Li. A New List Compaction Method. *Software Practice and Experience*, 16(2):145–163, February 1986.

[Li, 1986b] Kai Li. *Shared Virtual Memory on Loosely-coupled Multiprocessors*. PhD thesis, Yale University, October 1986. Tech Report YALEU-RR-492.

[Li, 1988] Kai Li. IVY: A Shared Virtual Memory System for Parallel Computing. In *Proceedings of the 1988 International Conference on Parallel Processing*, volume Vol:II Software, pages 94–101, August 1988.

[Thakkar *et al.*, 1990] S. Thakkar, M. Dubois, A.T. Laundrie, G.S. Sohi, D.V. James, S. Gjessing, M. Thapar, B. Delagi, M. Carlton, and A. Despain. New Directions in Scalable Shared-Memory Multiprocessor Architectures. *IEEE Computer*, 23(6):71–83, June 1990.

Toward Large-Scale Shared Memory Multiprocessing

John K. Bennett
John B. Carter
Willy Zwaenepoel

Computer Systems Laboratory
Rice University

Abstract

We are currently investigating two different approaches to scalable shared memory: Munin, a distributed shared memory (DSM) system implemented entirely in software, and Willow, a true shared memory multiprocessor with extensive hardware support for scalability. Munin allows parallel programs written for shared memory multiprocessors to be executed efficiently on distributed memory multiprocessors. Unlike existing DSM systems, which only provide a single mechanism for memory consistency, Munin provides multiple consistency protocols, matching protocol to data object based on the expected pattern of accesses to that object. We call this approach *type-specific coherence*. Munin also employs a relaxed consistency model to mask network latency and to minimize the number of messages required for keeping memory consistent. Willow is intended to be a true shared memory multiprocessor, providing memory capacity and performance capable of supporting over a thousand commercial microprocessors. These processors are arranged in cluster fashion, with a multi-level cache, I/O, synchronization, and memory hierarchy. Willow is distinguished from other shared memory multiprocessors by a layered memory organization that significantly reduces the impact of *inclusion* on the cache hierarchy and that exploits locality gradients. Willow also provides support for *adaptive cache coherence*, an approach similar to Munin's type-specific coherence, whereby the consistency protocol used to manage each cache line is selected based on the expected or observed access behavior for the data stored in that line. Implementation of Munin is in progress; we are still designing Willow.

MUNIN

Introduction

Shared memory programs are generally easier to develop than distributed memory (message passing) programs, because the programmer does not

---

This work was supported in part by the National Science Foundation under Grants CDA-8619893, CCR-8716914, and CCR-9010351 and by NASA and NSF Graduate Fellowships.

need to explicitly initiate data motion. Distributed memory machines, however, scale better in terms of the number of processors that can be supported. Hence, our goal is to provide the best of both worlds: the relative ease of programming of the shared memory model and the scalability of a distributed memory machine. Our performance goal is to provide execution efficiency nearly equal to that of hand-crafted distributed memory (message-passing) code for the same application.

Munin is a distributed shared memory (DSM) system that allows parallel programs written for shared memory multiprocessors to be executed efficiently on distributed memory multiprocessors. Munin's user interface is a consistent global address space, with thread and synchronization facilities like those found in shared memory parallel programming systems. Munin provides this interface via a collection of runtime library routines that use the system's underlying message passing facilities for interprocessor communication and that use kernel support for page fault handling. Munin is unique among existing DSM systems [Cha89, Li86, Ram88] both in that it provides *type-specific coherence* and in that it uses a relaxed model of consistency for shared memory.

Munin provides a suite of consistency protocols so that individual data objects are kept consistent by a protocol tailored to the way in which that object is accessed. Several studies of shared memory parallel programs have indicated that no single consistency protocol is best suited for all parallel programs [Ben90a, Egg88, Egg89]. Furthermore, within a single program, different shared data objects often are accessed in fundamentally different ways [Ben90a], and a particular object's access pattern can change during the execution of a program. Existing DSM systems have not taken advantage of these observations, and have limited their functionality to providing a single consistency protocol for all programs and all objects. Munin uses program annotations, currently provided by the programmer, to choose a consistency protocol suited to the expected access pattern of each object, or to change protocols during execution.

DSM systems such as Ivy, Clouds, and Amber [Li86, Ram88, Cha89] are based on *sequential consistency* [Lam79]. Sequential consistency requires that each modification to a shared object become visible immediately to the other processors in the system. In a DSM system, this means that the system is required to transmit at least one message to invalidate all remote copies of an object and then must stall until these messages are acknowledged. Recently, several researchers in the shared memory multiprocessor community have advocated the use of relaxed consistency models that force the programmer to make synchronization events in the program visible to the memory consistency mechanism. By requiring this visibility, the memory hardware is able to buffer writes between synchronization points, thus reducing the latency of processor stalls [Dub86, Sch87, Gha90]. Munin achieves similar advantage by using a software *delayed update queue* to buffer pending outgoing write operations. Use of the delayed update queue allows the runtime system to merge modifications to the same object transparently, which greatly reduces the number of messages required to maintain consistency and causes Munin programs to combine data motion and synchronization as is done in hand-coded message passing programs. All objects use the same delayed update queue, so updates to different objects destined for the same remote processor can be combined as well. The delayed update queue is flushed whenever the consistency semantics in force require strict ordering of write operations, e.g., when a local thread releases a lock or arrives at a barrier.

Munin differs from recent scalable shared memory multiprocessors [Aga90, Len90] that have used relaxed consistency models to minimize processor stalls during writes to shared memory. These multiprocessors can suffer from frequent read misses, which significantly affect performance. Munin's use of type-specific coherence addresses this problem of excessive read misses. We have found that an update-based consistency protocol is superior to an invalidation-based protocol if the invalidate protocol will result in an excessive number of reloads after invalidation (reloads are read misses). By taking advantage of semantic hints, Munin can frequently load shared data before it is accessed, for example, by moving the data protected by a lock when lock ownership is transferred. This allows us to reduce or hide the latency associated with the corresponding read misses.

In addition to the delayed update mechanism, Munin employs several other well known consistency mechanisms as part of its multiple protocol approach to type specific coherence [Ben90b]. These mechanisms include replication, migration, invalidation, and remote load/store. We use each of these mechanisms for the particular types of shared data objects for which they are most appropriate.

We have based many of our design decisions on the results of a study of sharing and synchronization behavior in a variety of shared memory parallel programs, in which we observed that a large percentage of shared data accesses fall into a relatively small number of access type categories that can be supported efficiently [Ben90a].

Our approach to the design of Munin can therefore be summarized as follows:

1. Understand sharing and synchronization in shared memory parallel programs.

2. Exploit this understanding by developing efficient consistency mechanisms for the observed sharing behavior.

3. Match mechanism to type using user-provided information.

The remainder of this section describes our progress toward achieving these objectives.

Sharing in Parallel Programs

Type-specific coherence requires that there be a relatively small number of identifiable shared memory access patterns that characterize the majority of shared data objects, and for which corresponding consistency mechanisms can be developed. In order to test our approach, we studied a number of shared memory parallel programs written in C++ [Str87] using the Presto programming system [Ber88] on the Sequent Symmetry shared memory multiprocessor [Lov88]. The selected programs are written specifically for a shared memory multiprocessor so that our results are not influenced by the program being written with distribution in mind and accurately reflect the memory access behavior that occurs when programmers do not expend special effort towards distributing the data across processors. Presto programs are divided into an initialization phase, during which the program is single-threaded, and a computation phase.

Six programs studied in detail were: Matrix multiply, Gaussian elimination, Fast Fourier Transform (FFT), Quicksort, Traveling salesman problem (TSP), and Life. Matrix multiply, Gaussian elimination, and Fast Fourier Transform are numeric problems that distribute the data to separate threads and access shared memory in predictable patterns. Quicksort uses divide-and-conquer to dynamically subdivide the problem. Traveling salesman uses central work queues protected by locks to control access to problem data. Life is a "nearest-neighbors" problem in which data is shared only by neighboring processes. Other programs studied include parallel versions of minimum spanning tree, factorial, SOR, shellsort, prime sieve, and a string matching algorithm.

Methodology

We collect logging information for a program by modifying the source and the run-time system to record all accesses to shared memory (13 microseconds to record each access). These program modifications are currently done by hand. A call to a logging object is added to the program source after every statement that accesses shared memory. The Presto run-time system was modified so that thread creations and destructions are recorded, as are all synchronization events. The end of each program's initialization phase is logged as a special event so that our analysis tool can differentiate between the initialization and the computation phase.

A program executed with logging enabled generates a series of log files, one per processor. Each log entry contains an *Object ID*, a *Thread ID*, the *Type of Access*, and the *Time of Access*. Examples of *Type of Access* include creation, read, write, and lock and monitor accesses of various types. *Time of Access* is the absolute time of the access, read from a hardware microsecond clock, so the per-processor logs can be merged to form a single global log.

We can specify the granularity with which to log accesses to objects. The two supported granularities are *object* and *element*. At object granularity, an access to any part of an object is logged as an access to the entire object. At element granularity, an access to a part of an object is logged as an access to that specific part of the object. For example, the log entry for a read of an element of a matrix object indicates only that the matrix was read at object granularity, but indicates the specific element that was read at element granularity.

Our study of sharing in parallel programs distinguishes itself from similar work [Egg88, Sit88, Web89] in that it studies sharing at the programming language level, and hence is relatively architecture-independent, and in that our selection of parallel programs embodies a wider variation in programming and synchronization styles.

An important difference between our approach and previous methods [Sit88, So86] is that we only log accesses to shared memory, not all accesses to memory. Non-shared memory, such as program code and local variables, generally does not require special handling in a distributed shared memory system. A useful side effect of logging only accesses to shared memory is that the log files are much more compact. This allows us to log the shared memory accesses of relatively long-running programs in their entirety, which is important because the access patterns during initialization are significantly different from those during computation.

Logging in software during program execution combines many of the benefits of software simulation [So86] and built-in tracing mechanisms [Sit88], without some of the problems associated with these techniques. As with software simulation, with software logging it is easy to change the information that is collected during a particular run of the program. For example, if only the accesses to a particular object are of interest, such as the accesses to the lock protecting a central queue, only the logging associated with that object need be enabled. On the other hand, software-based logging does not slow down program execution to the extent that software simulation of the program and architecture does. Unlike with address tracing techniques, it is possible to collect higher-order information about particular accesses. For example, we can log an attempt to acquire a monitor, successful acquisition of the monitor, or sleeping on a monitor condition variable. This information is not easily recreated from a standard address trace.

The flexibility, power and low overhead of our system does not come without cost. Only accesses to shared memory performed by the applications program and run-time system are collected, so our system suffers from what Agarwal refers to as *omission distortion* [Sit88], the inability of a system to record the complete address stream of a running program. The omission distortion is not significant in this case because we are not trying to determine how any particular cache consistency mechanism will perform, but rather are attempting to characterize patterns of sharing that are common in parallel applications programs. Also, because only accesses to shared memory are collected, our logs may experience *temporal distortion* in the sense that periods with frequent accesses to shared memory will be slowed down to a greater extent than periods when accesses to shared memory are infrequent. Since the temporal distortion in this case is limited by synchronization events, which constrain the relative ordering of events, temporal distortion is also not a serious problem.

Categories of Sharing: Intuitive Definitions

The results of our study support our approach, in that we have identified a limited number of shared data object types: *Write-once, Write-many, Producer-Consumer, Private, Migratory, Result, Read-mostly,* and *Synchronization*. We classify all shared data objects that do not fall into one of these categories as *General Read-Write*.

Write-once objects are read-only after initialization. *Write-many* objects frequently are modified by several threads between synchronization points. For example, in Quicksort, multiple threads concurrently modify independent portions of the array being sorted. *Producer-Consumer* objects are written (produced) by one thread and read (consumed) by a fixed set of other threads. *Private* objects, though declared to be shared data objects, are only accessed by a single thread. Many parallel scientific programs exhibit "nearest neighbors" or "wavefront" communication whereby the only communication is the exchange of boundary elements between threads working on adjacent sub-arrays. The boundary elements are *Producer-Consumer* and the interior elements are *Private*. *Migratory* objects are accessed in phases, where each phase corresponds to a series of accesses by a single thread. Shared objects protected by locks often exhibit this property. *Result* objects collect results. Once written, they are only read by a single thread that uses the results. *Read-*

mostly objects are read significantly more often than they are written. *Synchronization* objects, such as locks and monitors, are used by programmers to force explicit inter-thread synchronization points. Synchronization events include attempting to acquire a lock, acquiring a lock, and releasing a lock. The remaining objects, which we cannot characterize by any of the preceding classes, are called *General Read-Write*. The categories define a hierarchy of types of shared data objects. When we identify an object's sharing category, we use the most specific category possible under the following order (from most specific to least specific): *Synchronization*, *Private*, *Write-once*, *Result*, *Producer-Consumer*, *Migratory*, *Write-many*, *Read-mostly*, and *General Read-Write*.

Results of Sharing Study

The general results of our analysis can be summarized as follows:

General Results

- There are very few *General Read-Write* objects. Coherence mechanisms exist that can support the other categories of shared data objects efficiently, so a cache consistency protocol that adapts to the expected or observed behavior of each shared object will outperform one that does not.

- The conventional notion of an object, as viewed by the programmer, often does not correspond to the appropriate granularity of data decomposition for parallelism. Often it is appropriate to maintain consistency at the object level, but sometimes it is more appropriate to maintain consistency at a level smaller or larger than an object. Thus, a cache consistency protocol that adapts to the appropriate granularity of data decomposition will outperform one that does not.

- Type-specific coherence significantly reduces the amount of bus traffic required to maintain consistency. This improvement is caused by the fact that many programs perform a large number of writes to shared data objects between synchronization points, so many updates to the same data object are combined before they are eventually propagated. Additionally, type-specific coherence requires the same amount of bandwidth as write-invalidate, but when the cache line size is small, it does so with fewer messages (thus, the average message is proportionally larger).

Specific Results

- With object-level logging, *Write-many* accesses dominate other forms of shared data access. The other sharing category into which a large portion of the accesses fall at object-level granularity is *Write-once*.

- Parallel programs in which the granularity of sharing is fine tend to have their underlying fine grained behavior masked when the logging is performed on a per-object basis. The access behavior of many programs are considerably different when examined per element. For example, in the Life program, when examined on a per-object basis, virtually all shared accesses are *Write-many*. However, when examined by element, 82 percent of the shared data is in fact *Private* (the interior elements of the board) and 17 percent is *Producer-Consumer* (the edge elements).

- The average number of different objects accessed between synchronization points indicates the average number of delayed updates that will be queued up at a time. If this number is small, as the data indicate, managing a queue of delayed updates (thus providing a relaxed model of memory consistency) does not require significant overhead.

- *Write-many* objects are written about one-half as many times as they are read. Large numbers of accesses occur between synchronization points. We call a series of accesses to a single object by any thread between two synchronization points in a particular thread a "no-synch run". The large size of the no-synch runs indicate that delayed update offers substantial performance improvement. No-synch runs differ from Eggers's "write-runs" [Egg88] in that they do not end when a remote thread accesses the object, but rather whenever a thread synchronizes. Intuitively, write-runs end when a standard consistency mechanism, such as a write-invalidate or write-update scheme that enforces sequential consistency, would enforce consistency. No-synch runs end when the programmer requires consistency.

- The data recorded for locks indicate that the same thread frequently reacquires the same lock, thus facilitating local optimization of lock acquisition. Also, the number of threads waiting on the same lock is usually quite small, indicating that lock arbitration will not require excessive network traffic.

Type-specific Coherence Mechanisms

Existing software distributed shared memory systems [Cha89, Li86, Li89, Ram88] have provided only a single memory consistency protocol. These systems typically use either an invalidation-based or an update-based consistency protocol, but not both. Munin allows a separate consistency protocol for each shared data object, tuned to the access pattern of that particular object. Moreover, the protocol for an object can be changed over the course of the execution of the program. We have shown that a large number of shared memory accesses can be captured by a small set of access patterns, for which efficient consistency protocols exist, indicating that this approach is both manageable and advantageous [Ben90a]. We have developed memory consistency techniques that can efficiently support the observed categories of shared data objects [Ben90b]. This section briefly describes these mechanisms in the context of the sharing categories that they serve.

Write-many objects appear in many parallel programs wherein several threads simultaneously access and modify a single shared data object between explicit synchronization points in the program. If the programmer knows that individual threads access independent portions of the data, and the order in which individual threads are scheduled is unimportant, the program can tolerate a controlled amount of inconsistency between cached portions of the data. The programmer uses explicit synchronization (such as a lock or monitor) to denote the points in the program execution at which such inconsistencies are not tolerable. *Delayed updates* allow *Write-many* objects to be handled efficiently. When a thread modifies a *Write-many* object, we delay sending the update to remote copies of the object until remote threads could otherwise indirectly detect that the object has been modified. In this manner, by enforcing only the consistency required by the program's semantics, we avoid unnecessary synchronization and reduce the number of network packets needed for data motion and synchronization.

If the system knows that an object is shared in *Producer-Consumer* fashion, it can perform *eager object movement*. Eager object movement moves objects to the node at which they are going to be used in advance of when they are required. In the nearest neighbors example, this involves propagating the boundary element updates to where they will be required. In the best case, the new values are always available before they are needed, and threads never wait to receive the current values.

Migratory objects are accessed by a single thread at a time [Web89]. Typically, a thread performs multiple accesses to the object, including one or more writes, before the next thread starts accessing the object. Such an access pattern is typical of shared objects that are accessed only inside a critical section or through a work queue. The consistency protocol for migratory objects *migrates* the object to the new thread, provides it with read and write access (even if the first access is a read), and invalidates the original copy. This protocol avoids a write fault and a message to invalidate the old copy when the new thread first modifies the object.

Synchronization objects are supported by distributed locks. More elaborate synchronization objects, such as monitors and atomic integers, can be built on top of this. When a thread wants to acquire or test a global lock, it performs the lock operation on a local proxy for the distributed lock, and the local lock server arbitrates with the remote lock servers to perform the lock operation. Each lock has a queue associated with it that contains a list of the servers that need the lock. This queue facilitates efficient exchange of lock ownership. This mechanism is similar to that proposed by Goodman, et al [Goo89b].

Several categories of shared data objects can be handled in a straightforward fashion. *Private* objects are only accessed by one thread, so keeping them coherent is trivial. Replication is used for *Write-once* objects. *Read-mostly* objects are also candidates for replication since reads predominate writes. *Result* objects are handled by maintaining a single copy and propagating updates to this copy using the delayed update mechanism. Finally, *General Read-Write* objects are handled by the most convenient of the available consistency mechanisms.

Status

We are currently implementing Munin on an Ethernet network of SUN workstations. This implementation will allow us to assess the runtime costs of the delayed update queue and the other type-specific coherence mechanisms, as well as their benefits relative to standard consistency mechanisms.

In the Munin prototype system, the server associated with each processor is a user-level process running in the same address space as the threads on that processor. This makes the servers easier to debug and modify, which serves our goal of making the prototype system expandable, flexible and adaptable. We will be able to add mechanisms should we discover additional typical memory access patterns. We will be able to profile the system to evaluate system performance, and determine the performance bottlenecks. Running at user-level, the Munin servers will have access to all operating systems facilities, such as the file server and display manager, which will facilitate gathering system performance information.

The Munin prototype currently supports only six sharing types: *Read-only*, *Migratory*, *Producer-Consumer*, *Concurrent-write-shared*, *Result*, and *Reduction*. The sharing types *Write-once* and *Write-many* have been renamed *Read-only* and *Concurrent-write-shared*, respectively, since these terms more closely describe the manner in which objects of these types are accessed. *Reduction* is a new category for objects that are accessed via Fetch_and_Φ operations. Such operations are equivalent to a lock acquisition, a read, a write, and a lock release. Reduction objects are implicitly associated with a lock, and this lock is created automatically by the system at the time that the reduction object is created. An example of a *reduction* object is the global minimum in a parallel minimum path algorithm, which would be maintained via a Fetch_and_min. Reduction objects will be be treated as migratory objects, but Munin will execute the operation in-place at a fixed location.

WILLOW

Overview

Although we believe that Munin will provide an effective computing environment for a large class of shared memory applications, programs that exhibit fine-grain parallelism and synchronization cannot be adequately supported due to the high latency associated with accessing remote memory. However, with true shared memory multiprocessors, contention for shared memory usually becomes a limiting bottleneck above a few tens of processors. Recent research efforts have begun to address this issue, and to investigate the feasibility of providing shared memory on large-scale multiprocessors [Len90, Aga90, Che91, Goo88, SCI90]. The Willow project at Rice University represents one of these efforts. It is our belief that large-scale multiprocessors, providing both shared memory and fine-grain parallelism, will offer an advantage, in terms of both cost and ease of programming, over existing approaches to large-scale multiprocessing. Therefore, the research question that we have posed is: Is it possible, using available technologies, to design a true shared memory machine capable of supporting on the order of 1000 processors? Our work to date suggests that an affirmative response is indicated.

We are currently designing a sixty-four processor prototype of Willow, a shared memory multiprocessor intended to ultimately provide memory capacity and performance capable of supporting over a thousand commercial microprocessors. These processors are arranged in cluster fashion, with a multi-level cache and memory hierarchy. Willow is distinguished from other shared memory multiprocessors by several characteristics:

- a layered memory organization that significantly reduces the impact of *inclusion* [Bae88] on the cache hierarchy, and that exploits locality gradients (variations in locality between "local" and "remote"),

- support for *adaptive cache coherence*, an approach similar to Munin's type-specific coherence, whereby the consistency protocol used to manage *each cache line* is selected based on the expected or observed access behavior for the data stored in that line,

- an efficient distributed update protocol that supports both read combining and write merging in the cache hierarchy,

- support for a range of relaxed consistency protocols so as to avoid the adverse performance impact of unnecessary synchronization, and to allow aggressive buffering and reordering of write operations,

- the use of layered I/O to provide symmetric multiprocessing, and

- hardware support for hierarchical synchronization.

Our goal in the design of Willow is to provide hardware support in those areas where such support is most beneficial to performance, and to relegate to software those areas of system support requiring greatest flexibility. Thus, in the design of Willow, we take particular care to provide efficient support for lightweight threads, simple synchronization (locks and barriers), fast context switching, and low-latency memory access. One of Willow's novel features is the manner in which cache consistency is supported. Instead of attempting to devise a single protocol best suited for all applications, we employ an adaptive scheme. With adaptive caching, each cache line can be managed with a consistency protocol most appropriate to the manner in which the cache line is being used. Cache lines can employ any of the following update mechanisms: write-through, write-back on any synchronization (lock release or acquire), write-back on release, write-back on acquire, write-back whenever convenient, or no write-back (i.e., read-only). Supporting different update mechanisms allows us to provide a range of consistency models:

Sequential all reads and writes are totally ordered [Lam79]

Processor allows reads to bypass buffered writes [Goo89a]

Weak allows reads and writes to be buffered, but all must complete prior to any synchronization (e.g., a lock release or acquire) [Dub86]

Release allows reads and writes to be buffered, but all must complete prior to release [Gha90]

Status

We have identified and addressed what we believe to be the most serious impediments to scalability: enforcing sequential consistency, inefficient synchronization, memory latency and bandwidth limitations, bus saturation, memory contention, the necessity to enforce inclusion on lower-level caches, and non-symmetric I/O. We are evaluating the preliminary design of Willow, a scalable shared memory multiprocessor whose design addresses each of these issues in a substantive manner. We have defined a basic system architecture and are validating this design using detailed simulation and analytic techniques. This architecture is depicted in Figure 1.

Willow has a tree-like bus hierarchy that contains two types of modules. At the processor level, the leaves of the tree are processor-cache modules. All other levels consist of cache-memory modules. Figure 1 depicts Willow with a clustering factor of four, that is, four processor-cache modules are arranged in a cluster that share the processor-level bus with a memory-cache module. Four memory-cache modules on this level are arranged in a cluster that shares a bus with a memory-cache module on the second level. This fan-in continues until the lowest level is reached where only one memory-cache module exists. At this level, a global interconnect provides direct communication between the cache component of the lowest level module and all of the memory components of all the memory-cache modules. In a symmetrical Willow system of 1024 processors, a clustering factor of four implies one level of processors and five levels of memory-cache modules.

Each memory-cache module contains memory, a cache, and control and synchronization hardware. Each memory communicates with the level above it (i.e., toward the processors) via an intracluster bus, and communicates with any other memory using the global interconnect. Physical memory is divided among the memory-cache modules. These modules are uniformly addressed via a global address space. When a request appears on a bus, the memory and cache components of the module simultaneously look up the address. The address space is partitioned so that a memory module can determine if it can satisfy a memory request. If the data is not located in the memory or cache of the module, the request is propagated down to the next level. If data is not

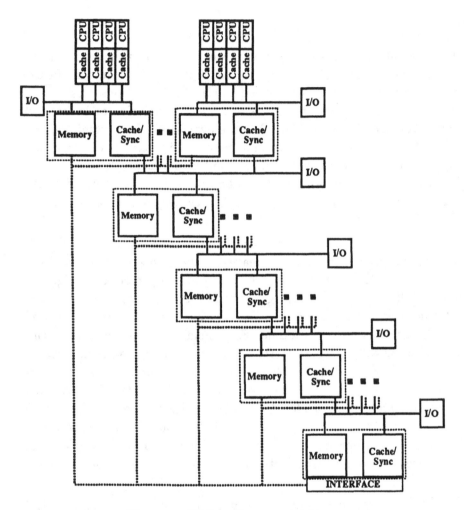

Figure 1: Willow System Architecture

found on the path from the processor to the memory module at the root of the hierarchy, the request is satisfied by the correct module over the global interconnect. Since all of the processors can access any part of the address space, Willow is a true shared memory system.

Data placement assumes special importance in Willow. Because we expect most parallel programs to exhibit strong locality, we have optimized the Willow architecture to be able to exploit this locality. Examples of this optimization include distributing memory over the levels, using adaptive caching, and placing I/O on the intrasystem busses. Part of our approach has been to try to build upon our relevant experience with Munin, a distributed shared memory system developed at Rice, by exploiting information about shared data access behavior and by incorporating our ideas about adaptive caching and relaxed consistency.

CONCLUSIONS

We have described two different approaches to scalable shared memory that we are currently developing at Rice University: Munin, a distributed shared memory system implemented entirely in software, and Willow, a true shared memory multiprocessor with extensive hardware support for scalability. Munin is designed to allow parallel programs written for shared memory multiprocessors to be executed efficiently on distributed memory multiprocessors. Willow is intended to be a true shared memory multiprocessor providing memory capacity and performance capable of supporting over a thousand commercial microprocessors. Implementation of Munin is in progress; we are still designing Willow.

We have described our goals and methods in the design of both systems, and we have described their distinguishing features. For Munin, these features include support for multiple consistency protocols, matching protocol to data object based on the expected pattern of accesses to that object (type-specific coherence), and a relaxed model of memory consistency to mask network latency and to minimize the number of messages required for keeping memory consistent.

The distinguishing features of Willow include a layered memory organization that significantly reduces the impact of *inclusion* on the cache hierarchy and that exploits locality gradients, and support for *adaptive cache coherence*, an approach similar to Munin's type-specific coherence, whereby the consistency protocol used to manage each cache line is selected based on the expected or observed access behavior for the data stored in that line.

ACKNOWLEDGEMENTS

Other members of the Computer Systems Laboratory have participated in the development of many of the ideas that we have presented. We thank Jim Carson, John Mellor-Crummey, Valerie Darbe, Elmootaz-bellah Elnozahy, Kathi Fletcher, Jay Greenwood, David Johnson, Pete Keleher, Mark Maxham, Rajat Mukherjee, and Peter Ostrin for their contributions.

REFERENCES

[Aga90]   Anant Agarwal, Beng-Hong Lim, David Kranz, and John Ku-biatowicz. APRIL: A processor architecture for multiprocess-ing. In *Proceedings of the 17th Annual International Sympo-sium on Computer Architecture*, pages 104–114, May 1990.

[Bae88]   Jean-Loup Baer aand Wen-Hann Wang. On the inclusion property for multi-level cache hierarchies. In *Proceedings of the 15th Annual International Symposium on Computer Ar-chitecture*, pages 73–80, May 1988.

[Ben90a] John K. Bennett, John B. Carter, and Willy Zwaenepoel. Adaptive software cache management for distributed shared memory architectures. In *Proceedings of the 17th Annual In-ternational Symposium on Computer Architecture*, pages 125–134, May 1990.

[Ben90b] John K. Bennett, John B. Carter, and Willy Zwaenepoel. Munin: Distributed shared memory based on type–specific memory coherence. In *Proceedings of the 1990 Conference on the Principles and Practice of Parallel Programming*, pages 168–175, March 1990.

[Ber88]   Brian N. Bershad, Edward D. Lazowska, and Henry M. Levy. PRESTO: A system for object-oriented parallel program-ming. *Software—Practice and Experience*, 18(8):713–732, August 1988.

[Cha89]   Jeffrey S. Chase, Franz G. Amador, Edward D. Lazowska, Henry M. Levy, and Richard J. Littlefield. The Amber sys-tem: Parallel programming on a network of multiprocessors. In *Proceedings of the Twelfth ACM Symposium on Operating Systems Principles*, pages 147–158, December 1989.

[Che91]   David R. Cheriton and Hendrik A. Goosen. Paradigm: A highly scalable shared-memory multicomputer architecture. *Computer*, 24(2):33–46 , February 1991.

[Egg88]   Susan J. Eggers and Randy H. Katz. A characterization of sharing in parallel programs and its application to coherency protocol evaluation. In *Proceedings of the 15th Annual International Symposium on Computer Architecture*, pages 373–383, May 1988.

[Egg89]   Susan J. Eggers and Randy H. Katz. The effect of sharing on the cache and bus performance of parallel programs. In *Proceedings of the 3rd International Conference on Architectural Support for Programming Languages and Systems*, pages 257–270, April 1989.

[Gha90]   Kourosh Gharachorloo, Daniel Lenoski, James Laudon, Phillip Gibbons, Anoop Gupta, and John Hennessy. Memory consistency and event ordering in scalable shared-memory multiprocessors. In *Proceedings of the 17th Annual International Symposium on Computer Architecture*, pages 15–26, May 1990.

[Goo88]   James R. Goodman and Philip J. Woest. The Wisconsin Multicube: A new large-scale cache-coherent multiprocessor. In *Proceedings of the 15th Annual International Symposium on Computer Architecture*, pages 422–431, May 1988.

[Goo89a]   James R. Goodman. Cache consistency and sequential consistency. Technical Report Technical report no. 61, SCI Committee, March 1989.

[Goo89b]   James R. Goodman, Mary K. Vernon, and Philip J. Woest. Efficient synchronization primitives for large-scale cache-coherent multiprocessor. In *Proceedings of the 3rd International Conference on Architectural Support for Programming Languages and Systems*, April 1989.

[Lam79]   Leslie Lamport. How to make a multiprocessor computer that correctly executes multiprocess programs. *IEEE Transactions on Computers*, C-28(9):690–691, September 1979.

[Len90]   Dan Lenoski, James Laudon, Kourosh Gharachorloo, Anoop Gupta, and John Hennessy. The directory-based cache coherence protocol for the DASH multiprocessor. In *Proceedings of the 17th Annual International Symposium on Computer Architecture*, pages 148–159, May 1990.

[Li86]   Kai Li. *Shared Virtual Memory on Loosely Coupled Multiprocessors*. Ph.D. thesis, Yale University, September 1986.

[Li89]   Kai Li and Paul Hudak. Memory coherence in shared virtual memory systems. *ACM Transactions on Computer Systems*, 7(4):321–359, November 1989.

[Lov88]   Tom Lovett and Shreekant Thakkar. The Symmetry multiprocessor system. In *Proceedings of the 1988 International Conference on Parallel Processing*, pages 303–310, August 1988.

[Ram88]   Umakishore Ramachandran, Mustaque Ahamad, and M. Yousef A. Khalidi. Unifying synchronization and data transfer in maintaining coherence of distributed shared memory. Technical Report GIT-CS-88/23, Georgia Institute of Technology, June 1988.

[Dub86]   Michel Dubois, Christoph Scheurich, and Fayé A. Briggs. Memory access buffering in multiprocessors. In *Proceedings of the 13th Annual International Symposium on Computer Architecture*, pages 434–442, May 1986.

[Sch87]   Christoph Scheurich and Michel Dubois. Correct memory operation of cache-based multiprocessors. In *Proceedings of the 14th Annual International Symposium on Computer Architecture*, pages 234–243, May 1987.

[Sit88]   Richard L. Sites and Anant Agarwal. Multiprocessor cache analysis using ATUM. In *Proceedings of the 15th Annual International Symposium on Computer Architecture*, pages 186–195, June 1988.

[So86]   K. So, F. Darema-Rogers, D. George, V.A. Norton, and G.F. Pfister. PSIMUL: A system for parallel simulation of the execution of parallel programs. Technical Report RC11674, IBM Research, 1986.

[SCI90]   P1596 Working Group of the IEEE Computer Society Microprocessor Standards Committee. SCI: An overview of extended cache-coherence protocols. Draft 0.59 P1596, February 5, 1990.

[Str87]   Bjarne Stroustrup. *The C++ Programming Language*. Addison-Wesley, 1987.

[Web89]   Wolf-Dietrich Weber and Anoop Gupta. Analysis of cache invalidation patterns in multiprocessors. In *Proceedings of the 3rd International Conference on Architectural Support for Programming Languages and Systems*, pages 243–256, April 1989.

Local-area Memory
in PLUS

R. Bisiani and M. Ravishankar
School of Computer Science
Carnegie Mellon University
Pittsburgh, PA 15213 USA
rb@cs.cmu.edu

Abstract

This paper describes the architecture and the design of a distributed-memory machine that supports a shared-memory programming model at a speed that is competitive with bus-based systems. This paper also includes the measurements of the amount of time required for memory accesses and synchronization operations on a two-node prototype of the architecture.

1. Introduction.

There are a few good reasons for using a distributed-memory architecture to implement a shared-memory multiprocessor, namely scalability, simplicity of construction and increased memory bandwidth. This is why we are building an experimental distributed-memory machine, called PLUS, that uses a combination of software and hardware techniques to support a shared-memory model at a speed that is competitive with bus-based multiprocessors.

Although PLUS is a full-fledged multiprocessor, the techniques introduced by PLUS can also be useful to interconnect existing machines like workstations and mainframes by extending their internal memory across a network. Therefore, we call PLUS's distributed shared-memory: *local-area memory*.

The main problem faced by any distributed-memory architecture is the latency of remote memory operations, which are often an order of magnitude slower than accesses to local memory and two orders of magnitude slower then accesses to the primary cache. Caching, in one form or another, is the obvious answer to this problem.

At one extreme, we have purely software-based caching and coherency protocols [2,3]. In these, memory is cached on a page-basis, with the main memory itself serving as a cache, and coherency is usually maintained by manipulating read and write permissions to the page. For example, if a given page is cached at many processors, each of them has read permission, but not write permission to the page. Whenever one writes to the page, it encounters a page fault and the fault handler executes a protocol that invalidates copies on other nodes, giving it sole ownership of the page. This scheme can be implemented virtually on any collection of processors interconnected by a network, but applications must require a limited amount of sharing and communication in order not to incur the overhead of the protocol too often.

At the other extreme, there are hardware-based caches that employ demand-caching and complex coherency protocols [1]. These are designed and built at considerable expense and their complexity increases significantly with the size of the system.

In the PLUS system, we combine the flexibility of software-based caching policies with the efficiency of coherence maintenance in hardware. The performance of the prototype seems to support the hypothesis that a software/hardware solution is feasible and competitive when compared with bus-based systems. A comparison of PLUS's solution with other techniques, e.g. demand caching with direct-mapped caches, is still unfeasible since these systems are not yet available.

In Sections 2 and 3 we describe the architecture of the machine. In Section 4 we explain the communication and coherence protocols. Finally, in Section 5 we present some measurements performed on a two-node prototype of the machine.

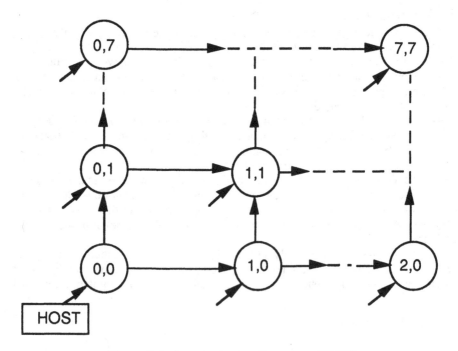

Figure 2-1. Communication Structure of PLUS.

2. Description of PLUS.

PLUS is a general-purpose, medium-scale multiprocessor which can have up to 64 processor nodes (see Figure 2-1).

Each node in the system is built around the Motorola 88000 processor and cache chip-set and contains up to 32 Mbytes of main memory, all of which are accessible from any node. The nodes are interconnected by a scalable, mesh-topology network for the purpose of integrating the distributed memory modules into a single, globally shared memory. The bandwidth of the mesh interconnection (as measured in the prototype) is about 30 Mbytes per second in each direction for each pair of nodes.

Each node can be connected to the outside world by means of an interface containing a Motorola DSP56001 and a SCSI controller; the interface processor can read and write the memory of the node it is connected to and has access to detailed performance information like cache hit-rate and a per-page trace of memory references. Typically, a system needs only one interface, although multiple interfaces can be useful to collect detailed performance information or to connect peripherals.

A logical page, which is 4 Kbytes in size, can be stored, under software control, in the main memory of several nodes. This action is called *replication* to distinguish it from the connotations associated with the word *caching*. System software can choose any one of the physical copies for mapping into the virtual address space of a given process; usually, picking the geographically nearest copy gives the best results. In this way, page replication reduces both the cost of remote memory references and contention for that logical page.

The software makes the replication scheme visible to the hardware via special *translation tables* maintained on each node, and the hardware is responsible for the consistency of all copies. Unlike most cache and memory consistency protocols which rely on invalidation, PLUS uses an update protocol for this purpose. That is, whenever a processor writes to a logical page, the consistency maintenance mechanism sends messages to update each copy; the granularity of an update can be as small as a byte.

The update protocol has the following advantages over an invalidation protocol:
- it eliminates the need for additional bits in memory to record if data are valid;
- since copies are never invalidated, the nodes that own a copy never have to incur the overhead of remote memory references;
- compared to a purely software-based scheme, the time-consuming layer of consistency protocol implemented in software is eliminated.

Obviously, write operations to replicated logical pages will usually take a relatively long time to complete. In PLUS, this cost is hidden by adopting a *weak-ordering* memory model [4]. When a processor writes to a replicated page, the task of updating all copies is carried out by independent, dedicated hardware and the processor can continue its task immediately after issuing the write operation. As a result, several write operations issued by a single processor can be concurrently in progress within the system, and they may even complete out of order. (In a strong-ordering model, write operations to memory take place and complete in the order in which they are issued.)

The PLUS coherency protocol guarantees that in the quiescent state, all memory copies will be consistent. In the dynamic state, however, one sometimes needs to explicitly ensure strong ordering of certain memory operations. For instance, a process may set a semaphore, update shared data structures, and then clear the semaphore, thus exposing the updated variables to other processes. Even in a weakly ordered memory system it is somehow necessary to ensure that a semaphore is cleared only after all earlier memory operations have completed. The PLUS system provides a *fence* mechanism for this purpose. That is, after a process executes a fence operation, any subsequent write or synchronization operation is suspended until all earlier memory operations have completed. The fence enforces strict ordering between operations preceding and following it. It is the programmer's (or the compiler's) responsibility to invoke this operation explicitly whenever necessary.

The last focus of research in PLUS concerns synchronization. The main problem here is to minimize the time spent by any process in a critical region, thus maximizing the amount of concurrent activity. In order to accomplish anything that is moderately involved, such as inserting or extracting an element from a shared queue, one has to execute a certain amount of code within a critical region; the simpler the synchronization operations, the larger the code. The conclusion is that simple synchronization operations are acceptable when they can be implemented efficiently, but providing a set of complex operations is better. In PLUS, we have identified about half-a-dozen such operations that are needed frequently.

Synchronization variables can be anywhere in memory, they can even be in replicated pages; the operations are carried out atomically at the location of the variable and all copies are kept consistent. The complex operations often eliminate several round-trip network transits between the invoking processor and the memory location, that would otherwise be necessary with simpler schemes. These semaphore operations are not part of the native instruction set of the Motorola 88000 processor, but have been defined by extending the processor's standard atomic-swap instruction (*xmem*).

There is one final optimization with respect to the extended operations in PLUS. The synchronization operations (such as *fetch-and-add*) return one 32-bit word result. As we shall see later on, synchronization operations almost always require remote memory access; replication is of no help in this case. Consequently, the result is available only after some delay. In order hide this latency, the processor that issued an extended operation is not required to wait for the result. Rather, the operation is carried out atomically and asynchronously by independent hardware, while the processor continues with normal instruction execution. It later issues a special *verify* operation to synchronize with the extended operation and retrieve its result. We call these operations *delayed* operations.

3. Implementation.

Figure 3-1 is an overview of a PLUS node, consisting of a Motorola MC88100 processor, a data Cache/Memory Management Unit (CMMU), a code CMMU, 512 Kbytes of fast SRAM memory, the Mbus subsystem, a network interface, and a host interface.

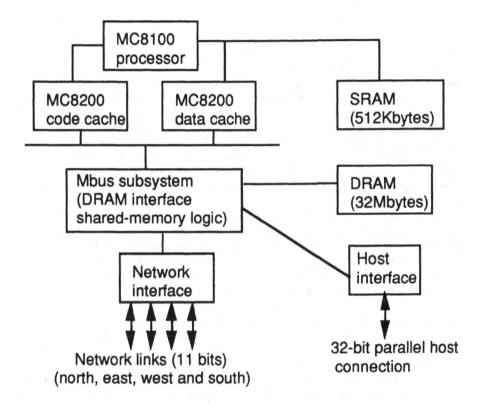

Figure 3-1. A PLUS Node.

The Mbus subsystem is the heart of the global shared-memory logic. It has up to 32 Mbytes of DRAM main memory which is part of the global shared-memory space, and it contains all the necessary logic for maintaining consistency of replicated pages, as well as executing the extended operations. This requires a number of special functional units, such as an ALU for carrying out the extended operations, and tables for maintaining replication information. Most of these units can be addressed as I/O-space devices. A substantial portion of the Mbus subsystem control logic is implemented in microcode.

The Network Interface connects the Mbus subsystem and the PLUS interconnection network, which is a 2-D mesh network. The network topology is not part of the focus of this research project. Our implementation employs an existing router (designed at Caltech) that can be connected in any rectangular mesh shape.. PLUS's implementation limits the size along either dimension to a maximum of 8 nodes. This configuration has sufficient bandwidth and speed for our purposes so that nodes are able to access remote memory locations. Whenever a node makes a remote memory reference, or updates a local memory location that is replicated on another node, the shared-memory control logic sends packets through the network to carry out the operation and keep all copies consistent. At the other end, the receiving node's shared memory control logic carries out the request and sends back a reply packet if necessary. The network interface provides an autonomous interface for buffering, and actually transmitting and receiving these network packets.

The host interface is a generic 32-bit interface between the node and a general-purpose workstation or *host*. This external host can address any location that the node processor can address via the Mbus, including the local as well as remote main memory, and other local functional units. A host is necessary to configure certain programmable logic array devices on the PLUS nodes, to download initialization code into the system, and to carry out physical I/O operations on behalf of the PLUS system. There is also a FIFO buffer in this interface, in which memory accesses made by the local processor are recorded. The host can monitor the dynamic memory access patterns via this buffer, in order to tune the page replication structure and thus improve performance.

The 512 K-bytes of SRAM memory reside on the data P-bus of the processor. Since the code and data caches are relatively small (16K bytes each), one can greatly improve the performance of selected applications with the help of the fast SRAM memory. However, there are a couple of limitations to it: this memory is virtually addressed, and it is private to the node. That is, it has to be explicitly managed by the user, and it cannot be addressed from other remote nodes.

4. Replication and Coherency Mechanisms.

Given that a logical page can be replicated on multiple nodes, and given the assumption of a weakly-ordered memory system, there are three basic requirements:

- The first is that in the quiescent state, all copies of any replicated page should be consistent. That is, if all processors stop writing to memory, eventually (when the pending write operations have finished propagating through the system) all copies of any replicated page should become identical. In a replicated, weakly-ordered memory system, write operations may finish out of order, and there can be transient inconsistencies among replicated copies.

- The second requirement of the PLUS system is that a single processor still sees its own actions in a strongly-ordered way. That is, whenever it reads any memory location, it receives the latest value that it wrote to that location, assuming no other processor wrote to the same location in the meantime. Without this assumption (*write-read consistency*) writing meaningful and understandable programs would be extremely tedious.

- Finally, if a node executes the *fence* operation, all its operations succeeding the fence should be strongly ordered with respect to its operations preceding the fence. That is, the former can proceed only after all of the latter have completed. Whenever necessary, the fence mechanism allows a user to selectively impose a strong ordering on the actions of one processor as seen by other processors.

In addition, one must not forget the need to keep *cached* locations consistent with replicated memory. This is especially tricky as caching policies and consistency mechanisms are totally different from the replication scheme. This Section describes the basic ideas behind the solutions to these issues in the PLUS architecture.

The consistency maintenance protocol in PLUS is quite straightforward: First, all physical copies of a given logical page have to be ordered (by software) in a linear list called the *copy-list*, the first copy is called the *master copy*. Any write or synchronization operations to the logical page by any processor must always begin at the master copy and propagate down the copy-list. This is sufficient to guarantee that the memory system is weakly coherent.

In order to allow the hardware to maintain consistency of replicated pages, the replication structure is exposed to the hardware by means of special *translation tables* distributed among all the nodes. Each node includes a *master-copy* table and a *next-copy* table, each containing one entry per local physical page. The first table contains pointers (i.e., node address and physical page location on that node) to the master copy for each local physical page, while the latter points to the next copy, if any, along the physical page's copy-list. Note that as far as the hardware is concerned, the replication structure is static. It can only be modified by software, and whenever this happens, the tables must be updated.

For any given logical page, a processor is free to map any convenient physical copy, local or remote, into its address space. The physical address obtained after a logical address undergoes address translation identifies both a physical node and the physical address of the location on that node.

The 32-bit physical address is decoded into three regions, depending on address bits 31-20, as shown in Table 4-1.

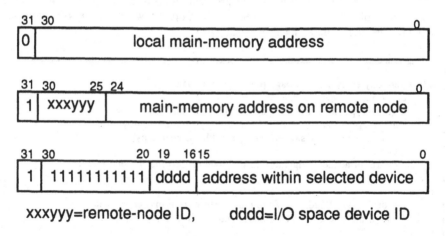

xxxyyy=remote-node ID,   dddd=I/O space device ID

Table 4-1. Structure of the Physical Address.

Bits 30-25 of a remote main memory address, shown as *xxxyyy* above, are actually the 6-bit remote node ID. This field is further divided into two 3-bit subfields: bits 30-28 (*xxx*) and bits 27-25 (*yyy*), forming an <*x,y*> coordinate address in the 2-D mesh topology. If the processor executes a read operation, it is performed on the addressed node. If it is a write or an extended operation, however, the coherence maintenance hardware carries out the algorithm of Table 4-2.

```
if (physical address points to local copy) {
        if (master-copy entry for this page points to local page) {
        carry out the operation;
        if (next-copy entry for this page points to a valid next copy) {
                get the physical address of the next copy from next-copy table
                send an update message to the node with the next copy;
                }
        } else {
        get the physical address of the master copy from master-copy table;
        forward the operation to the node with the master copy
        }
} else {
        /* physical address points to remote node and location on that node */
        /* NOTE -- this may not be the master copy!! */
        forward the operation to the remote node;
}
```

Table 4-2. Write and Synchronization Protocols.

When a node receives a write or synchronization operation request from a remote node as a result of the above, it executes the steps shown in Table 4-3. Note that such a request must be to a local physical page.

```
if (master-copy entry for this page points to local page) {
        carry out the operation;
        if (next-copy entry for this page points to a valid next copy) {
            get the physical address of the next copy from next-copy table;
            send an update message to the node with the next copy;
        } else {
            return an acknowledgement to the node originating the operation;
        }
} else {
        get the physical address of the master copy from master-copy table;
        forward the operation to the node with the master copy;
}
```

Table 4-3. Remote Request Protocols.

Finally, when a node receives an update request, it performs the steps of Table 4-4. Note that such a request must be addressed to a local physical page.

The reason for the acknowledgement messages will become clear in a moment. Following a quick examination, it should be obvious that the above mechanism guarantees that the memory system is weakly-coherent (assuming that the network preserves the chronological ordering of messages between any given pair of nodes).

The remaining two requirements of write-read consistency and strong ordering of operations around a fence are met by means of a hardware *write tag buffer* (WTB) on each node. Whenever a processor writes to a remote location, or a location that is replicated on other nodes, the physical-address presented by the processor is captured in the WTB. (If no free WTB entry is available, the operation is suspended.) The same thing happens if the processor invokes an extended operation. The WTB entry is freed after the operation is carried out on all the copies and an acknowledgement is finally received. The WTB enables write-read consistency to be achieved by suspending the processor whenever it reads a location that matches a valid entry in the WTB. The fence mechanism is implemented by suspending any write or extended operation issued after a fence, until the WTB is empty, i.e., all outstanding entries are acknowledged.

```
write (update) local memory;
if (next-copy entry for this page points to a valid next copy) {
        get the physical address of the next copy from next-copy table;
        send an update message to the node with the next copy;
} else {
        return an acknowledgement to the node originating the operation;
}
```

Table 4-4. Update Requests Protocols.

PLUS can also support execution in a completely strong-ordering mode. In this mode (which is enabled by a control bit that can be turned on selectively by software) every write or extended operation to memory by a given node must complete before the next such operation by that node is allowed to start. This ensures that memory always reflects the true ordering of operations as issued by the processor, and is useful for running programs or portions of programs that rely on a strong-ordering memory model.

Finally, note that while the master-copy and next-copy tables capture the static replication structure, in the PLUS architecture it is impossible to track the dynamically cached entries in order to keep the caches coherent with replicated memory. For this reason, we rely on software-enforced restrictions on caching policies to keep both cached and replicated copies coherent. If a node has no physical copy of a given logical page, it cannot cache the page at all. The coherency mechanism in PLUS relies on the page's copy-list to keep everything consistent, but the copy-list is not concerned with nodes that have no physical copy of the page. If a node has a physical copy of a replicated page, it should cache it only in write-through mode. This ensures that whenever the processor on the node writes to that page, the operation comes through the cache where it is visible to the coherency maintenance hardware. In addition, whenever some other node writes to this logical page, any cached entry should be either updated or invalidated when the physical memory on the node gets written. In a PLUS node, the caches are part of the Motorola MC88200 CMMU devices, which monitor or *snoop* writes to their local memory requested by remote processors, and invalidate any cached entry for that memory location.

5. Cost of Basic Operations.

At this time we have two working nodes and we could measure the cost of some of the basic operations. Although we have a few applications already running, it would be premature to report on their performance because the operating system software that handles replication is still not completely functional.

reads	local	520
	remote, locally replicated, one hop	520
	remote, not replicated, one hop	3560
	each extra hop	add 200
writes	local, not-replicated	330
	local, replicated	680
	remote, not replicated, weak ordering	640
	remote, not replicated, strong ordering	3410
synchronization	fetch&add, local	3100
	fetch&add, remote, immediate	5450
	fetch&add, remote, delayed	2750
	enqueue, local	4300
	enqueue, remote, immediate	6480
	enqueue, remote,delayed	2860
	dequeue, local	4320
	dequeue, remote, immediate	6340
	dequeue, remote, delayed	2900

Table 5-1. Cost of Basic Operations in Nanoseconds, Stride 4 (Always a Cache Miss).

We measured the number of operations that a node can sustain when reading, writing, updating a replicated page and synchronizing (see Table 5-1). All of these operations but read are pipelined. The timings are representative of the maximum peak rate at which the machine can perform these operations; in practice, many programs require a lower access rate. Measurements were performed by using an internal μsecond timer and averaged over a long sequence of operations in order to smooth all the possible discontinuities. The stride of the read and write operations was set in order to always cause a cache miss; the data cache write policy was write-through. The *delayed synchronization* entry does not include the latency between the issuing of an operation and the reading of the result; this is representative of the cost of synchronization using PLUS's *delayed* operations.

6. Conclusions.

We have described the structure of a distributed-memory machine that implements a shared-memory model in hardware. The emphasis of this machine is on simple protocols, on hardware that could be easily integrated and on independence from the topology and technology of the interconnection network.

The measurements performed on the prototype show that a weak-ordering memory model is necessary in order to get reasonable performance of write operations. Synchronization is quite fast but only measurements on real applications will be able to show if these operations are fast enough.

Non-demand caching is possible and efficient, at least in those cases when the memory allocation can be suggested to the system by the programmer (or by a tool).

The performance of replication depends heavily on the load of the system and the technique must be used sparingly. We feel that replication should be handled automatically by means of tools that measure the remote-access rate and merge the user knowledge of the application with the measurements.

References.

1. Agarwal, A., Simoni, R., Hennessy, J., and Horowitz, M. An Evaluation of Directory Schemes for Cache Coherence. In *15th Int. Symp. on Comp. Arch.*, IEEE, May 1988, pp. 280-289.

2. Forin, A., Barrera, J., and Sanzi, R. The Shared Memory Server. In *Intl. Winter USENIX Conference*, USENIX Association, San Diego, CA, February 1989, pp. 229-244.

3. Lee,K. and Hudack,P.. Memory Coherence in Virtual Shared-Memory Systems. *In Proceedings of the Fifth Annual Symposium on the Principles of Distributed Systems.*, ACM, 1986, pp.229-239.

4. Scheurich, C.E. *Access Ordering and Coherence in Shared-memory Multiprocessors*, Ph.D. dissertation, Also published as Tech, Rep. No. CENG 89-19, Computer Engineering - University of Southern Califirnia, May 1989.

A Dynamic Memory Management Scheme for Shared Memory Multiprocessors

Tam M. Nguyen [1,2]

Vason P. Srini [2]

[1] IBM T.J. Watson Research Center
P.O. Box 704
Yorktown Heights, NY 10598

[2] Computer Science Division
University of California
Berkeley, CA 94720

Abstract

In contrast to message-based systems, shared memory multiprocessors allow for (both time and space) efficient data sharing, and thus are more suitable for execution models that exploit medium grain parallelism. Automatic and efficient management of the limited globally shared address space allows larger programs to run in shorter time. In this paper, we propose a hybrid heap-stack mechanism, called ELPS (Explicitly Linked Paging Stack), for dynamic allocation and deallocation of space. ELPS allows the space of each parallel task to expand and contract dynamically, resulting in much more efficient sharing of space than static partitioning. The distributed link storage scheme allows a higher degree of scalability than the centralized table approach.

ELPS can be implemented with or without hardware support. It has been used to manage the memory space for parallel execution of Prolog. Simulation results show that our current implementation of ELPS incurs an average of 2% overhead (11% without hardware support), while satisfying the memory requirement of parallel execution to keep pace with the potential speedup.

INTRODUCTION

Parallel processing on multiprocessors involves partitioning a problem for execution on two or more processors. Correspondingly, the memory space (either virtual or physical) must be partitioned to provide work spaces required for parallel processing. In contrast to message-based systems, shared memory multiprocessors allow for more efficient data sharing.

Memory management generally contains two aspects: space and time. Sufficient space must be available to store code and data being processed. The stored code and data must also be quickly accessible to keep up with the processing power of the system. As the number of processors increases, memory becomes a more critical resource that needs to be properly managed for efficient parallel execution.

Static partitioning offers the simplest solution to managing the data space globally shared among the parallel tasks or processors. However, static partitioning is inadequate for parallel execution models with unpredictable memory usage. In this paper, we present a hybrid heap-stack mechanism, called ELPS (Explicitly Linked Paging Stack), for dynamic allocation and deallocation of space. ELPS is a two level memory management scheme that provides both the flexibility of the heap and the efficiency of the stack. The space of each parallel task may expand and contract dynamically, thus resulting in much more efficient sharing of the available space. ELPS is particularly suitable for managing the globally shared memory space for parallel execution of Prolog, since Prolog programs are generally memory intensive and have unpredictable memory usage patterns.

In this paper, we first briefly discuss the characteristics of Prolog and the conceptual view of its parallel execution. We then review the various memory models proposed for parallel execution on a shared memory space. We provide the details of ELPS and discuss how it overcomes the limitations of static partitioning. Finally, we present some simulation results on the efficiency of this dynamic memory management scheme.

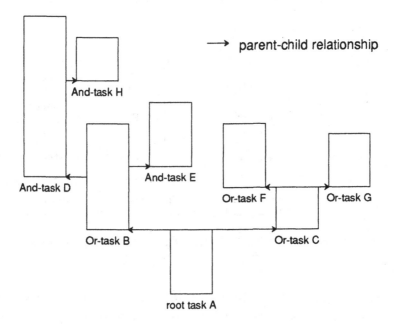

Figure 1: Conceptual View of a Cactus Stack

PARALLEL EXECUTION OF PROLOG

Prolog

Prolog is a programming language based on the theoretical foundation
of logic [5]. It has the following unique combination of features: logical
variables (single-assignment), unification (pattern matching), and non-
determinism (via backtracking). Due to the non-deterministic nature of
Prolog programs, a stack mechanism is the most efficient for reclaiming
unused space upon backtracking, as demonstrated by the Warren Abstract Machine (WAM) [9]. The WAM stack model greatly reduces the
need for expensive garbage collection [8].

Memory Models for Parallel Execution

Various parallel execution models have been proposed to exploit the
AND-parallelism and OR-parallelism that inherently exists in Prolog
programs [3, 10, 6, 4]. These parallel models use an extended stack
mechanism, called the *cactus stack*. *Figure 1* shows a conceptual view
of the cactus stack, which is a tree structure with a stack at each node.

316

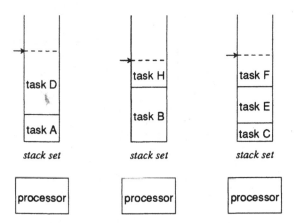

Figure 2: Stack Set per Processor Memory Model

Execution begins with the *root* stack. A new stack is created for each task spawned and is branched out from the current stack. Depending on the model, execution on the parent stack can either suspend or continue in parallel with execution on the child stack.

Implementation of a stack requires a chunk of memory, a stack base pointer, and a stack top pointer. In actual implementation, each branch of the conceptual cactus stack may be an independent stack or several branches may share the same stack, since all branches are not active at the same time. The sequential WAM requires a set of three stacks, which will be referred to as a *stack set*. The WAM-based parallel execution models designed for shared memory systems use three general types of memory models: a stack set for each *processor*, a stack set for each *task*, and a stack set for *one or more tasks*. In the first type, multiple tasks are allowed to share the same stack, interleaving the data space onto the same stack (*figure 2*). Execution models that use this memory model include RAP-WAM [3] and APEX [4] for AND-parallelism, and the SRI Model [10] and Aurora [6] for OR-parallelism.

In this scheme, the space previously occupied by a terminated task cannot be reclaimed if it lies below the space of an active task. To prevent leaving dead spaces in a stack and to ensure that the space of the executing task is at the top of the stack, various ordering schemes are used in the scheduling of the tasks for parallel execution at the cost

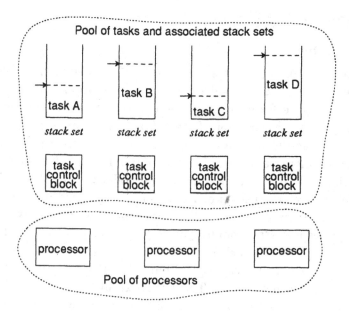

Figure 3: Stack Set per Task Memory Model

of some restriction on parallelism (e.g., the various *steal rules* described in [1, 3, 4]).

In a stack set for each task, the task space is independent of the processors (shown in *figure 3*), thus allowing for more flexible scheduling and a higher degree of parallelism. For example, the PPP [2] assign one stack set to each AND-task and each OR-task. The entire stack set can be discarded when a task terminates.

The third type of memory model is a relaxation of the first type, allowing for more stack sets than the number of processors. This relaxation has been shown to increase the degree of parallelism, resulting in faster execution in APEX [4]. Borgwardt's model [1] for AND-, OR-, and stream parallelism also falls under this category, allowing the AND-tasks to share the stack set, while creating a new stack for each OR-task.

STATIC PARTITIONING

The Problem

Static partitioning is the simplest way of managing the globally shared space. The space is divided into equal partitions, one for each stack set. The space for each stack set is further subdivided for each of the stacks. When the number of stack sets is very large, the space reserved for each stack is very small and thus the the chance of stack overflow is greatly increased. This is particularly true of the stack-set-per-task models, such as the PPP Execution Model [2]. In the PPP execution model, tens of thousands of tasks may be spawned over the life time of a program to exploit the medium grain parallelism. Many of these tasks go into sleeping state, holding on to their execution stat and data spaces for potential future backtracking. These sleeping tasks accumulate over time, tying up statically assigned but unused memory space that could be used to spawn new tasks. The PPP Execution Model takes the simple approach of reverting to sequential execution when no more space is available for spawning new tasks.

Potential Solutions

Three well known techniques may be used individually or together to reduce the problems of static partitioning. While they are very useful for some situations, they each have shortcomings of their own. They are as follow:

- *Virtual Memory:* Extending the virtual address space reduces the chance of overflow. The globally shared address space can be extended up to the smaller of the widths of the processor's memory address register and the internal processor datapath. The virtual address space, which is typically 32-bit in present technology, is insufficient when it is divided for tens of thousands of tasks.

  Segmentation techniques that use a segment register (or a segment table) to extend the global address space do not extend the *shared* address space, since not all segments are accessible at any given time, without reloading the segment base registers.

- *Garbage Collection:* Normal execution is suspended while reclaiming unused space. Parallel garbage collection is difficult to perform efficiently. If the statically partitioned space containing valid data is exceeded, it cannot be further compacted. Furthermore, if a task terminates in the near future, its entire space can be quickly discarded. In this case, the time spent to garbage collect before the task terminates can be saved by obtaining new free space and delaying garbage collection until no more free space is available.

- *Copy When Overflow:* When a stack overflows, a larger area of free space may be used to copy over the old stack. The complexity and cost of this operation are similar to those of parallel garbage collection, since the pointer data must be updated to point to new addresses. Furthermore, copy-when-overflow does not deal with the underflow problem. When the stack usage shrinks, the unused space on top of the stack remains allocated to that stack.

An alternative approach to static partitioning is dynamic allocation. It may stand alone as the memory management technique for parallel execution. It may also be integrated with one or more of the three techniques described above for more completely memory management. In the next section, we will describe a scheme for dynamic allocation and deallocation which allows for more efficient sharing of the global address space.

THE ELPS MODEL

Model Overview

The schemes previously described maintain a contiguous address space for each stack. An alternative would be to allocate address space in small ranges as needed, and linking these segments to form a conceptual stack. This section presents such a scheme, called *ELPS (Explicitly Linked Paging Stack)*, which is basically a heap management mechanism adapted to provide dynamically sized stacks.

The concept of linked segments of memory is a classic one. Operating systems manage pools of free pages to be allocated to user processes. Support libraries for the C programming language contain memory allocation/deallocation functions for storage of dynamic data. One important distinction is that in these memory management support, allocation and deallocation of space must be explicitly requested by the programmer. ELPS provides automatic (implicit) memory management support for stacks in a parallel execution environment.

Page Partitioning

In ELPS, the globally shared address space is divided into many small (thousands of words) chunks of equal size, called *pages*. Since it is difficult to determine at compile time (or task creation time) how much space a task will need, equal sized chunks are adequate and require less bookkeeping than variable sized chunks. Each task may need one or more stacks. Initially, one page is allocated to each stack. The use of the stack occurs in the usual fashion, with the top of stack pointer being modified at each push or pop operation. As the stack overflows, additional pages are allocated and linked with existing pages. As the stacks underflows into a page below, the page on top can be unlinked and put back into the free-page-list. In virtual memory, the mapping of a contiguous virtual space onto discontiguous physical pages is implicit in that a hardware mechanism automatically translates every virtual address into a physical one. The ELPS links are explicit in that no address translation is required. If it is implemented on top of virtual memory, then the links are virtual addresses. If there is no virtual memory, then the links are physical addresses.

Link Management

Figure 4 compares fix-sized stacks with ELPS variable-sized stacks. The free pages are linked together in the *free-page-list*. A processor requesting for a free page must lock the head of the list. To reduce contention for the lock, one free-page-list may be kept for each processor and a processor may be allowed to pick up a page from another processor's free-page-list. Each page has two links, pointing to the page above and the page below it in the stack. Each page may also contain additional information regarding the page, such as page size or relative ordering of pages in a stack.

The links and information fields may be stored separately in the page itself or combined together in a table. *Figure 5* shows two possible implementations. In both implementations, an address consists of two parts: the page number p and an offset to the data area d. In the first implementation (figure 5(a)), the links are stored together with the data

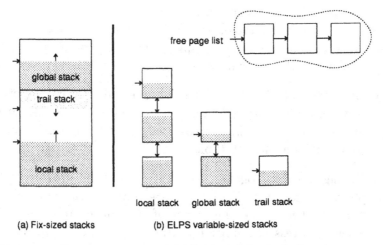

Figure 4: Fix-sized versus ELPS Variable-sized Stacks

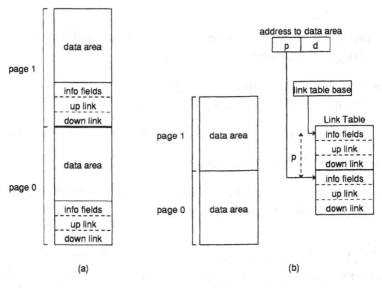

Figure 5: Two Link Storage Schemes for ELPS

in each page. In the second implementation (figure 5(b)), the links are collected in a central table, separate from data storage. An indexing scheme is needed to access the link table. We choose to implement the first scheme for the following reasons:

- Since the links for each page are accessed only by the owner task, distributed link storage allows interference free access to the links by parallel tasks, while centralized storage introduces unnecessary contention on the link table.

- Having the links together with the data would provide better cache performance. A task that accesses data at the bottom of a page is more likely to be the owner of that page, and thus would also need to access the links for that page. On the other hand, the centralized scheme would require the links of each page to be stored in a separate cache blocks to avoid extraneous contention on the cache block, thus wasting much of the space in each cache block.

Qualitative Evaluation

Advantages

The dynamic memory management style of ELPS has a number of advantages over other schemes. They are:

- more efficient sharing of the global address space than static partitioning, reducing the need for garbage collection.

- much less expensive overflow handling than copy-when-overflow.

- more efficient handling of underflow.

- much simpler hardware support than virtual memory and does not require address translation which adds complexity to the cache system.

The heap style management may also be quite appropriate for garbage collection [8]. Garbage collection typically involves copying valid data to a new section of memory, and deallocating the old section which include invalid data. Due to the link structure in ELPS, any free page can be readily obtained for copying data from pages in current use, and pages in current use can easily be replaced by other pages.

Challenges

This heap-style management scheme introduces complexity which can potentially affect performance. They are as follows:

- *Efficiency of overflow/underflow checking.* Hardware support can be used to monitor access to a stack data area or changes to the stack pointer. If so, overflow/underflow checking can be done concurrently with the stack push/pop operations. Without any hardware support, the efficiency of overflow/underflow checking depends largely on program behavior: the frequency in which items are put on and removed from the stack.

- *Frequency of page crossing.* Crossing a page boundary on an overflow takes additional time to follow the link. It is expected that the page size is chosen to be large enough such that overflow is infrequent. A potential problem would exist in the case where stack storage and removal occur frequently at the page boundary.

- *Fragmentation.* In ELPS, there are two types of internal fragmentation that can occur. (Since the pages are of equal size and may be assigned to any task, there is no external fragmentation.) The first type of internal fragmentation occurs at the end of each non-top-most page, where some space is left unused because a contiguous data object does not fit and must be placed on the next page. The second type occurs at the end of the top-most page on the stack, the space is left unused when a task goes to sleep. If the page size is properly chosen, the internal fragmentation can be minimized and may be insignificant. Compared with static partitioning, internal fragmentation of ELPS pages is much smaller than internal fragmentation of the fixed address range. From that view, reduced fragmentation is the biggest advantage of ELPS.

SIMULATION RESULTS

An event-driven multiprocessor simulator was written to evaluate the performance of ELPS for the PPP Execution Model [2]. This simulator allows for complete system simulation: from the instruction set level to the memory architecture level with caches and communication protocols. The simulated multiprocessor has VLSI-PLMs [7] as the processing units and a single bus with coherent caches. Proper synchronization is enforced among the processors.

Seven Prolog benchmark programs were chosen for our study of ELPS in parallel execution. These programs exhibit a variety of parallelism characteristics and memory usage. *Table 1* lists the benchmarks, their static code sizes, and a brief explanation for each. Prolog programs are annotated for parallel execution, compiled into assembly code, and loaded into the simulator.

Table 1: Benchmark Code Sizes and Descriptions

Benchmark	lines of Prolog code	Description
boyer	396	Boyer-Moore theorem prover
chat	1196	natural language parser
ckt4	48	circuit design for a 2-to-1 mux
compiler	2271	a Prolog compiler
qsd200	18	quicksort on list of 200 data items
query	71	multiple queries of a simple database
tp3	763	Overbeek's theorem prover

Execution Time Overhead

Table 2 shows the execution times of the programs for three configurations: static partitioning, ELPS with hardware support, and ELPS with software only. The overhead percentage is computed by $(\frac{ELPS\ time}{static\ partitioning\ time} - 1) \times 100$. To study the overhead of ELPS, the number of tasks is set to a maximum of 64 for all configurations. ELPS page size is set at 4K words so that overflow does not occur in most programs[1]. Furthermore, the multiprocessor system is configured to single cycle memory to factor out the cache effects. No time is charged for checks with hardware support, and two cycles are charged for each overflow check with software only. Without any overflow, the overhead of ELPS includes the extra time incurred by: (a) the checks for page overflow (if software only), and (b) the checks for variable locality (for OR-parallelism and always done in software). A variable is local (or internal) to a task if it exists on one of the stacks of that task. The linked

---
[1] Overflows occur only in boyer and tp3.

Table 2: Overhead of ELPS Checking and Overflow Handling

benchmark	static partition (cycle)	ELPS with hardware support (cycle)	(%*)	ELPS with software only (cycle)	(%*)
query	34757	35969	3.5	39142	12.6
qsd200	67050	67610	0.8	75788	13.0
compiler	1088084	1101923	1.3	1190858	9.4
ckt4	1468717	1516685	3.3	1670465	13.7
chat	2290302	2347801	2.5	2580181	12.7
tp3	3213414	3254666	1.3	3449535	7.3
boyer	51370794	52008092	1.2	56096531	9.2
arith mean			2.0		11.1
geom mean			2.0		10.9

* percentage of overhead in execution time

list of pages forming the stack may need to be traversed to determine if the variable lies in one of the pages.

With hardware support for overflow checking, the overhead for all programs ranges from 0.8% to 3.5% (2% on average). With software-only checking, the overhead is quite a bit higher, ranging from 7.3% to 13.7% (11% on average). Thus hardware support provides an average of 9% improvement in total execution time over software-only checking.

Table 3 shows a breakdown of ELPS behavior. In this table, the page size is set to 1K for greater overflow frequency. The first column shows the average number of cycles between checks. The average over all programs, except query, is 87 cycles between checks. Query requires very infrequent overflow checks (one every 4831 cycles) because it spends most of the time reading a database and writes very infrequently to the stacks. The next two columns show the number of overflows and the average time required to handle an overflow. The number of overflows depend greatly on the page size. An advantage of ELPS is very fast overflow handling which is in tens of cycles.

The new page request percentages (number of new page requests/number of overflows) indicate the degree of stack pointer movement across page boundaries. When a page overflow occurs for the first

Table 3: Behavior of ELPS Checking and Overflow Handling

benchmark	cycles between checks	number of over-flows	avg overflow handling time	new page requests (%)	times cannot spawn*
ckt4	126	0	-	-	0
query	4831	0	-	-	23
qsd200	84	1	31	100.0	137
compiler	73	26	26	69.2	0
tp3	80	129	15	52.7	279
chat	68	357	2	2.5	0
boyer	92	1851	23	98.3	93993

* under static partitioning

time, a new page is obtained. When the stack underflows to the previous page, the current page is retained (lazy deallocation) so that subsequent overflows do not require new pages. Boyer and chat are examples of opposite extreme behaviors. The stacks in boyer primarily grow upward (98.3% new page requests), while the stacks in chat backtracks very frequently (only 2.5% new page requests). For chat, lazy deallocation is clearly advantageous. It results in an average overflow handling time of only 2 cycles.

The last column in table 3 shows the number of times that new tasks could not be spawned because the number of tasks is limited (to 64), with all unused space statically allocated to other tasks. This column shows the key advantage of ELPS. With ELPS, memory is efficiently distributed to keep up with the demand for a very large number of tasks. For ELPS, this unable-to-spawn column would typically be zero. While ELPS provide memory space support for a high degree of parallelism, the resulting speedup depends on the ability of the scheduler to efficiently exploit parallelism (i.e., to spawn a parallel task only when the amount of work to be done by the new task is sufficiently higher than the overhead of task creation, communication, and termination).

Fragmentation is another performance measure of ELPS. *Internal* fragmentation occurs when the space at the top of each page is insufficient to store the data object. *External* fragmentation is the amount of space unused on the section of the page beyond the top of stack pointer. Compared to a smaller page size, a larger page size will tend to have greater external fragmentation but less internal fragmentation. For the chosen set of benchmark programs, internal fragmentation is consistently very small, averaging less than 10 words per 1K word page (less than 1%). External fragmentation varies greatly from program to program. Compared with static partitioning, ELPS has slightly more internal fragmentation (none in static partitioning), but much less external fragmentation (ELPS page size is much smaller than a static partition).

Parallelism Gained

A key point of ELPS is efficient sharing of the global address space to allow a very large number of tasks to be spawned. The significant potential of advantage of ELPS over static partitioning can be illustrated by a specific example. Consider a 32-bit address space and a set of programs that use tens of words up to 1M words for each stack. For static partitioning, stack must be configured to the largest possible size to avoid overflow. If each stack is sized at 1M words, there can be at most $\frac{2^{32}}{2^{20}} = 2^{12} = 4096$ *stacks*. Suppose that only 20% of the stacks are near the 1M-word usage while the others are less than 1K (such unpredictable usage is often the case for parallel execution of Prolog under the PPP model). Thus 20% of the space can be partitioned into pages of 1M word each, while the other 80% can be partitioned into pages of 1K word each. Hence, there can be at most $\frac{2^{32}}{2^{20}} \times 0.2 + \frac{2^{32}}{2^{10}} \times 0.8 = 3356262$ *stacks*, or almost 3.4 million more stacks with ELPS than with static partitioning. While the exact number varies with each program, ELPS can potentially support millions more tasks (each with one or more stacks) than static partitioning without the need for garbage collection or other schemes to handle overflow, while allowing the tasks to fully share the global address space.

CONCLUDING REMARKS

We have presented a two-level dynamic memory management scheme called ELPS, which is suitable for parallel execution models with unpredictable memory usage. In the first level, this hybrid mechanism is a heap which allows efficient sharing of the global space. In the second level, it is a stack which allows efficient space reclamation.

The memory model has been simulated for parallel execution of Prolog programs. The detail simulations indicate the feasibility of the model and provide its performance measurements. The average overhead of ELPS is 2% with hardware support and 11% with software only. ELPS provides the memory management needed to keep up with the memory demand for parallel execution, thus increasing the degree of potential parallelism. To obtain a high overall speedup, proper scheduling and granularity control must be coupled with this potential for a very large (millions) number of tasks.

For more complete memory management, ELPS may be integrated with a garbage collector to reclaim unused space within each page. Due to the memory usage nature and the highly dynamic life times of the parallel tasks, a local garbage collector should do well in reclaiming unused space and not interfere with the execution of other tasks.

References

[1] P. Borgwardt. Parallel prolog using stack segments on shared-memory multiprocessors. In *Proceedings of the 1984 International Symposium on Logic Programming*, Atlantic City, NJ, Feb. 1984.

[2] B.S. Fagin and A.M. Despain. Performance studies of a parallel prolog architecture. In *14th International Symposium on Computer Architecture*, June 1987.

[3] M. Hermenegildo. An abstract machine for restricted and-parallel execution of logic programs. In *Proceedings of the 3rd International Conference on Logic Programming*, London, 1986.

[4] Y.-J. Lin. *A Parallel Implementation of Logic Programs*. PhD thesis, University of Texas, Austin, August 1988. Technical Report AI88-84.

[5] J.W. Lloyd. *Foundations of Logic Programming*. Springer-Verlag, 2nd edition, 1987.

[6] E. Lusk, R. Butler, T. Disz, R. Olson, R. Overbeek, R. Stevens, D.H.D. Warren, A. Calderwood, P. Szeredi, S. Haridi, P. Brand,

M. Carlsson, A. Ciepielewski, and B. Hausman. The aurora or-parallel prolog system. In *Proceedings of the Int'l Conference on 5th Generation Computer Systems*, Tokyo, Japan, November 1988.

[7] V.P. Srini, J. Tam, T. Nguyen, B. Holmer, Y. Patt, and A. Despain. Design and implementation of a CMOS chip for prolog. Technical Report UCB/CSD 88/412, CS Division, UC Berkeley, March 1988.

[8] H. Touati and T. Hama. A light-weight prolog garbage collector. In *International Conference on Fifth Generation Computer Systems 1988 (FGCS'88)*, Tokyo, Japan, 1988.

[9] D.H.D. Warren. An abstract prolog instruction set. Technical report, SRI International, Menlo Park, CA, 1983.

[10] D.H.D. Warren. The sri model for or-parallel execution of prolog - abstract design and implementation issues. In *Proceedings of the 1987 IEEE Symposium on Logic Programming*, pages 92–102, San Francisco, September 1987.